The Hero and the Perennial Journey Home in American Film

The Hero and the Perennial Journey Home in American Film

SUSAN MACKEY-KALLIS

PENN

University of Pennsylvania Press   Philadelphia

Copyright © 2001 University of Pennsylvania Press
All rights reserved
Printed in the United States of America on acid-free paper

10 9 8 7 6 5 4 3 2 1

Published by
University of Pennsylvania Press
Philadelphia, Pennsylvania 19104–4011

Library of Congress Cataloging-in-Publication Data
Mackey-Kallis, Susan.
The hero and the perennial journey home in American film /
Susan Mackey-Kallis.
p. cm.
Includes bibliographical references and index.
ISBN 0-8122-3606-8 (cloth : alk. paper) —
ISBN 0-8122-1768-3 (pbk. : alk. paper)
1. Home in motion pictures.   2. Heroes in motion pictures.
3. Myth in motion pictures.   I. Title.
PN1995.9.H54 M33   2001
791.43′652—dc21   00-069950

To Janice Rushing and Thomas Frentz, whose scholarship in the area of mythic criticism of film has made mine possible, and to my children, William and Alexander, and to my husband, Kyriakos Kallis

The problem is nothing if not that of rendering the modern world spiritually significant — or rather . . . nothing if not that of making it possible for men and women to come to full human maturity through the conditions of contemporary life. — Joseph Campbell, *The Hero with a Thousand Faces*, p. 388

Contents

1 Introduction

Many of the top-grossing films in the American cinema have been based, however loosely, on the hero quest. Such a quest does not involve simply the hero's discovery of some boon or Holy Grail, however; it also involves finding him- or herself, which ultimately means finding a home in the universe. Home is often the literal home from which the hero sets out, but more significantly, it is a state of mind or a way of seeing not possible before the hero departs. The hero's journey, in Joseph Campbell's words, "is a labor not of attainment but of reattainment, not discovery but rediscovery. The godly powers sought and dangerously won are revealed to have been within the heart of the hero all the time." [1] The hero's quest, then, is a double quest that often requires a journey home not only to the place from whence the hero departed but to a state of being or consciousness that was within the hero's heart all along. To put it simply, the hero's journey outward into the world of action and events eventually requires a journey inward—if the hero is to grow—and ultimately necessitates a journey homeward—if the hero is to understand his or her grail or boon and is to share it with the culture at large. This book is an attempt to trace the story of this quest and its various permutations as it has been told and retold again and again in some of the most popular films in contemporary American cinema.

Some of the films discussed in this book trace the circular path taken by protagonists as they journey from home and back. The most obvious examples are Dorothy in *The Wizard of Oz*, E.T. in *E.T.: The Extra-Terrestrial*, Roy Hobbs in *The Natural*, Ray Kinsella in *Field of Dreams*, Scarlett O'Hara in *Gone with the Wind*, and Simba in *The Lion King*. Other films take their protagonists to a transcendent home, a home often not of this world, but a home, nevertheless, for which they have been searching and to which they have been moving all along. Some examples are Ellie Arroway in *Contact*, Ada in *The Piano*, Luke Skywalker in the "Star Wars" trilogy, Dave Bowman in *2001: A Space Odyssey*, and Thelma and Louise in *Thelma and Louise*. And, in the strangest of all quest films, *It's a Wonderful Life*, although the protagonist George Bailey never actually leaves home, he goes questing in his hometown and endures many arduous tests before learning the value of home and what it represents in his life.

The films explored in this book fall into diverse genres and cover many historical periods. *The Wizard of Oz*, *Field of Dreams*, and the "Star Wars" trilogy, for example, are fantasy films. *The Lion King* is a children's animated feature-length film. *Contact*, *E.T.*, and *2001* are science-fiction films. Other films such as *It's a Wonderful Life* and *Gone with the Wind* are coming-of-age films. The films discussed in the book were made from the 1930s through the 1990s. As such, the book demonstrates that the quest for home in American film is not located in any particular genre or historical period, but instead transcends all genres by its universal appeal to wholeness and cultural evolution. The protagonists of these films share an overriding desire to find their way "home" on a journey that involves either a glimpse or an attainment of a transcendent way of knowing and being in the world and a chance to offer that vision to the culture at large.

The hero quest is a much documented and frequently cited universal myth.[2] Theorists and critics have noted its links to Perennial philosophy[3] as well as psychology and human development.[4] Theorists have also explored both the mythic and Jungian dimension of film and the film-viewing experience.[5] There is a limited amount of scholarship, however, that draws together the elements of quest mythology, Perennial philosophy, and Jungian psychology in the criticism of Hollywood cinema.[6] In its application of theory, this book is similar to Janice Rushing and Thomas Frentz's *Projecting the Shadow: The Cyborg Hero in American Film.* While Rushing and Frentz's book focuses primarily on science fiction, this book offers a more wide-ranging analysis of Hollywood cinema. Although this book also shares some similarities with Joel Martin and Conrad Ostwalt, Jr.'s *Screening the Sacred: Religion, Myth, and Ideology in Popular American Film*, particularly the middle section on mythological criticism, this book expands this framework to include a number of other popular films in the American cinema, it emphasizes the "home" motif found in all of these films, and it explores the role of myth in discourse and the value of mythic criticism.

There are a number of reasons why I chose to write this book. First, while I would never claim possession of some interpretive key to meaning, the mythic models employed in this book provide ways of thinking about some of the most popular Hollywood films that may account for their power, popularity, and longevity. Second, mythic criticism has recently been maligned as overly simplistic. Some of the worst examples of mythic criticism epitomize this claim, some of the best examples—the work of Rushing and Frentz comes to mind—reveal the complexity, flexibility, and analytical beauty of mythic criticism done well. It is hoped that the interpretations of various films offered in Chapters 4–8 of this book do likewise. Third, in the hopes of offering some middle ground between the two camps in mythic criticism,[7] although ultimately asserting the liberating and transcendent power of many of the films discussed, each chapter acknowledges how various films' mythic interpretations of the world might invite problematic perceptions of, for example, women, or minorities, or notions of privilege and hierarchy. Accordingly, many chapters conclude with a section that problematizes either mythic models generally (see, for example, the discussion of the sacred marriage quest at the end of Chapter 4) or their applications in particular films (see, for example, the discussion of *Gone with the Wind* at the end of Chapter 6). In sum, this book, it is hoped, will illuminate the power of a number of significant Hollywood films while making sense of what these films are "about" from a mythic perspective, provide a testament to the lasting interpretive value of mythic models of criticism while demonstrating these models' elasticity in application, and offer some middle ground between competing theoretical assessments of myth as ideological/false consciousness and myth as liberating/enlightened consciousness. Ultimately, the book asserts the transformative power of mythic ways of being in the world, particularly as we make sense of ourselves in an increasingly fractured and alienating postmodern world.

The remainder of this chapter introduces the analytic model of the perennial journey home used throughout, it asserts the urgent need for mythic understandings of the world in the current postmodern moment, and it concludes with a discussion of the book's method and organization.

The Perennial Journey Home

In Jungian terms, the history of humanity's evolution is the history of the emergence of the ego from a pre-egoic state and its inevitable reexploration of this state—through an examination of the collective unconscious—in order to achieve individuation. This return to the realm of the pre-egoic is not regressive, however, because, in Jung's words, "the unconscious has a Janus-face: on the one side its contents point back to a preconscious, prehistoric world of instinct, while on the other side it potentially anticipates the future—precisely because of the instinctive readiness for action of the factors that determine man's fate." [8] The journey homeward, in other words, is to a "home" that we have never known. Although it has elements of preconsciousness—particularly in its emphasis on spiritual unity (the Garden of Eden before the Fall)— it does not truly represent a state of innocence, for, as a result of our journey outward into the realm of consciousness and experience, we have known sin. Such knowledge of both good *and* evil, therefore, makes a return to innocence no longer possible.[9] To truly reach individuation, as individuals and as a culture, we must go "home" fully prepared to face our collective Shadow and to fashion a new home in the universe.

This circular or mandalic pattern is most clearly articulated in Homer's *Odyssey* where Odysseus (literally "the traveler"), after leaving Ithaca to fight the Trojan War, both wittingly and unwittingly travels for another ten years before finally arriving home. Along the way he and his shipmates encounter numerous challenges that ultimately result in Odysseus' edification and growth. He alone of all his companions, however, does not succumb to the appeals of the unconscious, and thus returns to Ithaca where he must battle the numerous suitors for his wife's hand who have moved in and polluted his hearth and home.

Odysseus' quest, however, is more than a literal journey. In one interpretation, it represents the evolution of consciousness and the development of civilization from preconsciousness (represented by the Garden before the Fall—a perfect state of unity, innocence, and harmony) to consciousness (represented by the rise of modern civilization, science, and technology— an imperfect or imbalanced state without god/spirit) to transconsciousness (represented by the "return" to the spiritual plane of harmony and unity with god/spirit).[10] From the perspective of world mythology and Perennial philosophy, Odysseus' development, or the evolution of humanity, is our movement toward some ultimate telos or unity, which can be interpreted as our attempt to find our place in the universe, or our striving toward "home." [11]

Thomas Wolfe says that we can never go home again. What this may mean is not that we can never go home again, but that home, once reached, will never be the same. Because we are changed, it will have changed as well. So whether we return to Kansas (*The Wizard of Oz*), Ithaca (the *Odyssey*), or the

Pride Lands (*The Lion King*), such a return is premeditated in our departure and represents our evolution toward a more perfect state or a new Eden only dimly prefigured in our memories of home before the Fall. And such a return is never regressive or simply nostalgic; although home is the place we have "always been," it remains a place that we could not have either recognized or attained before our "departure" or journey outward. Transconsciousness, paradoxically, is both a being and a becoming.

The Contemporary Moment

Contemporary culture's disillusionment with positivism—the predominant strain of thought over the past five hundred years since the Scientific Revolution—coupled with fin-de-siecle thinking, or in the case of the close of the twentieth century, "fin de millennium" thinking, has resulted in the increasing influence of both postmodernism and transcendentalism. As Rushing and Frentz note, however, postmodernism, "with a trenchant rasp of the sinister, but with no sense of the sacred," has tended to "produce reactions of hopelessness in its subscribers." [12] Frentz and Farrell, speaking of transcendental movements, note that however "crude" or "inarticulate" their messages, their proliferation is "symptomatic of a collective disenchantment with Positivism." [13] Tony Kushner's critically acclaimed plays *Angels in America: The Millennium Approaches*, and *Angels in America: Perestroika*, for example, seem to have tapped into both our fears about the widening gyre that is societal and semantic disintegration and our fascination with all things angelic and nonrational.

Rushing, in reference to such diverse philosophers as Carl Sagan, Robert Pirsig, Joseph Campbell, and Mircea Eliade, notes that all have spoken of culture's universal need for transcendence.[14] She explains that in the contemporary era this need or exigency is driven by our "sense of separation from self, society and the universe." [15] As I argue elsewhere, "the 'felt fragmentation' of the modern age is a result of our desire for the next stage of evolutionary consciousness being stymied by our inability either to give up ego identity or to see it as a part rather than a whole, as a transition rather than a final stage in the development of consciousness. This exigency invites individuals and cultures to search for stories that offer transcendence and freedom from the fear of ego death." [16] But, as Rushing notes, just "as death is 'beyond the capacity of any symbolism whatever ultimately to assuage,' so is the lack of wholeness. And yet, as we respond to death with funerals, so we respond to division with rituals and words." [17]

Films, and perhaps much of cultural discourse in general, may offer answers to questions of being and non-being, separation and connection. Space fiction or fantasy film in particular, as Rushing asserts, is a particularly significant genre "for presenting and responding to the rhetorical exigency of fragmentation." [18] Rushing, in her analysis of transcendence in *E.T.*, notes that the film, a modern hero myth, provides a provocative example of such a response. She goes on to assert, however, that "a theory of the modern hero myth at the height of the age of consciousness" requires "a careful comparison of many like stories." [19] This book attempts to provide such a comparison.

If the role of art, as Jung asserts, is to "dream the myth outward," to continually offer new interpretations of the archetypes of the collective unconscious as we attempt to find our way home,[20] then the films that this book explores "dream the myth outward." They offer new interpretations of the hero's mandelic quest, continually interpreting this quest in terms of our teleological evolution toward transconsciousness. The popularity of such seemingly diverse films as *E.T.*, *The Lion King*, *Field of Dreams*, and the "Star Wars" trilogy rests in their ability to reinterpret the quest for home in a fashion that speaks to our collective unconscious while also reinvigorating our private and collective searches for meaning and growth in an era of separation and fragmentation.

My approach to these films can broadly be defined as rhetorical and psychomythological. Rhetorical criticism of film is a mode of analysis that "regards the work not so much as an object of aesthetic contemplation but as an artistically structured instrument for communication." [21] This concern places the emphasis not on the work itself but on the way it interacts with an audience inside of a context to produce meaning. As a psychomythological critic I explore "the mythic dimensions of film, focusing on archetypes, both historical and literary, in their relation to the viewer's experience." This involves looking at "how a film's mythic structure, viewed as cultural or universal, draws upon the audiences unconscious (psychoanalytic) structures as they are played out in a larger social context." [22]

Audience-based film criticism has become over the last two decades a widely anticipated development. An appeal for such a criticism, for example, was made by Grogg and Nachbar in their introduction to the 1982 book *Movies as Artifacts: Cultural Criticism of Popular Film*. They write:

If the clamor of our critics is to ever provide insight, it must be stimulated by a grasp of the essential relationship of American movies with the mass audience of moviegoers. The elemental nature of our movies is grounded in the people. The critic must throw out his credo of "I know what I like" and consider closely what *they* like. . . . Audience-based film critics have emerged, not surprisingly, to be among the few writers whose ideas about film remain valuable reading decades later.[23]

This book provides a close analysis of each of the films discussed while also building an argument about the films collectively. The individual film and its invitations to meaning are always forefront in the analysis, thereby avoiding the danger of overreading any particular film in order to "fit" it into the analytical framework. The larger purpose of the book, however, is to provide an understanding of the audience appeal of these extremely successful films, accounting for that appeal primarily through their reflection of powerful unconscious mythic structures, specifically the perennial journey outward, inward, and homeward undertaken by so many mythological heroes throughout time.

As a psychomythic critic, I also make moral judgments about the films discussed. Mythic criticism is frequently assailed for being apolitical in nature. The charges often leveled are that, by assuming universal qualities to human experience, mythic criticism risks erasing awareness of difference (i.e., class, race, and gender); by focusing on spiritual transcendence, mythic criticism potentially ignores the impact of material conditions (i.e., wealth and poverty); by exploring visions of unity, mythic criticism may ignore the existence of power and dominance structures that divide (i.e., political, economic, and religious systems). Although, like many psychomythological critics, I ultimately view universal or "deep structure" myths as liberating non-literal "truths," I acknowledge that archetypes, as they are inflected through cultural myths, may contain elements that work against cultural evolution by, for example, reifying dominance structures that create or maintain repressive relationships between and among individuals and groups. Each of the chapters of film analysis, therefore, concludes with a discussion that problematizes the films discussed in light of, for example, ideology, race, ethnicity, class, gender, and sexual orientation.

Overview of the Book

Part I of the book develops a model of the universal hero's circular quest and explores this quest myth in a number of top-grossing Hollywood films. More specifically, Chapter 2 develops the model using quest mythology, Perennial philosophy and Jung's theory of the personal and collective unconscious. Chapter 3 traces this model in Odysseus' homeward journey in the *Odyssey*. One of the earliest Western models of the hero's perennial journey home, the *Odyssey* not only provides an exemplar telling of the journey home, it also offers an explicit model for analyzing *The Natural* (examined in Chapter 4) and an implicit model for many of the other films discussed in the book. Although the hero quest is a universal myth, various interpretations often emphasize such elements as the "father" quest, the "sacred marriage" quest, or the "Grail" quest. Accordingly, Chapter 4 explores the "sacred marriage quest" in such seemingly diverse films as *The Natural, Bull Durham, The Piano*, and *Thelma and Louise*. Chapter 5 looks at the "father quest" as it appears in *The Lion King* and *Field of Dreams*. These two permutations of the hero myth are discussed at greater length in each of the chapters where they are applied.

Joseph Campbell and others theorists of myth have asserted that although myths are universal in nature they are always inflected through cultural myths —stories specific to a society at a given point in time. Even if universal elements dominate the telling of a myth, any interpretation is always grounded in the particular socio-historical moment out of which it arises and to which it speaks. Mythic criticism of film, in other words, does not treat a film as if it operated in a vacuum. Thus, although the universal qualities of the hero quest are emphasized in Part I of the book, Part II attempts to deepen and complexify the discussion of the hero quest by looking at films in terms of their particular socio-historical moment. Specifically, Part II further develops the model of the hero quest by focusing on films that address the American character and the American journey home at a particular point in time. Chapter 6, for example, explores the nature of the quest for home during the 1930s Depression era as evidenced in such Hollywood blockbusters as *The Wizard of Oz, It's a Wonderful Life*, and *Gone with the Wind*. Chapter 7 takes this same sociohistorical approach by looking at a contemporary manifestation of the quest myth—the current era's attempt to reconcile scientific and technological ways of knowing with spiritual/nonrational ways of knowing. This theme is played out, not surprisingly, in a number of science fiction films such as *E.T., Close Encounters of the Third Kind, 2001: A Space Odyssey*, and *Contact*.

Part III of the book provides a synthesis of the analytical model developed throughout. Specifically, Chapter 8 examines the universal quest for home in one of the top grossing quest trilogies of all times, George Lucas'

"Star Wars" films. The "Star Wars" trilogy, perhaps more than any films in the history of Hollywood cinema, is the quintessential hero quest film.[24] This analysis not only explores various permutations of the quest myth—specifically the father quest and the Grail quest—it also grounds the films in their particular sociohistorical moment, viewing them in light of such cultural myths as the Western cowboy hero, Arthurian legend, and the contemporary quest to reconcile technology/science with humanity/spirit. In its conclusion, the chapter problematizes the "trilogy" in light of gender, race, and ideology. The final chapter of Part III examines the value of myth and mythic criticism by placing them in the debate over the progressive/regressive role of myth in discourse. This chapter also confronts ways in which some of the films discussed in the book construct the hero quest in a fashion that reinforces traditional class, gender, and ethnic stereotypes. As Rushing and Frentz explain, "Narratives may implicitly advocate any number of courses of moral action in relation to the end point of cultural individuation. Those that imply a movement toward individuation would be judged as morally superior to those that imply a movement away from it." [25] Thus with an eye toward "cultural individuation," the chapter concludes with a discussion of the types of myths necessary as we move into the new millennium.

Mythological Criticism

2 The Perennial Journey Home

The elemental [myth] for spiritual instruction is called *marga* which means "path." It's the trail back to yourself.

—Joseph Campbell, *The Power of Myth*, p. 59

To view an American film is to witness the dreams, values and fears of the American people, to feel the pulse of American culture.

—Sam Grogg and John Nachbar, *Movies as Artifacts*, p. 5

Joseph Campbell and other theorists of myth argue that the collective development of human consciousness (Perennial philosophy) parallels the developing consciousness of the individual (Jungian psychology). Both types of evolution are explained in myth as an individual (hero's) journey. This journey moves the individual out from known territory (the parochial/the home/ego-consciousness) to unknown territory (often a descent into strange or terrible lands/unconsciousness) where the individual is sometimes aided (mentors/gods/shamans/dreams), and is often sorely tested (demons/Shadow-self), in a search for a treasure or boon (gold/grail/enlightenment/individuation) that the individual then shares with the culture upon returning home (cultural enlightenment/awareness of the undivided nature of being/transconsciousness). Campbell in *The Hero with a Thousand Faces* explains that the nuclear units of this hero quest, which he refers to as the monomyth, are separation, initiation, and return.[1]

This movement outward, downward, inward, and homeward, although teleological or evolutionary, as Campbell also points out, is ultimately cyclical or mandalic since the home to which the hero returns, although the "same," cannot be truly known or grasped until the journey outward. Such a departure from home, which ultimately constitutes the birth of drama, only becomes necessary with our movement out from preconsciousness (caused in mythic time by our expulsion from the Garden/paradise—a place before time or consciousness). Such an expulsion creates the profound feeling of loss or lack and provides the motive for the journey "home." For what else is a journey but an attempt to discover something that is missing or lost, something dimly intuited but not yet fully grasped? Such a journey offers a chance for change, growth, and possibly transcendence, that although evolutionary, ultimately represents, as Zen Buddhism tells us, a longing to be reunited with an energy or way of being always already present; a longing, in other words, for home.

This chapter details at greater length this relationship among the hero quest, the journey home, and cultural and individual evolution. Specifically, the chapter provides a working definition of myth, discussing myth's origins, purpose, and relationship to dreams, art, film, and culture. It then develops a model of the perennial journey home in quest mythology, discussing a number of permutations of the hero quest as they appear in the various films analyzed at greater length in later chapters.

What Are Myths?

According to Campbell, myths are "the secret opening through which the inexhaustible energies of the cosmos pour into human cultural manifestations." [2] They are "the world's [archetypal] dreams." Myths "deal with great human problems" while providing "clues to the spiritual potentialities of the human life." [3] They "offer a way of experiencing the world that will open us to the transcendent that informs it, and at the same time forms ourself within it"; [4] the transcendent, in Campbell's usage, referring to "that which is beyond all concept . . . beyond the categories of being and non-being." [5]

Although myths may vary somewhat from culture to culture, they draw on a surprisingly universal storehouse of archetypal information about what it means to be human and how to live a meaningful human life. And although these archetypal stories offer dark and unsettling images and recount difficult and often terrifying experiences, [6] they ultimately affirm the value of life and provide a primer, a set of instructions, for living. As Curtin notes, when myths "are epic—that is, when they express the crucial experiences, ideals, and aspirations of any culture—then they help to keep that culture alive and healthy, in touch with its values and hopes. Living myths become the antidote to cynicism." [7]

Myths, contrary to the common understanding of a myth as a falsehood, are neither true nor false in the traditional sense of those terms. Versenyi, for example, explains that in Homer's era mythos "did not mean fable . . . the tale was not something mythical, fabulous, fictional, and therefore untrue. Myth meant simply word of mouth, a story told rather than written down, winged words not fixed in an enduring medium but orally related and transmitted from generation to generation." He goes on to explain that "that is why living myth is always true; true, that is, to the experience, ideals, and aspirations of each generation." [8] Myths, therefore, neither true nor false, are instead more or less functional for interpreting the "truth" of human experience and giving life shape, substance, and meaning. Jung goes so far as to argue that myths, or more specifically the "archetypal foundations" of the unconscious upon which they are based, are so important for a culture that "in reality we can never legitimately cut loose from them. . . unless we are prepared to pay the price of a neurosis, any more than we can rid ourselves of our body and its organs without committing suicide." [9]

Where Do Myths Come From?

Campbell explains that "the earliest evidence of anything like mythological thinking is associated with graves. . . . There was a person who was alive and warm before you who is now lying there cold, and beginning to rot." [10] Faced with such an event, premodern humans were compelled to ask such essential questions as, if there was something there that isn't there now, "Where is it now?" [11] If there is such a thing as a soul that makes the body lively, where did it come from? Did someone create it? And if there is a creator or creators, does that mean that humans have a divine purpose? If so, what then is that purpose? From such questions as these, many mythologists assert, religion and myth were born.

A particularly fascinating question for many mythologists relates to the universal nature of many myths. Five strains of theory have developed to account for these universal qualities.

The first is experiential; because we all are born, mature, face questions of procreation, unification, and separation, because we all eventually face death, myths speak to these elemental human experiences. As a result, we have creation stories, coming-of-age stories, stories of death and life after death, and stories of humanity's fall from grace and of the hope in resurrection/reunification with spirit/God.[12]

A second theory for explaining the universal qualities of many myths is diffusion; myths that effectively accounted for the human experience were told again and again and eventually spread around the world and throughout time from culture to culture. This would mean that most contemporary cultural permutations of myths can be traced back, in some form or another, to a set of elemental mythic stories told in antiquity.

A third theory is environmental; a culture's specific geographical environment and their experiences of that environment shapes the stories they tell. To the extent, for example, that all agricultural cultures have faced similar experiences—the cycle of sowing the crops in spring, their growth, maturation, and harvest, dormancy in winter, and regrowth in spring—they have responded with similar stories about fertility, creation, and the resurrection of life from death. And by comparison, to the extent to which all hunting cultures have faced similar experiences—the wandering of the tribe in search of food, the power of the animal as both threat and source of life, the vagaries of the hunt—they have responded with similar stories about animal deities as creators, similar cleansing rituals in preparation for the hunt, and similar rituals of thanks for the life of the animal as willing sacrifice.[13] More recently, to the extent to which contemporary cultures have been impacted by the rapid development of technology—from the Industrial Revolution onward—they have responded with a cultural myth about the relationship between technology/science and humanity/spirituality. This myth has been played out most predominantly in science fiction, from Mary Shelley's *Frankenstein* to Stanley Kubrick's *2001: A Space Odyssey*.

A fourth explanation for the existence of archetypic myths is biological. Just as human beings are "hard-wired" to do many things, such as breathe, suck mother's milk, and recognize shapes, they are also "programmed" to articulate and respond to certain archetypic material, such as mandalas, "ascent" and "descent" motifs, and images of lightness and darkness, the sun, the sea, and fire. Advocates of this position argue that archetypes are ahistorical and transcultural and are not tied to experiences, environments, or cultural diffusion.[14] Although this is the most controversial position, it has a number of adherents in the communication field.[15]

A fifth explanation is spiritual. Proponents of this position assert that mythic structures articulate divine inspirations from God/spirit. Mythic archetypes thus represent the language of God. Nonliteral Bible scholars, for example, assert that Old Testament stories such as the expulsion of Adam and Eve from the Garden and the slaying of Abel by his brother Cain are spiritual truths conveyed to the people by God through prayer or divine inspiration.[16]

What Purposes Do Myths Serve?

Related to the question of where myths come from, is the question of the functions they serve. Mythologists argue that there are two different, although related types of myths — universal and cultural/sociological — and that these two types serve different, although related purposes.[17] The universal myth, according to Campbell, is the "mythology that relates you to your nature and to the natural world, of which you're a part." [18] Universal myths transcend cultural and historical conditions to speak to the elemental and identical nature of the human condition. The hero quest, for example, is a universal story that appears in numerous cultures across time. By contrast, the cultural/sociological myth relates the individual to his/her particular society and "affirm[s] that you are an organ of the larger organism." [19] The American myth of "settling the West" or "manifest destiny" is an example of a cultural myth. Although cultural myths may vary widely from culture to culture, they are usually grounded in a larger or deeper universal mythic structure that informs them and gives them power. So, for example, the western expansion myth is grounded in and draws upon such myths as the universal hero quest and the Garden of Eden myth.

Both universal and cultural myth can serve diverse functions.[20] Theorists and critics who specifically view myths from a functionalist/structuralist perspective often talk about their sociological or "sociofunctional" role. Robert Rowland, for example, argues that myths perform three interrelated functions: they offer pragmatic, "how to live" advice, they help make intellectual sense of the world, and they provide cultures and individuals with psychological adjustments to change (for example, growth and maturation) and crisis (for example, murder or social upheaval).[21] Other theorists who take this structural/functionalist approach to myth include Claude Lévi-Strauss,[22] Bronislaw Malinowski,[23] and Theodore Gaster.[24] Other theorists of myth, such as Houston Smith,[25] Mircea Eliade,[26] Aldous Huxley,[27] and Ken Wilber[28] focus on the sacred or religious functions of myth, while others, like Sigmund Freud and Carl Jung, focus on myths' psychological functions. Still others critics, such as Roland Barthes[29] and Jacques Ellul,[30] view myths, particularly political myths, as "false consciousness," or ideology in the negative sense of the word. These critics focus on the way myths limit freedom, assert power relationships, and maintain inequalities.[31] And finally, there are theorists like Joseph Campbell and critics like Janice Rushing and Thomas Frentz who take a multifaceted approach to understanding the functions of myth.[32] Theorists and critics applying this multiperspectival orientation often integrate insights from Perennial philosophy, Jungian psychology and the structural study of myth in order to illuminate the rhetorical power and evolutionary thinking of mythic structures while also acknowledging the ideological implications of certain cultural constructions of myth in discourse.[33] My approach, in the analysis of films in this book, falls into this last camp.

How Are Myths Related to Dreams, Art, and Film?

According to Campbell, although "myths and dreams come from the same place . . . from realizations of some kind that have then to find expression in symbolic form," [34] he then goes on to say that "a dream is personal experience of that deep dark ground that is the support of our conscious lives, and a myth is the society's dream. The myth is the public dream and the dream is the private myth." [35]

Consistent with Campbell's distinction between myth and dream is Jung's elucidation of two types of dreams, the personal dream and the archetypal or mythic dream. According to Jung, the personal dream arises from the personal unconscious, which consists of repressed personal memories and experiences, including the shadow. The mythic dream, by contrast, arises from the collective unconscious, which is made up of archaic or "primordial types," "universal images that have existed since the remotest times" and which are shared by all.[36] The collective unconscious is made available to the culture and the individual through archetypes that are expressed in myths, fairy tales, and dreams.[37]

Myths, however, like the unconscious, have a life of their own. They are "spontaneous productions of the psyche" and, as such, "cannot be ordered, invented, or permanently suppressed." [38] As Campbell explains,

The unconscious sends all sorts of vapors, odd beings, terrors, and deluding images up into the mind—whether in dream, broad daylight or insanity; for the human kingdom, beneath the floor of the comparatively neat little dwelling that we call our consciousness, goes down into unsuspected Aladdin caves. There not only jewels but also dangerous jinn abide: the inconvenient or resisted psychological powers that we have not thought or dared to integrate into our lives. And they may remain unsuspected, or, on the other hand, some chance word, the smell of a landscape, the taste of a cup of tea, or the glance of an eye may touch a magic spring, and then dangerous messengers begin to appear in the brain. These are dangerous because they threaten the fabric of the security into which we have built ourselves and our family. But they are fiendishly fascinating too, for they carry keys that open the whole realm of the desired and feared adventure of the discovery of the self.[39]

Psychoanalysis, the "modern science of reading dreams" Campbell asserts, is primarily responsible for drawing our attention to these unconscious impulses and images. Campbell explains, however, that myths are more than simply manifestations of the unconscious in conscious life. Myths are also manifestations "of certain spiritual principles, which have remained as constant throughout the course of human history as the form and nervous structure of the human physique itself." [40]

The mythic unconscious not only reveals itself through dreams, visions, and psychoanalysis; it also asserts itself in various cultural art forms. Despite the universal qualities of the unconscious, myths must constantly be reborn and reinterpreted for every generation or they will die. "Myths," Campbell asserts, "are so intimately bound to the culture, time, and place that unless the symbols, metaphors, are kept alive by constant recreation through the arts, the life just slips away from them." [41] Accordingly, it is the artists and writers of a culture who are responsible for keeping myths lively and relevant for a people.[42] Jung, in fact, argues that the primary role of art is to "dream the myth outward," to continually find new interpretations of the archetypes of the collective unconscious.[43]

The initial inspiration for the creative act—the artist's muse—can even be attributed to myth. As Campbell notes:

Anyone writing a creative work knows that you open, you yield yourself, and the book talks to you and builds itself. To a certain extent you become the carrier of something that is given to you from what have been called the Muses, or in biblical language, "God". . . . Since the inspiration comes from the unconscious, and since the unconscious minds of the people of any single small society have much in common, what the shaman or seer brings forth is something that is waiting to be brought forth in everyone. So when one hears the seer's story, one responds, "Aha! This is my story. This is something that I had always wanted to say but wasn't able to say." [44]

Film, in particular, can be a powerful conduit for archetypal material. Davies, Farrell, and Matthews, for example, claim that film sequences can take the form of "memories, reflections, or dreams, where images combine, fade, or dissolve, contrary to physical restrictions of time, space, object constancy, and causality." [45] As a result, they argue that "stylistic elements inherent in cinema make it especially amenable to the communication of archetypal material." [46]

According to Jung, archetypes "arise in a state of reduced intensity of consciousness (in dreams, delirium, reveries, visions, etc.). In all these states the check put upon unconscious contents by the concentration of the conscious mind ceases, so that the hitherto unconscious material streams, as through from opened side-sluices, into to the field of consciousness." [47] The film-viewing state is also marked by passive receptivity. One's body is relatively inert while one's mind is open to the audio-visual stimulation presented. As such, the viewer, like the dreamer, may be more conducive to the unconscious and its archetypes.

The entire film-viewing experience can actually be seen as a metaphor for dreaming. For example, just as the viewer moves from light to dark as he enters the cinema, so does the dreamer as sleep begins. When the lights come up on the screen/inner eye, the dream/film begins. The viewer/dreamer often finds himself in a liminal world where fantasies or fears can be played out before his eyes — voyeurism (the pleasure in secret looking), scopophilia (the vicarious pleasure in being "looked" at), fetishism (the investing of objects with special powers), nightmares (the harbingers of deep-seated fears) — all are possible. The viewer's/dreamer's visions are also realized in a drama that is visual, auditory, and often viscerally moving. At its best the cinema can invoke either the cold sweat and rapid pulse of the dream or the critical reflection that often renders dreams psychic guides to life. And, just as the dreamer feels that he cannot control the direction in which the dream takes him, the same is obviously so for the filmviewer. Both can only decide whether they want to hang on for the ride. Even the movement of the camera in the film can be likened to the point of view experienced by the dreamer. The camera's mobility mimics the dreamer's, which can be omniscient or naive, have a bird's-eye view or a ground-level perspective. Time is also fluid and relative for both the dreamer and the viewer, who can experience, for example, slow motion, flashbacks, flashforwards, repeated sequences, and rapid, montage-like shifts in time and space. To the extent, then, that films are like dreams, and dreams, as Jung argues, are windows to the unconscious realm of the archetypal, films can also tap the latent mythic energy of the unconscious.

Myths, then, neither true nor false, are instead portals to the unconscious realm of archetypes that are continually produced and reproduced in all cultures in all ages. Manifest in dreams and psychoanalysis as well as in art and film, myths—whether universal or cultural—speak to human experiences while providing guides for living the fully human life. What, then, are some of these archetypal stories? How have they evolved? To what urgencies do they speak?

The Cosmogonic Cycle in Myth

Perennial philosophy, Jungian psychology, and much of the scholarship on myth asserts that humanity is collectively experiencing a teleological evolution; a movement, in other words, toward a more perfect state of being.[48] The history of this evolution, according to Janice Rushing and Thomas Frentz, is the history of the emergence of consciousness from preconsciousness and the contemporary striving of humanity toward transconsciousness.[49]

In psychological terms, as Rushing and Frentz point out, this evolution is the process both of "becoming an individual" and "becoming undivided." [50] For the developing individual, this involves the emergence of ego from a pre-egoic state of being. The child, for example, develops a growing sense of herself as separate from the mother as she moves from childhood into adulthood. Erik Erikson refers to this as the achievement of ego-identity. It represents the "comprehensive gains which the individual, at the end of adolescence, must have derived from all of his preadult experiences in order to be ready for the task of adulthood." [51] Ego-consciousness, however, is not a final stage in the individuation process, simply a stop along the way. Full adult maturity implies a movement beyond ego-identity toward awareness of the collective, undivided nature of being and our unity with all things.[52] According to Jung, "As the individual is not just a single, separate being, but by his very existence presupposes a collective relationship, it follows that the process of individuation must lead to more intense and broader collective relationships and not isolation." [53]

In the evolution from one stage to the next it is often the heroes of myth, as I argue elsewhere, who are best "able to try out the next stage of human consciousness—to act as philosophical test pilots for an entire culture." [54] In order to do this, however the heroes of each age are depicted as needing to slay or overcome the gods or goddesses of their age. In the era of preconsciousness, for example:

the hero's main feat is to overcome the monster of darkness: it is the long-hoped-for and expected triumph of consciousness over the unconscious. So in the Golden Age of heroes in Greek mythology . . . male figures such as Pericles, Jason, Achilles, Hector and Odysseus had to face the monsters and villains of preconsciousness in order to liberate the ego identity just beginning to emerge. These monsters or villains were represented by the "Great Mother" or "Great Goddess" worshipped during the era of preconsciousness. These female figures became the dragons to be slain, however, because they represented obstacles impeding the emergence of ego consciousness and thus the rise of civilization.[55]

In the modern era of consciousness, when the age of great heroes has passed, the gods of rationality and science—the saviors of the previous age—become the demons and monsters that must either be overcome or better integrated into our collective psyche. The ego, no longer the hero, is now the villain to be defeated. This is because science, technology, and rationality, which represent the ego phase of development, separate us from the irrational, the mythical, and the spiritual—the realm with which we must be reunited in order to advance to the next phase of teleological development.[56]

The emergence of consciousness from preconsciousness, argues Jung, was most likely a "tremendous experience for primeval times, for with it a world came into being whose existence no one has suspected before." [57] Jung asserts, however, that since the first act of the emerging individual consciousness from preconsciousness was matricide, this act brought with it a profound sense of guilt or longing for the loss of the mother and the irrational realm she represents. As a result, what may have only been an inkling of guilt or sin over the loss of the irrational and the matricide of the "Great Mother" or "Great Goddess" of preconsciousness in Homer's era, in the contemporary era has become a profound longing or angst over the meaninglessness of the modern condition. The realm of ego-consciousness, dominated by First World cultures' reverence for, even worship of, the "sovereign rationale subject" has resulted in our inability to explore the archetypal realm of the unconscious in order to "go home." [58]

There may be multiple reasons why individuals and cultures fail to explore the realm of the unconsciousness in order to complete their trip "home" to transconsciousness. The first is guilt over our loss of the Mother and the realm of the unconsciousness. In the Christian tradition, this guilt translates as sin related to our expulsion from paradise and our separation from God. It is not only guilt or sin, however, that has separated us from the realm of the unconscious and the Mother. Fear of the loss of ego identity also provides a powerful deterrent to experiencing the transcendent. The central event, in fact, of modernism is "the perfection of the ego until it becomes strong enough to dominate the rest of the psyche. Thus, instead of becoming one with Spirit, the ego tries to substitute for Spirit; as Wilber put it, 'instead of becoming one with the cosmos, he [egoic man] tries to possess the cosmos.' " [59] According to Perennial philosophy, as I argue elsewhere, "although the individual or the culture may desire transcendence, this transcendence implies the 'death' of the isolated self. [As a result,] instead of attempting evolution, in the age of ego consciousness we repress or sublimate our awareness of trans-consciousness to ego identity by finding ways to leave our mark, build bigger buildings or claim our fifteen minutes of fame." [60] Despite this, as Campbell asserts, the hero's real task, and hence that of the culture at large, is "losing yourself, giving yourself to some higher end, or to another." [61] He goes on to explain that "when we quit thinking primarily about ourselves and our own self preservation, we undergo a truly heroic transformation of consciousness." [62]

Rushing and Frentz assert that this "truly heroic transformation of consciousness," or the hero's "return" to unity with the cosmos, is not a regressive return to preconsciousness in which the ego is destroyed or infantalized. Instead, rather than being dissolved, in a transmodern view, the ego is simply displaced from its central position "in favor of recentering the psyche in a larger, transcendent self that encapsulates the ego . . . a transmodern view posits a level of the psyche beyond the ego which is not unconscious, not conscious, but *transconscious*." [63]

In this view, transconsciousness is not, nor can it ever be, identical with unconsciousness/preconsciousness. Because the hero is changed by his descent into the realm of unconsciousness, when he returns "home," paradoxically it is to a place he has never been. Because he has changed, it has changed as well. Hence, because we have known sin, death, and separation such a return to preconsciousness is no longer possible. Because we have known self (ego), such a return is no longer desirable. What is possible, indeed what may be necessary, as Rushing and Frentz assert, is a displacement of self (the sovereign rationale subject that modernism canonizes and postmodernism vilifies) that allows us to consider the soul rather than the ego as "the seat of the self." [64] Thus transconsciousness, or the state of unity with Spirit sought by the heroes of all ages, is an evolution, paradoxically to a place that has always existed (soul-knowledge) but which could never be fully realized without our questing in the realm of consciousness (ego), unconsciousness (pre-ego), and imperfect human activity (Shadow/sin, death, and separation).

Birth of the Hero and the Quest

The birth of the hero quest, according to Campbell, occurs with a historical and mythological "shift of consciousness from the consciousness of identity to the consciousness of participation in duality." For then, as Campbell puts it, "you are in the field of time." [65] In the beginning of most creation myths, for example, the world is undivided or undifferentiated, there is no good or evil, male or female, darkness or light, past or future. But with God's first act division takes place and time begins, immortality for humanity ends, and, in Western mythology, death, sin, sadness, and separation enter the world. The darkness is separated from the light, the day is separated from night, the man is separated from the woman, and, in Judeo-Christian mythology, in the betrayal and expulsion from the Garden of Eden the man and woman are separated from God.

At this point a dramatic change has occurred, a new consciousness of duality (male/female, mortal/immortal, good/evil) and separation from God has emerged, time and becoming come into existence, and the first quest, or journey outward, begins. In Campbell's words:

It started with the sin . . . moving out of the mythological dreamtime zone of the Garden of Paradise, where there is no time, and where man and woman don't even know that they are different from each other. The two are just creatures. God and man are practically the same. God walks in the cool of the evening in the garden where they are. And then they eat the apple, the knowledge of the opposites. And when they discover that they are different, the man and the woman cover their shame. You see, they had not thought of themselves as opposites. . . . Then comes the idea of good and evil in the world. And so Adam and Eve have thrown themselves out of the Garden of Timeless Unity, you might say, just by that act of recognizing duality. To move out into the world, you have to act in terms of pairs of opposites.[66]

The Garden of Eden, then, a mythic representation of the realm of preconsciousness, in Campbell's words, "is a metaphor for that innocence that is innocent of time, innocent of opposites, and that is the prime center out of which consciousness then becomes aware of the changes." [67]

But "life really began with that act of disobedience" [68] — metaphorically speaking, it is the eating of the apple. This tension of opposites, or the duality of being, becomes the catalyst for drama and the hero quest since the primary task of the hero and the culture at large will be seeking unity from a place of separation, transcendence from duality.[69]

According to Campbell, there are two types of quests: intentional and unintentional. An intentional quest would be Telemachus in search of his father, sent on the quest willingly by the goddess Athena. An unintentional quest would be that undertaken by Han Solo in *Star Wars*, when Han, initially against his will, is thrown into the "thick of things" by a series of mishaps and adventures.

Just as there are two types of quests, according to Campbell, there are two types of deeds, physical and spiritual. The physical deed often involves the slaying of a dragon, a courageous act in battle, or the saving of a life. The spiritual deed is the experiencing of transcendence in the face of duality and the sharing of this message with the culture. Popular tales usually emphasize physical acts of bravery and strength while the higher religions tell the story of the hero facing moral and philosophical challenges and tests. Despite the differences in the two types of quests, however, "there will be found astonishingly little variation in the morphology of the adventure, the character roles involved, the victories gained." [70]

Campbell, in *The Hero with a Thousand Faces*, explains that the nuclear units of the hero quest, which he refers to as the monomyth, are separation, initiation, and return; "a separation from the world, a penetration to some source of power, and a life-enhancing return":[71]

The usual hero adventure begins with someone from whom something has been taken, or who feels there's something lacking in the normal experiences available or permitted to the members of his society. This person then takes off on a series of adventures beyond the ordinary, either to recover what has been lost or to discover some live-giving elixir. It's usually a cycle, a going and a returning.[72]

Examples of such a cycle of separation, initiation, and return are Prometheus ascending into the heavens, stealing fire from the gods, and returning to bestow this boon upon mortals; Aeneas descending into the underworld, conversing with the shade of his dead father, and returning with a new knowledge about the destiny of souls and the destiny of Rome, the city he is about to found; Jason sailing through the Clashing rocks, circumventing the dragon who guards the Golden Fleece, and then returning with it, giving him the power to regain his throne.

Decent and initiation into some source of power is always a significant element in the hero quest. A cave or a womb-like space is often representative of the underworld to which the hero descends. According to Jung, "The cave is the place of rebirth, that secret cavity in which one is shut up in order to be incubated and renewed. . . . Anyone who gets into that cave, that is to say into the cave which everyone has in himself, or into the darkness that lies behind consciousness, will find himself involved in an—at first—unconscious process of transformation. By penetrating into the unconscious he makes a connection with his unconscious contents." [73]

Although the unconscious represents a liminal space of growth, change, and enlightenment, and the hero must descend into it, as does Odysseus when he enters Hades to speak with the shades of his mother and other dead heroes, the individual must not dwell there indefinitely. To remain in the unconscious is to lose touch with reality and the world of human activity and events. Dwelling in the unconscious, in other words, represents the abandonment of the human evolution project and the infantilization/destruction of the self. A descent into the unconsciousness, therefore, must be followed by an ascent into consciousness if the hero is to share her boon with the culture at large and if the culture is to move to a new level of enlightenment or transconsciousness. As a result, the end of the hero's journey is not the aggrandizement of the hero, rather "the ultimate aim of the quest must be neither release nor ecstasy for oneself, but the wisdom and power to serve others." [74] The goal of the hero quest, or the boon provided by the hero to the people, is to see beyond the division of the here and now of consciousness and to realize, as Campbell explains, that "You and [the] other are one, that you are two aspects of one life, and that your apparent separateness is but an effect of the way we experience forms under the conditions of space and time. . . . The hero is the one who has given his physical life to some order of realization of that truth." [75] The hero of the hero quest, in other words, "suggest that behind that duality there is a singularity over which this plays like a shadow game." [76] Just as Christ, in Judeo-Christian mythology, provides Christians with the ability to recognize unity in the face of the separation represented by the Fall, Mohammed does the same for Muslims as does Buddha for Buddhists.

Essentially, it might even be said there is but one archetypal mythic hero whose life had been replicated in many lands by many, many people. A legendary hero is usually the founder of something—the founder of a new age, the founder of a new religion, the founder of a new city, the founder of a new way of life. In order to found something new, one has to leave the old and go in quest of the seed idea, a germinal idea that will have the potentiality for bringing forth that new thing.[77]

Campbell provides a more complete summary of the hero quest and the events that occur along the way:

The mythological hero . . . is lured, carried away, or else voluntarily proceeds, to the threshold of adventure. There he encounters a shadow presence that guards the passage. The hero may defeat or conciliate this power and go alive into the kingdom of the dark (brother-battle, dragon-battle, offering, charm), or be slain by the opponent and descend in death (dismemberment, crucifixion). Beyond the threshold, then, the hero journeys through a world of unfamiliar yet strangely intimate forces, some of which severely threaten him (tests), some of which give magical aid (helpers). When he arrives at the nadir of mythological round, he undergoes a supreme ordeal and gains his reward. The triumph may be represented as the hero's sexual union with the goddess-mother of the world (sacred marriage), his recognition by the father creator (father atonement), his own divinization (apotheosis), or again—if the powers have remained unfriendly to him—his theft of the boon he came to gain (bride-theft, fire-theft); intrinsically it is an expansion of consciousness and therewith of being (illumination, transfiguration, freedom). The final work is that of return. If the powers have blessed the hero, he now sets forth under protection (emissary); if not, he flees and is pursued (transformation flight, obstacle flight). At the return threshold the transcendental powers must remain behind; the hero re-emerges from the kingdom of dread (return, resurrection). The boon that he brings restores the world (elixir).[78]

In sum, the hero quest, or the monomyth as Campbell often refers to it, is the central universal story in which the archetypic events of separation, initiation, and return are acted out. The hero, acting as cultural visionary/prophet/messiah, moves through these phases with the primary goal of healing the culture by her ability to transcend the dualities of human existence, seek unity from separation, and move culture to the next level of consciousness.

Types of Quest Myths

Myths, then, are about the elemental experiences and desires in life such as birth, growth, separation, death, rebirth, and redemption. All myths, according to Campbell, draw on the monomyth or the universal quest myth. But, as Campbell notes, "Many tales isolate and greatly enlarge upon one or two of the typical elements of the full cycle (test motif, flight motif, abduction of the bride), others string a number of independent cycles into a single series (as in the *Odyssey*). Differing characters or episodes can become fused, or a single element can reduplicated itself and reappear under many changes." [79] Extrapolating from Joseph Campbell's writing on mythology in an application to contemporary American film, we can identify four different permutations of the quest myth: the creation/re-creation quest, the father quest, the sacred marriage quest, and the Grail quest. All of these permutations, however, still focus on an individual's journey outward (often downward), inward, and homeward. The remainder of this chapter briefly discusses these four versions of the quest myth and illustrates them with examples from a number of films.

Creation/Re-creation Myths

Cultures often have myths and rituals, which are the enactments of myths, about birth; not only about the birth of the individual, but the birth or creation of the culture and world.[80] These creation myths often explain the origin of the universe or the planet, where the particular culture came from, and the role of the creator(s) in the lives of his creations. They ask such questions as where did we come from? Where are we going? Is there intrinsic value to being human? Are we mortal or immortal?

Campbell argues that creation/re-creation stories not only attempt to explain primal origins, but they also deal with the first crime of killing in order to live, what Campbell calls the "brutal precondition of all life, which lives by the killing and eating of life." [81] The snake, in particular, is a central image in creation myths and points to the life/death element of the circle of life. The snake often symbolizes resurrection or transformation. In ancient Crete, for example, the serpent was often depicted on burial stones. In Greek mythology, the soul was said to leave the body in the form of a snake, thus emphasizing its connection with the afterlife and immortality. As Campbell explains:

The serpent sheds its skin to be born again. . . . Sometimes the serpent is represented as a circle eating its own tail. That's an image of life. Life sheds one generation after another, to be born again. The serpent represents immortal energy and consciousness engaged in the field of time, constantly throwing off death and being born again. . . . Life lives by killing and eating itself, casting off death and being reborn.[82]

The film that best illustrates a creation/re-creation component in the quest myth, and which will be explored at greater length in a Chapter 5, is *The Lion King*. The by now famous phrase "circle of life" directly acknowledges the birth, death, rebirth cycle central to the condition of all living things. Significantly, the film begins and ends with a birth: the film opens with Simba the lion cub, as he is proudly displayed for all the animal kingdom to see, and finally, the birth of Simba's own cub ends the film, as she is heralded as the next link in the chain of life. In between these two births, however, are a series of deaths—that of Simba's father, Scar, and the Pride Lands through a wasting away disease of neglect and overconsumption. Simba's father also represents a type of messiah figure who dies not only to save his son, but also to ensure the future of the Pride Lands. After his death he is resurrected in the form of a vision that appears to Simba and guides him in his quest to save the Pride Lands from destruction. As is particularly obvious in the "circle of life" example from *The Lion King*, creation/re-creation myths are clearly mandalic and often tell the story of a cyclical journey home.

Some other films discussed in this book that employ versions of the creation/re-creation myth, and that will be discussed in Chapter 7, include *2001* and *Contact*.

Coming-of-Age Myths

Just as cultures tells myths about creation/re-creation, they also often have myths and rituals about growth and separation, or "coming of age," as the individual is initiated into her culture and/or is separated from society and sent on a quest for maturation. The father quest and the sacred marriage quest are often predominant myths told in reference to growth and coming of age or sexual maturity. In the specific telling, both quests are usually composed of a separation, an initiation into a source of power, and a return home.

The sacred marriage quest for males involves the hero's sexual union with a goddess figure who represents the culmination of his quest. For a female hero, the union is usually with a godlike figure who also offers her the same blissful triumph.[83] The marriage quest in myth and literature is often different for men and women. Males are often the active seekers of their identity, which is usually achieved in more public and extroverted ways. For females, the coming of age, as Anthony Stevens points out, is often "an introverted dawning of awareness of herself as a woman. In many cultures this new feminine consciousness is marked by no rites at all, for it is the initiated male who brings it about by his recognition and pursuit of her womanhood; it is the man who puts the child to rest and awakens the woman." This helps to explain, Stevens adds, "the ubiquitous existence, in myth, legend, and fairy-tale, of the heroine who lies sleeping until her prince comes to waken her." [84] Fairy tales, such as Cinderella, Sleeping Beauty, Snow White and the Seven Dwarfs, and Rapunzel best exemplify the conservative enactment of women's sacred marriage quest in literature. Joseph Campbell, in his interpretation of the sacred marriage quest in myth and legend, gives a somewhat more positive spin to this seemingly passive (read, negative) interpretation of the female's role. As he explains:

Women, in the picture language of mythology, represents the totality of what can be known. The hero is the one who comes to know. As he progresses in the slow initiation which is life, the form of the goddess undergoes for him a series of transfigurations: she can never be greater than himself, though she can always promise more than he is yet capable of comprehending. She lures, she guides, she bids him burst his fetters. And if he can match her import, the two, the knower and the known, will be released from every limitation.[85]

Some contemporary films that best illustrate the sacred marriage quest for both men and women, and which are discussed at greater length in Chapter 5, include *The Natural*, *Bull Durham*, *Thelma and Louise*, and *The Piano*.

A second coming-of-age myth is the father quest. This quest requires the hero to find the father, or to find the father-potential existing inside of him or even her. The core assumption of this myth is that to truly know oneself, the individual must come to recognize the father or to be atoned (to become "as one") with him.[86]

The father quest, for example, is a central motif in the "Star Wars" trilogy, where Luke Skywalker, although he may not know it at the outset, is questing to find his father, and thus to find himself. In *The Natural*, Roy Hobbs is also questing, in part, to find the father figure inside him. In *Contact*, although Ellie's explicit quest is to discover extraterrestrial life by scanning the heavens for radio signals, her implicit quest is to "find" her father and mother. Since her father died when she was eleven years old, the film can be viewed, in part, as her attempt to rediscover her father, as she ultimately does when she is transported to the solar system Vega. It is on Vega that the alien she meets takes the form of her father as the easiest way for her to cope with this strange new reality. The father quest also appears in the film *Field of Dreams* where Ray Kinsella, needing to reconcile his relationship with his long-dead father, is offered a chance to do so on the magical field of dreams. In *The Lion King*, although Simba the lion already knows his father, upon his father's death, Simba rejects his destiny and refuses to take his father's place. Simba's quest, therefore, is to find his father again and thereby find his own father-potential.

Some of the films, discussed at length in Chapter 5, that best exemplify the father quest include *Field of Dreams* and *The Lion King*.

The Grail Myth

Cultures also often have myths about redemption from evil, sin, or destruction. The Grail quest or stories of crucified and resurrected heroes, such as that told in the Christ story, are representative of these types of myths.[87] In the Christian tradition, Jesus Christ, a Grail king in his own right, also offers the literal origin of the Grail quest. Indeed, legend has it that the Grail vessel, the object of all Grail questing in Western literature, is the cup of Joseph of Arimathea, the chalice of the Last Supper and the chalice that caught the blood from Christ's wounded side as he hung on the cross. Perhaps the most well-known Grail quest in Western literature is the myth of King Arthur, in which the Knights of the Round Table go in search of the Holy Grail, first witnessed by Percival in a vision. Their hope is that the Grail will restore Camelot to its ancient glory and will remove the magic spells that have devastated the land. As Evola puts it, "The Grail is the symbol of that which has been lost and must be found again."[88] Thus, on a larger level, Arthur himself is the Grail (or wounded Grail king) who attempts to heal a divided Britain (a "wasteland" of rival tribes). In his battles abroad to create a just empire, however, his nephew Mordred, who remains at home, usurps Arthur's rule and steals his wife Guinevere. In the ensuing battle between the forces loyal to Arthur and those loyal to Mordred, Arthur is mortally wounded. He is taken to the island of Avalon where he is healed by the magic wrought there by the women of the island. In the legend, however, his wounds open again every year while his people wait anxiously at home for his return. Thus, the hope remains that Arthur will one day return, resume his reign, and restore peace and tranquility to the land.[89] The triumphant return of Jesus Christ in the Christian tradition (known as the Second Coming) can also be likened to the long hoped-for return of the wounded Grail king. In Campbell's words, "the theme of the Grail romance is that the land, the country, the whole territory of concern has been laid waste. It is called a wasteland. And what is the nature of a wasteland? It is a land where everybody is living an inauthentic life." [90] It is a land longing for the redemption that only an enlightened hero or savior can provide.

An obvious modern-day example of the Grail quest is *Indiana Jones and the Last Crusade*. In this film Indy is questing for the cup of Joseph of Arimathea. The country that is a wasteland is Hitler's Germany where everyone is living an inauthentic life, following orders, creating a world order based on discipline and lack of individual courage or initiative. The Grail is needed to change the wasteland. Indy succeeds in finding the Grail, however, only when he is able to walk the higher spiritual way, to take a literal "leap of faith" and to negotiate the narrow path between fear and desire (represented by greed) and good and evil (represented by the difference between the devout and the nondevout man).

A number of the films discussed in the book employ the Grail quest in a somewhat less obvious fashion. In *The Lion King*, for example, the Pride Lands have become a wasteland under the dominion of Scar, Simba's evil uncle, and peace, tranquility, and bounty are restored to the land only when Simba returns and fights for his rightful place as leader. The "Star Wars" trilogy also tells a version of the Grail quest by its use of Arthurian legend and by the pending destruction of the universe by the forces of the evil Empire.

It is possible, indeed it is often likely, that various representations of the universal quest myth tell more than one version of the myth. The Star Wars trilogy, for example, tells a version of the father quest, the Grail quest, and, to a lesser degree, the sacred-marriage quest. As such, this trilogy is the focus of Chapter 8.

Probably one of the earliest Western models of the hero's perennial journey home, however, is Homer's *Odyssey*. The *Odyssey* not only provides an exemplar telling of the journey home, encompassing versions of the sacred marriage, the father quest, and the Grail quest; it also offers an explicit model for analyzing *The Natural* and an implicit model for many of the other films discussed in the book. Finally, the *Odyssey*, from an optimistic perspective, offers a significantly new way of thinking about the evolution of human consciousness, a move from a tribal worldview to a more global or ethically complete worldview. If, in other words, the history of evolution is the history of the emergence of consciousness from preconsciousness,[91] then the *Odyssey*, historically speaking, documents humanity's movement from preconsciousness to consciousness and presages, in many ways, our contemporary search for meaning and growth in an era of separation and fragmentation. More pessimistically, however, the *Iliad* and the *Odyssey* document the raging battle between two contrasting ways of life, the order of Mother Right, in which the goddess was "venerated as the giver and supporter of life as well as consumer of the dead" and the order of father rule, "with [its] ardor for righteous eloquence and a fury of fire and sword." [92] Ultimately, the *Odyssey* celebrates the triumph of patriarchy and father worship over matriarchy and mother worship and anticipates Western culture's collective guilt over such a matricide and their fear that although demoted or dismissed, the goddess-mother of the world, as Campbell explains it, "is to remain as an ever-present threat to their castle of reason, which is founded upon a soil that they consider to be dead but is actually alive, breathing, and threatening to shift." [93] The next chapter, therefore, reads the *Odyssey* in light of scholarly literature about the *Iliad* and the *Odyssey*, quest mythology, and Perennial philosophy.

3 Reframing Homer's *Odyssey*

"Odysseus then you are, O great contender,
of whom the glittering god with golden wand
spoke to me ever, and foretold
the black swift ship would carry you from Troy.
Put up your weapon in the sheath. We two
shall mingle and make love upon our bed.
So mutual trust may come of play and love."

To this I said:
                                    "Kirke, am I a boy,
that you should make me soft and doting now?
Here in this house you turned my men to swine;
now it is I myself you hold, enticing
into your chamber, to your dangerous bed,
to take my manhood when you have me stripped.
I mount no bed of love with you upon it.
Or swear me first a great oath if I do,
you'll work no more enchantment to my harm."
She swore at once, outright, as I demanded,
and after she had sworn, and bound herself,
I entered Kirke's flawless bed of love.

Homer, *Odyssey*, book X, 371–90

The *Odyssey* is probably one of the earliest Western models of
the hero's perennial journey home. As such, it offers not only
an exemplar version of the journey home, encompassing the
sacred marriage, the father quest, and the Grail quest, but also
an explicit model for analyzing *The Natural* in Chapter 4 and
an implicit model for discussing many of the other films explored in later chapters. Finally, the *Odyssey* documents a significant shift in the evolution of human consciousness, a movement away from matriarchy and the realm of preconsciousness
toward patriarchy and the realm of consciousness. The epic

poem, however, also intuits the dangers of consciousness and the guilt over the loss of the maternal and unconscious realm, while pointing toward the possibilities for transcendence to a higher state of consciousness that integrates rather than denies earlier phases of its construction. Such a move, as we will see, was central to the developing mythic consciousness of Western civilization.

In what follows I provide some brief history about Homer and the impact of both epic poems, I review scholarship that explores the cosmogonic cycle in the *Odyssey*, and I conclude with a discussion of the sacred marriage quest, the father quest, and the Grail quest in the *Odyssey*.

The impact of Homer's *Iliad* and *Odyssey* on the ancient world cannot be overestimated. As M. I. Finley asserts in *The World of Odysseus*:

No other poet, no other literary figure in all history, for that matter, occupied a place in the life of his people such as Homer's. He was their pre-eminent symbol of nationhood, the unimpeachable authority on their earliest history, and a decisive figure in the creation of their pantheon, as well as their most beloved and most widely quoted poet.[1]

Finley reports that of the 1,233 copies of books by authors with identifiable names found on fragments and scraps of papyrus in Egypt, 555 were copies of either the *Iliad* or the *Odyssey*. To put this in perspective, Plato was represented by only thirty-six papyri, while Aristotle was the author of six. In Finley's words, "If a Greek owned any books—that is, papyrus rolls—he was almost as likely to own the *Iliad* and *Odyssey* as anything from the rest of Greek literature."[2] Plato writes that many Greeks felt that Homer "educated Hellas and that he deserves to be taken up as an instructor in the management and culture of human affairs [and that] a man ought to regulate the whole of his life by following this poet."[3]

Despite these glowing assessments, very little is known of Homer. Although most scholars agree that he did exist—and that "Homer" was not just a name for anonymous—there is disagreement over whether he wrote one or both epics, or whether he was simply the recorder of long-lived stories that, until Homer's time, had been preserved by oral tradition. The date of the writing or recording of both poems, however, has been placed between 750 and 650 B.C.[4] The *Iliad* provides an account of the ten-year war between the Greeks and the Trojans, while the *Odyssey* offers a tale of Odysseus' ten years of wandering after the war and before his return to Ithaca and his wife and son.

The impact of both epic poems on Western civilization is so immeasurable that a complete listing of all of the scholarly and literary references to both works would be impossible. The following discussion of a number of scholarly essays about the *Odyssey*, therefore, is simply an attempt to frame some of the major issues invoked by the poem in reference to the developing mythic consciousness of Western civilization generally and to the hero quest specifically.

The Cosmogonic Cycle in Odysseus

Odysseus' quest—from Ithaca to Troy, around the Aegean and home again—as scholars have pointed out for decades, is more than a literal journey. It tells the story of Western civilization's evolution from preconsciousness (represented by matriarchy, the Garden before the Fall—a perfect state of unity, innocence, harmony, and unconsciousness) to consciousness (represented by the rise of modern civilization, law, and patriarchy—an imperfect or imbalanced state without God) to transconsciousness (represented by the "return" to the spiritual plane of harmony and unity with God and the feminine).[5] From the perspective of world mythology and Perennial philosophy, Odysseus' development, or the evolution of humanity, is our movement toward some ultimate telos or unity, which can be interpreted as our attempt to find our place in the universe, or our striving toward home. The epic poem also tells a version of the sacred marriage quest, in Odysseus' search for his wife Penelope; a version of the father quest, in Odysseus' son Telemachus' search for his father and for his own father-potential; and a version of the Grail quest, in its depiction of Ithaca as a wasteland in need of a returning Grail king.

Regardless of their specific analyses of the poem, most scholars agree that the *Odyssey* represents a significant shift in the developing consciousness of Western civilization. For George Lord, that shift was from a narrow tribal view of the world to a more global or ethically developed one. He asserts in "The *Odyssey* and the Western World," for example, that the *Odyssey* mediates between an old and a new conception of the hero. The old hero, Lord contends, is "the warrior hero with his narrow tribal loyalties, his jealous personal honor, and his fierce passions, who is, whatever his motives, the foe of reason, order and civilization." By contrast, the new hero is a "builder of civilization" who has "renounced personal glory and desperate courage." [6] Odysseus, over the course of the *Iliad* and the *Odyssey*, changes from the "old" hero to the "new" as he "grows in the course of his experiences from the shrewd 'sacker of cities' to the wise restorer of Ithaca." [7] Lord goes on to say that Odysseus' safe return and his triumph over his adversaries is not a coincidence, but rather is based "on his recognition and acceptance of his divine mission, and on harmonizing his own will with the divine will." [8] As such, "The *Odyssey* presents through the experiences of its hero the birth of personal and social ideals which are remarkably close to those of the Christian tradition and repudiates the old code of the heroic warriors at Troy as resolutely as does the *Aeneid*." [9]

George Dimock, Jr., in his essay "The Name of Odysseus," argues that the epic poem is about Odysseus' search for an identity, and thus implies that the historic shift in Western consciousness is the rise of individual consciousness from the realm of preconsciousness. Dimock traces such evolution through the analysis of a number of episodes in the *Odyssey*, focusing primarily, however, on Odysseus' adventures with Calypso. Calypso's and her island's allure can be likened, Dimmock argues, to the appeal of the maternal and the realm of preconsciousness or unconsciousness. He asserts, for example, that Calypso represents the danger of engulfment, as by a vast maternal sea. Even Calypso's name, as he points out,

suggests cover and concealment, or engulfing; she lives "in the midst of the sea" — the middle of nowhere, as Hermes almost remarks — and the whole struggle of the fifth book, indeed of the entire poem, is not to be engulfed by that sea. When the third great wave of Book Five breaks over Odysseus' head, Homer's words are: *ton de mega kyma kalypsen* — "and the great wave engulfed him." [10]

Dimock likens the safety and security of Calypso to a womb, but adds "as the Cyclops reminds us, the womb is after all a deadly place. In the womb one has no identity, no existence worthy of a name." [11]

Dimock argues that Odysseus' encounter with the Cyclops Polyphemus also represents the birth of identity as Odysseus goes from being "Nobody" — *outis* — to being able to shout his name to all: "To blind the son of Poseidon, and then to defy him, is both to challenge nature to do her worst, and to demonstrate her ultimate impotence to crush human identity." [12] Leaving Polyphemus' womb-like cave, like leaving Calypso's island, in Dimock's words, is "to pass from being 'nobody' to having a name, [it] is to be born. . . . We are born for trouble, the adventure of the Cyclops implies, yet to stay in the womb is to remain nobody." [13] The departure from Calypso and the blinding of the

Cyclops, in other words, represents humanity's separation from the realm of preconsciousness and the maternal, the rise of consciousness, and the birth of modern (male) civilization.[14]

Charles Taylor, Jr., in his essay "The Obstacles to Odysseus' Return," seems to concur with Dimock's assessment when he notes that Odysseus, facing many obstacles, is primarily dedicated to preserving his identity. Although the many temptations Odysseus faces appear, on the surface, to be sexual or moral in nature, they are more appropriately viewed as temptations to surrender his individuality.[15] Taylor points out that Odysseus' encounter with the lotus-eaters, for example, represents the attraction of forgetting his journey home: "The eater of the lotus becomes like an infant who is well-fed and contented, for the environment supports him without demanding anything in return. The lotus-eater loses all consciousness of self, of being an individual with origins of his own." [16] Although eating the lotus allows the individual to forget the cares and struggles faced in the world of action, it also erases any sense of individual consciousness. If, as Campbell reminds us, drama starts with the first act of disobedience (original sin) and stepping out of the dream time of the Garden of Eden,[17] then a permanent return to such a Garden would eliminate drama as well as the need for a protagonist and an antagonist. Such a return as the lotus-eaters invite, in other words, results in the death of drama, and hence, the death of identity.

The same type of engulfment and erasure of identity is represented in the *Odyssey* in the form of drowning at sea, which symbolically represents "the whole realm of the irrational . . . a compelling image of being overwhelmed from below, returning to the elemental." [18] As Taylor points out, such a threat represents vanishing "from the world of men . . . a fate far worse than death in battle." [19] Indeed, as he notes, Odysseus frequently laments not falling in battle with honor and acclaim at Troy since that would have been preferable to suffering an anonymous death by drowning at sea.

Despite the developing Western civilization's fear of preconsciousness and its accompanying erasure of identity—represented by Odysseus' individual quest for identity—there remains for the ancient Greeks a fascination with all things nonrational and unconscious. Taylor, for example, asserts that the many threats to Odysseus' identity symbolically suggest "the magnetic attraction of the unconscious in the human psyche":

In the picture of Odysseus clinging doggedly to the fig tree above Charybdis' whirlpool we find a striking representation of the struggle between conscious determination and the downward pull of subterranean forces . . . Odysseus' struggles for survival and identity convey more than the recognized Homeric values of fame and reputation as their ends. . . . part of the poem's appeal rest in the way it suggests the struggle for individual consciousness against the forces for primitive absorption in the instinctual world. This is a fundamental meaning of nearly every hero story. It is the struggle every human being experiences as he strives to achieve a degree of genuine individuality and self-awareness.[20]

Self-awareness, or the increased individuality that the hero, and hence the culture, gains can be equated with the rise of ego-consciousness. Such awareness, however, comes at a great price.

This emergence, although a necessary development for modern civilization, brings with it an "unconscious recognition that the earth-bound and all it stands for have been undervalued." [21] Ego-consciousness, in other words, invites a longing for the realm of the nonrational and the Mother, and a deep guilt over their loss. Odysseus, in other words, remains genuinely torn about the allure of Calypso's bed. (We will see such ambivalence, for example, played out, on the one hand, in Nuke LaLoosh's sexual attraction to Annie Savoy in the film *Bull Durham*, and on the other, his fear of getting lost in her all-consuming embrace. Drowning himself in the unconscious sea of her desire is seductive, yet Nuke remains conscious of the potential loss of himself (ego/fame) by that submersion.)

In the case of the *Odyssey*, the character of Odysseus stands in for pre-moderns' newly developing consciousness, their fear of falling back into matriarchal unconsciousness, but their guilt, nevertheless, over the loss of the mother/unconscious. Indeed, Jung asserts that the first act of the emerging individual consciousness from preconsciousness was matricide and that such an act brought with it a profound sense of guilt or longing for the loss of the mother and the irrational realm she represents. In Taylor's words, "The powerful feelings of guilt are derived ultimately from undue disregard for the claims of the non-rational . . . [which] springs essentially from the vengeance in the unconscious of the matriarchal Furies." [22]

Taylor asserts, however, that the guilt related to the rise of consciousness is not yet apparent in the *Odyssey* as it is in later works of literature that, with the rise of patriarchy, will exhibit a much clearer contempt for the feminine and the irrational. Taylor, citing Eric Neuman, also notes that "since the unconscious is generally given a feminine character, the depreciation of the unconscious in cultural development becomes confused with a belittling of feminine values." In the *Odyssey*, however, female characters, such as Penelope, Helen of Troy, Arete, Nausicaa, and the goddess Athena are treated with respect and admiration by Odysseus and his son Telemachus.[23] Taylor goes so far as to assert that Odysseus' quest for identity, as we will see, is actually "profoundly involved with the feminine." [24]

The Sacred Marriage Quest

Although Taylor does not directly refer to the sacred marriage quest mythology, it is apparent that he sees Odysseus' journey in light of this goal when he writes that "In seeking the wholeness of his being, he passes through intimate experience with various embodiments of archetypal women, each reflecting some aspect of what he as masculine hero lacks." [25] Although many of these encounters invite a return to matriarchal rule where his individual identity would be extinguished, and although he must undergo many trials related to these chthonic powers, the ultimate goal he seeks is reunion with his wife Penelope. We will see this story played out almost self-consciously in the film *The Natural* as we watch Roy Hobbs become "odyssied" by two different women, Harriet Bird and Memo Paris, who seek to extinguish his identity. It is only when he learns the lessons these women have to teach about overweening pride that he can finally make the sacred marriage with his childhood sweetheart Iris, who, like Penelope, waits many years for his return from the world of fame and fortune. Despite all the other women Roy encounters in his wanderings (like Odysseus), Iris is the one he seeks, she alone, as we will see, represents home and the true sacred marriage. Taylor notes, in speaking of the sacred marriage between Odysseus and Penelope:

Only Penelope shares Odysseus' intellectual alertness and is yet so alluring that she can represent the feminine counterpart of his heroic individuality. . . . In regaining Penelope Odysseus reclaims something of his own soul and so makes meaningful his resistance to the wiles of all the other women he meets on his way home. Having avoided submitting to the powers of the unconscious in a way which would destroy his identity, he is able finally to relate to them in the only way which will complete it.[26]

Thus, Penelope, his loyal wife, represents his true mate; she offers a balancing of darkness and light, consciousness and unconsciousness. Circe and Calypso signify the "lower feminine values" [27] — synonymous with the unconscious/preconscious — to which Odysseus must submit if he is to grow in consciousness. They represent, in other words, the cave or womblike cavern where the hero must spend time in passive reflection to possibly gain enlightenment. Odysseus must not remain in the realm of the unconscious forever, however, or risk the extinction of self. In seeking a higher level of consciousness (transconsciousness), however, he must be willing to submit to the "higher feminine values," [28] in order to displace or decenter self in favor of Self.[29] The sacred marriage with his wife Penelope, the goddess Athena's earthly representative, represents one means of achieving this higher consciousness. Campbell asserts something similar when he writes that "Since Penelope is the only woman in the book who is not of a magical category, it is clear . . . that Odysseus' meeting with Circe, Calypso, and Nausicaa represent psychological adventures in the mythic realm of the archetype of the soul, where the male must *experience* the import of the female before he can meet her perfectly in life." [30] Thus the *Odyssey* offers one of the earliest examples in Western literature of the sacred marriage quest, a mythic story that has been repeatedly told, in numerous shapes and forms, in the art and literature of the past 2,500 years. In the next chapter, we will see the sacred marriage quest played out in such contemporary films as *The Natural*, *Bull Durham*, *The Piano*, and *Thelma and Louise*.

The Grail Quest

Although somewhat less apparent than the sacred marriage quest, the *Odyssey* tells a version of the Grail quest as well. Odysseus, the wandering Grail king, like King Arthur in Arthurian legend, does battle with his country's enemies abroad (in the *Iliad*) only to face deceit and treachery at home. Odysseus' faithless neighbors and friends, assuming he was killed during or after the battle of Troy, have moved in to claim his house, his hospitality, and his wife are their own. Odysseus' son Telemachus, in the second book of the *Odyssey*, describes the wasteland that these faithless suitors have created to the Ithacan Assembly:

My distinguished father is lost, who ruled among you once, mild as a father, and there is now this greater evil still: my home and all I have are being ruined. Mother wants no suitors, but like a pack they came — sons of the best men here among them . . . these men spend their days around our house killing our beeves and sheep and fatted goats, carousing, soaking up our good dark wine, not caring what they do. They squander everything. We have no strong Odysseus to defend us, and as to putting up a fight our-selves — we'd only show our incompetence in arms. Expel them, yes, if I only had the power; the whole thing's out of hand, insufferable. My house is being plundered: is this courtesy? Where is your indignation? Where is your shame?[31]

It is clear from Telemachus' words that King Odysseus' home, possibly acting as a metaphor for Ithaca itself, has been turned into a wasteland that only the Grail king himself can put right. A version of the Grail quest, as we will see, is played out at length in *The Lion King*, when Mustafa, the reigning king at Pride Rock, is killed through treachery and deceit. The pretender to the throne, Scar (like Mordred in Arthurian legend), has turned the land into a wasteland, in this case through overgrazing and the unfair allocation of resources. It takes the self-exiled son Simba, returning as mature Grail king, to battle the usurper and put the land to rights. Although it is unclear in *The Lion King* whether Scar takes Mustafa's mate Sarabi as his own (the homosexual undertones in the film would certainly not make sense if he did), the parallels to the *Odyssey* and other versions of the Grail quest are otherwise unmistakable.

In the *Odyssey*, Odysseus' wife Penelope does not willingly submit to the attentions of the suitors who have taken over her house. Although she con-tinually refuses their offers of marriage, she is ultimately forced to chose one in a contest of archery skill and strength; she will marry whoever can bend and string Odysseus' mighty bow and successfully thread an arrow through a series of targets. Odysseus, however, returning in the disguise of an old beggar, together with his son Telemachus, develops a plan not only to gain revenge but also to eliminate the plague that these suitors represent. The dramatic scene in which Odysseus, still in disguise, strings his own bow, shoots the targets, and, with the help of his son, slaughters the unfaithful suitors, represents the triumphant return of the Grail king who demonstrates his prowess and ability to lead once again while also ridding his homeland of the treachery and deceit that have turned it into a wasteland. This early ver-sion of the Grail quest, predating the rise of Christianity and the actual devel-opment of the mythology surrounding the Holy Grail, signifies the enduring importance of this archetypal story in Western consciousness. Not surpris-ingly, we will see the Grail quest at work in such contemporary films as *The Natural* (discussed in Chapter 4) and *The Lion King* and *Field of Dreams* (the focus of Chapter 5).

The Father Quest

Odysseus' son Telemachus, like his father, is on a quest of his own—to find his wandering father, and, in the process, to discover the father-potential that will allow him to grow to full maturity as a man. He attempts the first when, with the help of the goddess Athena, he leaves Troy in search of news of his father. He attempts the second when he aids his returning father in eliminating the unwanted suitors from his home.

Athena explains Telemachus' father quest to him and the importance it holds for his own individuation when she tells him:

Then here's a course for you, if you agree: get a sound craft afloat with twenty oars and go abroad for news of your lost father, perhaps a traveler's tale, or rumored fame issued from Zeus abroad in the world of men. Talk to the noble sage at Pylos, Nestor, then go to Menelaos, the red-haired king at Sparta, last man home of all the Akhaians. If you should learn your father is alive and coming home, you could hold out a year. Or if you learn that he is dead and gone, then you could come back to your own dear country and raise a mound for him, and bury his gear, with all the funereal honors due a man, and give your mother to another husband. When you have done all this, or seen it done, it will be time to ponder concerning these contenders in your house—how you should kill them, outright or by guile. You need not bear this insolence of theirs, you are a child no longer. Have you heard what glory Orestes won when he cut down that two-faced man, Aigisthos, for killing his illustrious father? Dear friend, you are tall and well set-up, I see; be brave—you, too—and men in times to come will speak of you respectfully.[32]

Although Telemachus does not find his father, he does find his father-potential. His journey seasons him; it gives him great insight into his father's character and the respect that others have for Odysseus. Ultimately, his journey prepares him to assist his father in ridding Ithaca of the suitors that have polluted his home. As mentioned in Chapter 2, we will see the father quest emerge in such contemporary films as *Contact*, *Field of Dreams*, and *The Lion King*.

In sum, the *Odyssey*, not only offers fully articulated versions of the Grail quest, the sacred marriage quest, and the father quest; it also can be read in terms of the developing consciousness of Western civilization. Homer's masterpiece illuminates a dramatic shift in the understanding of humanity's relationship to the cosmos—a movement away from matriarchy and the realm of preconsciousness toward patriarchy and the realm of consciousness. Ultimately, according to Taylor, the lesson we learn from the *Odyssey*, and one that is surely still relevant today, is that "man must be conscious to be human, but he must come to terms with the unconscious to be whole. Divided as we have been since Homer's time by our awareness of the duality of human nature, the *Odyssey* continues to impress us with its vital image of an integrated man." [33] Odysseus' quest, in other words, is one of the first in a long line of epic stories in Western culture of what it means to be human, to find ourselves, and to go home.

4 The Sacred Marriage Quest in American Film

Nuke: Crash once called a woman's, uh . . . pussy—y'know how the hair kinda makes a "V" shape? —Well he calls it the Bermuda Triangle. He said a man can get lost in there and never be heard from again.

Annie: What a nasty thing to say.

Nuke: He didn't mean it nasty. He said that gettin' lost and disappearing from the face of the earth was sometimes a good thing to do—especially like that. But he also said there's a time for discipline, and I think this is one of those.

—*Bull Durham*

What a death!
What a chance!
What a surprise!
My will has chosen life!?
Still it has spooked me, and many others besides!

—Ada, *The Piano*

I feel awake, wide-awake. I don't think I ever remember feeling this way. Everything seems different.

—Thelma, *Thelma and Louise*

All of the films discussed in this chapter—*The Natural, Bull Durham, The Piano,* and *Thelma and Louise*—tell the story of the sacred marriage with a god/goddess consort. In each case a mythic hero or heroine makes a literal and a psychological journey from a place of ignorance/innocence to knowledge/transcendence guided by another male or female figure and is ultimately rewarded by a sexual/spiritual union with that figure. Roy Hobbs' journey in *The Natural* takes him more than sixteen years, Crash Davis in *Bull Durham* travels from town to town during the entire length of his baseball career. Ada's journey to New Zealand in *The Piano* takes place over the course of a season or two, while Thelma and Louise complete their road trip over a long weekend in *Thelma and Louise*. Despite the length of their journeys, however, only when the lessons to be learned are complete is the hero prepared to return home, whether home is a farm in rural Illinois (*The Natural*), the home of the beloved (*Bull Durham* and *The Piano*), or a transcendent home in the universe (*Thelma and Louise*). After a brief discussion of the sacred marriage quest and the mother quest implicitly embedded inside of this quest, I explore each of the above mentioned films, focusing primarily on the role of the sacred marriage in the hero or heroine's quest for home. The chapter concludes with a discussion that problematizes the sacred marriage quest as it applies to each of the films analyzed.

The Sacred Marriage Quest

The hero's sacred marriage with a god or goddess figure often represents a sexual union as well as a spiritual maturation. For the male hero, this "mystical marriage of the triumphant hero-soul with the Queen Goddess of the world," as Campbell explains it, is "the ultimate adventure, when all the barriers and ogres have been overcome."[1] The woman with whom the hero makes the sacred marriage, as "Queen Goddess," is often of supernatural origins. Since all women are the goddess's earthly representative, however, the sacred marriage can occur between mortals as well. Such a marriage is often a boon for the hero, since it can represent the culmination of his quest. Odysseus' reunion with his wife Penelope—the goddess Athena's earthly incarnation—for example, represents the goal of all of his wanderings.

Although the male hero is the active seeker in the world of unseen events, the goddess with whom he will make the sacred marriage represents the totality of all that can be known.[2] In Campbell's words, the goddess

is the paragon of all paragons of beauty, the reply to all desire, the bliss-bestowing goal of every hero's earthly and unearthly request. She is mother, sister, mistress, bride. Whatever in the world has lured, whatever has seemed to promise joy, had been premonitory of her existence. . . . For she is the incarnation of the promise of perfection; the soul's assurance that at the conclusion of its exile in a world of organized inadequacies, the bliss that once was know will be known again.[3]

According to Campbell, "the bliss that was once known" refers to the hero's return to the mother, both the personal mother known to the suckling child and the impersonal mother known to all in the era of preconsciousness. Thus, the sacred marriage quest, for male protagonists, has a mother quest embedded in it as well. The goddess/mother figure that he seeks, on the one hand, represents "the comforting, the nourishing, the 'good' mother—young and beautiful—who was know to us, and even tasted, in the remotest past." [4] This goddess/mother figure, however, has a Janus face. Not only nourishing and comforting, like the goddess Kali she can be the all-devouring destroyer as well. Thus she represents, in both a Jungian/Freudian sense and in a larger mythic sense:

the "bad" mother too— (1) the absent, unattainable mother, against whom aggressive fantasies are directed, and from whom counter-aggression is feared; (2) the hampering, forbidding, punishing mother; (3) the mother who would hold to herself the growing child trying to push away; and finally (4) the desired but forbidden mother (Oedipus complex) whose presence is a lure to dangerous desire (castration complex)—persists in the hidden land of the adult's infant recollection and is sometimes even the greater force. She is at the root of such unattainable great goddess figures.[5]

For this reason, the sacred marriage as a return to the mother, as much as it is desired by the male hero, may also be filled with fear and trepidation since such a return may represent a literal death, or at least the death of ego-consciousness, as the hero returns to the source of being beyond time and consciousness. Such a return, in other words, as discussed in Chapter 2, represented a double-edged sword for the emerging ego-consciousness of the pre-moderns. As Jung explains, in order to evolve to the next level of consciousness the hero must delve into the archetypal preconscious. He must not, however, remain there indefinitely. The hero's journey, in other words, is both a descent into the world of liminal and passive unconsciousness and an ascent into consciousness and the world of action.

Thus Odysseus' encounters with the goddesses Calypso and Circe can be viewed, in one interpretation, as incomplete sacred marriages, and, in another interpretation, as mother quests embedded in his larger quest for the sacred marriage. Both goddesses have much to teach him. They will nurture and comfort him and as well as test and punish him. Part of Odysseus' attraction to both figures is their offer of blissful forgetfulness from the pain of earthly struggles. Both goddesses represent the lure of the return to preconsciousness, to a state of oneness beyond the duality of the conscious plane of human action and events. If Odysseus is to complete his hero's journey, however, he must not remain with Circe or Calypso. He must be receptive and humble enough to learn the lessons only they can teach, but be strong enough to resist the temptation to remain with them for an eternity. It is only when he had learned these lessons and returns to his wife Penelope that the sacred marriage can be consummated.

By contrast, when the hero of the quest is female, "she is the one who, by her qualities, her beauty, or her yearning, is fit to become the consort of an immortal. Then the heavenly husband descends to her and conducts her to his bed, whether she will or no. And if she has shunned him, the scales fall from her eyes; if she has sought him, her desire finds its peace." [6] Such a sacred marriage for the heroine, for example, as Campbell points out, is celebrated by the Greek Orthodox and Catholic churches in the Feast of the Assumption, where "The Virgin Mary is taken up into the bridal chamber of heaven, where the King of Kings sits on his starry throne." [7] Another example is the Roman god Jupiter giving Psyche, at the completion of her tasks, the elixir of immortality that would allow her to unite with Cupid, her beloved, forever. Although there is very little scholarly discussion about the sacred marriage quest for women — most of the emphasis being on the hero's marriage quest — implicit in the sacred marriage quest for women is also the notion of a father quest. Finding the true mate for female protagonists, in other words, has echoes of finding the father as well.

This discussion of the sacred marriage quest for both male and female protagonists implicitly raises some questions about the relationship among the sacred marriage quest, the father quest, and the mother quest. Although the mother quest is the obvious counterpart to the father quest, it has received little attention in literature, art, and film, and the scholarship about them. Although numerous stories in antiquity tell versions of the mother quest, such as Persephone's marriage with the god of the underworld and her seasonal return to her mother Demeter, or various stories told about supplicants' return to the Egyptian goddess Isis, in the contemporary era, little attention has been paid to the notion of a mother quest as an end in itself. As a result, while the next chapter focuses specifically on the father quest in American film, there is no separate chapter in this book on the mother quest. Janice Rushing, in her analysis of the films *Alien* and *Aliens*, comes the closest of any scholar of myth to articulating what the mother quest looks like in contemporary film and culture. Her critique of these films is highly recommended for those interested in exploring this particular mythic manifestation further.[8] Thus, although what follows does not examine the mother quest in specific films, it explores the nature of the mother quest generally as well as several reasons why it has received so little attention since the close of the Bronze Age. This discussion, as we will see, rather than being tangential, is actually central to understanding the analysis of the sacred marriage quest in American film that constitutes the bulk of this chapter.

The Mother Quest

Why has so little attention been paid to the mother quest in the art and literature of Western culture over the past 2,000 years? One reason may be that, historically speaking, matrilineal lines have been much more certain that patrilineal. Proof of parentage, due in part to the biology of gestation, means that an infant's mother is often easy to discern while an infant's father may be less so. As a result, there may appear a less obvious need to go questing for a mother since she is already present and assured, while there is a more obvious need to find a possibly absent father.

Although the mother-origin on the surface seems well known, paradoxically, in so far as the mother-origin writ large is concerned, it may be the least well known. Living under the rule of the father—or patriarchy—has been as a direct result of the overthrow of mother rule—or matriarchy. This has resulted in the suppression or reinterpretation of myths related to the mother and mother worship. Such "mythic defamation," [9] as Joseph Campbell refers to it, occurred toward the end of the Bronze Age when, as he writes, "the old cosmology and mythologies of the goddess mother were radically transformed, reinterpreted, and in large measure even suppressed, by those suddenly intrusive patriarchal warrior tribesmen whose traditions have come down to us chiefly in the Old Testaments and in the myths of Greece." [10]

Prior to this suppression or eradication of mother myths and rites, mother worship was extensive throughout the ancient world. As Campbell explains:

The entire ancient world, from Asia Minor to the Nile and from Greece to the Indus Valley, abounds in figurines of the naked female form, in various attitudes, of the all-supporting, all-including goddess: her two hands offering her breasts; her left pointing to her genitals and the right offering her left breast; nursing or fondling a male child; standing upright among beasts, arms extended, holding tokens—stalks, flowers, serpents, doves or other signs. Such figurines are demonstrably related, furthermore, to the well-known Bronze Age myths and cults of the Great Goddess of many names.[11]

This mother goddess held sway over all creation, symbolizing both the life-giving powers of birth and the life-taking powers of death. As "undivided goddess," [12] she was mother, mistress, and virgin. In her earliest incarnations she was "one-in-herself," without creator or consort, who gave birth to all being through the Immaculate Conception and later consumed the dead as they returned to her bosom. In later incarnations she was made fertile by a male consort, often her son (since she was the creator of all) who was frequently killed and reborn ("The king is dead, long live the king"). Thus her consort, like she herself, was often represented by the moon, which waxes and wanes in its cycle, or by the snake, which sloughs its skin only to be made new, or eats its tail as a symbol of the endless circle of life.

The worship of this mother goddess, unlike the male god worship that was to succeed it, held "an essentially organic, vegetal, non-heroic view of the nature and necessities of life," a view that Campbell explains was directly opposed to the view of the male-dominated societies that were emerging.[13] Unlike their male counterparts who were concerned with war, glory, and plunder, these goddesses, Whitmont explains, "were not at all concerned with conquest and territorial expansion. Those were male obsessions. Rather, these goddesses monitored the life cycle throughout its phases: birth, growth, love, death, and rebirth." [14]

Thus, it became the primary mission for mythic heroes of the emerging Iron Age to eradicate goddess worship by killing or conquering her representatives. As Campbell explains:

The early Iron Age literatures both of Aryan Greece and Rome and of the neighboring Semitic Levant are alive with variants of the conquest by a shining hero of the dark . . . disparaged monster of the earlier order of godhood, from whose coils some treasure was to be won: a fair land, a maid, a boon of gold, or simply freedom from the tyranny of the impugned monster itself.[15]

Think, for example, of the victory of Zeus over Typhon, the youngest child of Gaea, which ensured the reign of the male gods on Olympus over that of the goddess mother. Or think of Perseus slaying Medusa, queen of the Gorgons, whose hair was of hissing serpents and whose glance could turn men to stone. Or think of Yahweh's victory, in the Old Testament, over the sea serpent Leviathan. Or remember the Greek sun god Apollo, who shot the python. In almost all of these cases the monster appears as a snake or a serpent — the serpent being the traditional symbol of the goddess and of her consort. Thus, in slaying the snake these heroes of the Iron Age were attempting to eradicate the goddess herself. Additionally, in each of these acts of matricide, as was discussed in Chapter 2, all that was vile or dark was attributed to the old mother worship, whereas all that was noble and good was attributed to the new gods. This was so, even though, as Campbell explains, in "mother myths and rites the light and dark aspect of the mixed thing that is life had been honored equally and together." [16]

To the extent then that the mother goddess of antiquity was reduced solely to her evil or murderous nature—a "divided goddess" [17]—it is not surprising that the mother quest in Western consciousness would have lost its mythic appeal as an end in itself, and would only be retained, in the sacred marriage quest, as a dark chamber through which the hero must pass, but where he should not, at his peril, linger or remain. To the extent, in other words, that a quest to find the mother is equated with a return to preconsciousness, such a journey may be perceived as regressive rather than transcendent, a stop along the way rather than a final destination. Such a meeting with the goddess mother, as we have seen in the *Odyssey*, was equated by the premoderns with being consumed by the preconscious forces that they had fought so desperately to escape.

In the time of the Homeric Greeks, however, mother worship, although subdued, was not entirely suppressed. Indeed, "numerous vestiges survive of a pre-Homeric mythology in which the place of honor was held, not by a male god of the sunny Olympic pantheon, but by a goddess, darkly ominous, who might appear as one, two, three or many, and was the mother of both the living and the dead." [18] Such worship is evidenced in the story of Demeter and Persephone, the classic Greek mother quest, in which Persephone, queen of the underworld, returns once yearly to her mother Demeter, goddess of the earth. This myth is reenacted in the Eleusian mysteries, itself a type of mother quest, in which Demeter's child and consort, Ploutos (or Plutus), "return[s] to her bosom in death (or, according to another image, in marriage), [and] the god is reborn." [19] This myth of a return to the goddess mother was reenacted when an initiate into the mysteries who contemplated the goddess mother, "became detached reflectively from the fate of his mortal frame (symbolically, the son who dies), and identifie[d] with the principle that is ever reborn, the Being of all being (the serpent father)." [20]

Unlike in Greece, where, according to Campbell "the patriarchal gods did not exterminate, but married, the goddess of the land," instead "in Biblical mythology all the goddesses were exterminated—or, at least, were supposed to have been." [21] Perhaps the Judeo-Christian deathblow to the mother comes in the book of Genesis, where Eve, a vestige of the mother of all, rather than creating Adam as her son and consort (the typical motif of goddess myths of antiquity), is created from him. In the story of the Garden of Eden, even the initial act of creation has been denied her. It is not so easy, however, as Campbell asserts, to completely eliminate the goddess. Speaking of this inversion of Eve's function, he writes:

"The man," we read, "called his wife's name Eve, because she was the mother of all living." As the mother of all living, Eve, herself, then, must be recognized as the missing anthropomorphic aspect of the mother-goddess. And Adam, therefore, must have been her son as well as spouse: for the legend of the rib is clearly a patriarchal inversion (giving precedence to the male) of the earlier myth of the hero born from the goddess Earth, who returns to her to be reborn.[22]

In one final insult to the goddess, the snake, rather than representing Eve's consort, betrays her to become the cause of her downfall.

The division of the goddess mother of antiquity was now complete. Her darker nature, represented by the mistress/harlot and devouring mother, was repressed into the realm of the unconscious, while her lighter nature, representing the virgin and the good and nurturing mother,[23] was celebrated, most prominently in Christianity, in the form of the Virgin Mary: "Queen of Martyrs," "Mystical Rose," "Gate of Heaven," and mother of God. The Virgin Mary is a goddess figure purged of any negative, destructive, or sexual impulses (such "bad" imagery is instead reserved for the prostitute Mary Magdalene before she repents her evil ways). Ultimately, the Christian reduction of mother worship to the figure of the Virgin Mary, a goddess figure stripped of a good deal of the yin/yang balance of earlier goddesses, may also account for the decreased emphasis on the mother quest in mythic art and literature; there is just not as much there, in other words, for which to search.

Although the mother quest in its contemporary manifestations, at its best, is depicted as a step along the way to the sacred marriage rather than as a destination in itself, the father quest, to the contrary, is implicitly viewed as a goal in itself. Finding the father or being atoned with him (i.e., to be "at one" with the heavenly father God in Judeo-Christian tradition) bears echoes of the transcendent. This is the case, paradoxically, despite the realization that, as Campbell notes, "the patriarchal point of view is distinguished from the earlier archaic view by its setting apart of all pairs-of-opposites—male and female, life and death, true and false, good and evil—as though they were absolutes in themselves and not merely aspects of the larger entity of life." [24] The father quest, in other words, is a partial or incomplete journey that does not reunite the opposites of life into a true unity of being.

Ultimately, both the father quest and the mother quest may best be viewed as steps along the path that may lead to the transcendent. Insofar as the transcendent represents the ultimately awareness of the unity of all things, it calls for the balancing of all energies—darkness and light, life and death, heaven and earth, male and female, and father and mother. Although early goddess worship seemed to offer this balance to the initiated, it may be that a full appreciation of this harmony is now no longer possible since, as a result of the rise of patriarchy we have fallen from grace and entered the imperfect and imbalanced realm of consciousness. A return to the mother of preconsciousness may no longer be possible. Since we have quested in the realm of sin, sadness, and separation, we can no longer go "home." As such, what is necessary is not a return to preconsciousness, but rather a questing after transconsciousness, a fashioning of a new home in the universe. Such a quest will surely require a reassertion of the value of the mother quest, and a balancing of this quest with the father quest and the sacred marriage quest as well. Unless such awareness pervades a Western culture so deeply imbued with the myths of the father, the mother quest, in all its complexity and depth, may be doomed to continued obscurity or bloodless and superficial interpretation. More problematically, however, if the mother quest is not reinvigorated with meaning and urgency, it may be that Western culture will "miss the boat" and fail to complete the journey for home, a journey that we were predestined to make, but may not be predestined to complete.

Although the sacred marriage quest, in one form or another, forms the basis of many Hollywood films, one is struck by the realization that two of the most beloved contemporary films about baseball, *The Natural* and *Bull Durham*, have less to do with baseball, per se, than they do with the importance of making the sacred marriage and receiving guidance from a goddess/mother's wisdom. In *The Natural* and *Bull Durham*, the male protagonists' task is not only to complete a mythic journey, but to be united in sacred marriage with a goddess/mother figure who reveals secrets that help them reach enlightenment and also share their boon with the culture at large. By contrast, in *The Piano*, the protagonist is female. Thus her hero task is to come to recognize and join in a sexual/spiritual union with an appropriate god/husband figure while also coming to terms with the goddess/great mother of preconscious-ness. *Thelma and Louise* provides an interesting twist on the sacred marriage insofar as both women in the film make various attempts at sacred marriages with various men over the course of the film; however, none are deemed ap-propriate. By the film's conclusion, in one interpretation, the women, sealing their fate with a passionate embrace, instead confirm the sacred marriage with each other (and possibly return to the goddess/great mother of preconscious-ness) when they sail their car over the edge of the cliff and into the cavernous womb/tomb of the Grand Canyon.

The remainder of this chapter explores the sacred marriage as a journey home in each of the aforementioned films. Although the focus of the analysis will be on the sacred marriage quest in each film, the discussion, at any given time, might include references to the Grail quest, the mother quest, the father quest, or other relevant mythic motifs. The reason is that although stories may emphasize certain elements of the hero quest, such as the sacred marriage, other elements are often present as well. Mythic themes, in other words, do not stand alone, but rather implicate each other. Although any interpretive lens emphasizes certain features of a discourse while de-emphasizing others, as an inductive critic my first allegiance is to the discourse rather than to the critical lens. Interpretations are often richer when they allow not chaos, or "anything goes," but rather a certain amount of critical play. As such, the fol-lowing readings remain open to the critical possibilities, suggested by each film, within the broader lens of mythic criticism. Finally, the chapter con-cludes with a discussion that problematizes the sacred marriage generally, and its development specifically in the various films discussed.

The Natural

The Natural (1984), directed by Phil Dusenberry and based loosely on the Bernard Malamud novel of the same name, was a slow-building commercial success. Although it generated only $25 million in box-office sales during its first year of release, it went on to become one of the most beloved baseball movies of all time and has achieved an extensive repeat viewership in video release.[25]

The Natural represents a self-conscious interpretation of Homer's *Iliad* and *Odyssey*. Roy Hobbs (Robert Redford) is the Odyssean hero. His jour-ney is from a small town where he plays baseball with his father to the major leagues in the big city, then back to that same town where he once again will play ball, but this time with his own son. The lessons that he learns, and that we as a culture are invited to learn, involve the value of a human life, the danger of ego-fulfilling pride, and the importance of giving back to the human community. Like Odysseus, Roy actually undertakes two journeys; the first is "a short-lived exploration for ego-gratifying fame." [26] Like Odysseus in the *Iliad*, for whom honor and glory on the battlefields of Troy are the markers of success, Roy attempts greatness through records, trophies and sexual conquests. This shallow quest leads him nowhere except into sixteen years of obscurity. This time in oblivion, however, gives him a chance to rethink his journey's goals. It is on his second journey, the equivalent of Odysseus' ten years of wandering, that Roy truly undertakes a heroic transformation when he lets go of ego-fulfillment and overweening pride, is redeemed in the human community, and returns home to make the sacred marriage with Iris (Glenn Close), his Penelope.

The Natural also tells a version of the father quest and the Grail quest. Roy Hobbs, who loses his own father at an early age, unconsciously spends most of the film searching for the father figure within him. By the end of the film he finally fulfills this role when he recognizes his own son and takes on the role of father-mentor that his own father had played so many years before. The Grail quest is represented by the success that Roy ultimately brings to the "wasteland" professional baseball team, the New York Knights. It is his phenomenal success at bat that brings the team out of a lengthy losing streak and puts them on the road toward capturing the pennant. Although both the father quest and the Grail quest will be discussed in what follows (since it would do violence to a mythic analysis of the film to simply ignore their presence), the emphasis is on the sacred marriage since it receives the greatest attention in the film.

The film begins at a train station, somewhere in America. Roy is waiting for the train that will carry him to his destiny—his tryout with the Chicago Cubs and a chance to play major-league ball. In mythological terms he has voluntarily moved to the threshold and has accepted the "call to adventure." [27] As he waits, the film flashes back to a slow-motion image of Roy as a young boy playing catch with his father in an Edenic setting of endless fields of alfalfa. His father speaks the first words of the film in voice-over when he intones, "You've got a gift, Roy. But it is not enough, you gotta develop it. Rely too much on your gift and you're gonna fail." In the brief series of scenes that follow we witness his father's sudden death, Roy's grief at his father's passing, and a lightning bolt striking the oak tree under which his father died. We then see Roy as a young boy fashioning a baseball bat from the wood of that tree and inscribing it with the name "Wonderboy."

The bat is a talisman, a gift from the Norse god of thunder, or more important, a legacy from his father who has actually given Roy three important gifts: the bat—a magical Excalibur that will bring him success no ordinary bat might bring, the love and support to believe in himself and what he can accomplish, and those words of wisdom—reminding him of the false promises of "natural" talent and the deadly sin of overweening pride. All three are gifts that will serve Roy well on his Odyssean journey to find himself and his worth, in both professional baseball and in life.

Along the way there will be three significant women in his life: Iris, his Penelope and the woman with whom he eventually makes the sacred marriage; Harriet Bird, his first temptress, the Circe who sends him off into Odyssean oblivion for sixteen years after attempting his murder; and Memo Paris, his Calypso, who lulls him into a sexual oblivion where he almost forgets himself and abandons his quest to "be the best there ever was" in baseball.

Iris, the first woman in Roy's life, is his hometown sweetheart. She is also the woman he loves and expects to marry, despite the fact that he has a dream of going to Chicago to play professional baseball. When that opportunity occurs there is never any question that Roy will go and that Iris, despite a promise of future marriage, will wait at home for his return like Odysseus' Penelope.

In a striking comparison of two of the women that will shape his life, the camera cuts from a romantic and soft-focused image of Iris dressed in white saying goodbye to Roy before that first train trip to Chicago, to Harriet Bird, Roy's first temptress, whom he meets on the train, literally "dressed to kill" in black. It is during this train trip that Roy meets "The Whammer," a young fame-monger who challenges Hobbs to a contest—to strike him out with three pitches. When Roy succeeds, he becomes a local hero for a crowd of onlookers while also getting the attention of Harriet Bird, who is also watching with keen interest. Later that evening, while Roy is eating dinner in the empty dining car, Harriet approaches him, saying, "Hello, I'm Harriet Bird. Have you ever read Homer?" To which Roy naively replies, "The only Homer I know has four bases on it." By these comments the film self-consciously acknowledges Roy as an Odyssean hero while placing Bird squarely in the role of a Calypso- or Circe-like temptress. It is clear, however, that like Odysseus succumbing to

Circe's power, Roy has been hypnotically seduced by Harriet's sexual charm and wit. Still flush with his victory over the Whammer, he tells her that all he wants from life is for people to say " 'There goes Roy Hobbs, the best there ever was.' What else is there?" Ego-fulfillment and overweening pride have become his central goals in life.

Harriet Bird, dressed in diaphanous black from head to foot, later appears at Roy's hotel in Chicago. Summoning him to her room, he stands in the doorway, surprised that she has found him. Like an ill-fated omen, she demands, "Roy, will you be the best there ever was in the game?" Upon his affirmative reply, she covers her face with a black lace "bridal veil," shoots him in the stomach, and then seems to disappear into thin air. (We later learn of her fetish for destroying successful sports figures and her previous success in murdering a star football player and an Olympic athlete.) Like the goddess Circe, Harriet Bird has "odyssied" Roy Hobbs; she has given him trouble that will sidetrack him and send him into obscurity for sixteen years of anonymous wandering, equivalent to the years Odysseus spends in unconscious revel on Circe's island. Harriet has succeeded in stealing his consciousness, his ego-identity, and his chance at fame. The "maternal" has cast him back into the realm of preconsciousness to teach him a lesson about hubris, and while his story might have ended here, Roy, like Odysseus, will struggle against this fate to emerge from his drowning humbled and strengthened by Circe/Harriet's lesson.

In the next scene, sixteen years later, we find ourselves on the practice field of the Knights, a professional baseball team managed by "Pop" Fisher (Wilfred Brimley). As we witness the hopeless attempts of team members to complete plays or pitch or bat like the professionals they supposedly are, Fisher complains to his assistant coach, "I'm wet nurse to a dead from the neck up, last-place team." As if to emphasize the talent drought that he faces, his attempts to drink from the rusted water fountain in the dugout are to no avail. We are witnessing the wasteland of T. S. Eliot's Fisher King. Everything is dead or dying, morale and hope are nonexistent, and the team, experiencing its worst losing streak in its history, is parched for a sip of success. This is a country deeply in need of a Grail.

At this exact moment, Roy Hobbs, like an unassuming savior, emerges quietly from out of the dark clubhouse entrance that leads to the field. Back-lit, he materializes in silhouette from shadowy darkness into the light of day. When asked by Pop Fisher where he is from, he replies, "Does it matter? It took me sixteen years to get here." Like a young King Arthur or a Jesus of Nazareth, Roy is the hero of obscure origins who has come to restore the wasteland and make it fruitful again. This motif will be repeated throughout the film as Roy's fame grows and other ballplayers, sportscasters, and sports columnists try unsuccessfully to discover who he is and where he comes from.

The first trial or obstacle that Roy must overcome, however, is Pop. Angry that a talent scout sent Roy, a middle-aged rookie with no record in either the minors or majors, Pop refuses to play Roy, instead forcing him to sit the bench for most of the season. Finally, after a major fight in which Roy threatens to leave the team, Pop agrees to play him. At the very next batting practice Roy wows everyone as he hits ball after ball into the stands. The import of this event is not lost on the film-viewing audience. When Pop goes to the water fountain, for perhaps the first time in years he is able to take a drink of water. Even though Pop may not yet realize it, it is as if the drought is over. The young Grail hero is about to breathe life into the desolate wasteland. Pop comments to Roy, "I don't believe it, all these years and you never played organized ball?" Roy responds, in typical Odyssean understatement, "Well, I sorta got sidetracked."

At the very next game, when all hope for a win seems lost, Pop sends Roy in to bat. Pop urges Hobbs to "knock the cover off the ball," little knowing that Roy will mythically oblige. As Roy steps to the plate the radio announcer tells the fans that although he knows nothing about the new batter, he will try to find out who he is. Roy, on the second pitch, in slow motion, connects with the ball and sends it spinning out of the field. Hobbs brings all of the runners on base home and the Knights win the game. Lightning strikes and rain pours down. The drought is officially over. The wasteland has been restored by the new "Wonderboy" of obscure origins and his magical bat that splits baseballs in two.

It is not long before Roy's magic spreads to the entire team. We soon see all of the players sporting a lightning-bolt patch on their uniform as they embark on one of the hottest streaks in the team's history. It is also not long, however, before Roy meets his second test, the temptress Memo Paris (Daryl Hannah). The two become romantically involved and her effect on his career is deadly. It is as if Roy has forgotten his mission to "be the best there ever was." Although the Knights start losing badly, Roy is too wrapped up in his affair with Memo Paris to care. Memo, like Calypso, has come the closest to casting Roy back into the obscurity of unconsciousness, where he was a nobody, without fame, identity, or purpose in life.

The name "Memo Paris" is also interesting since it also self-consciously echoes the *Odyssey*. "Memo" Paris, or "remember" Paris, is an admonition to Roy, or perhaps to the literate film audience, to remember the initial cause of the Trojan war, or what sent Odysseus on his journey in the first place —the mythological beauty contest between Aphrodite (representing sexual desire/beauty), Athena (representing wisdom), and Hera (representing marriage), judged by the young Adonis Paris. Paris awards the golden apple to Aphrodite (sexual desire/beauty) and receives her human counterpart, Helen of Troy, as his bride. As a trophy, Helen comes with a great deal of trouble since she already belongs to King Menelaus. Thus, the ten-year Trojan War begins and Odysseus is sent on his twenty-year odyssey. If Roy Hobbs can only "remember Paris" and Paris' choice of sexual desire over wisdom and marriage (represented by his childhood sweetheart Iris), he will also be able to remember that Memo Paris, like Harriet Bird, represents the very forces of sexual oblivion and unconsciousness that "odyssied" him for sixteen years and that have worked against his completion of the hero quest.

Early on in the film, for example, Memo asks him if they have met before. He replies that he does not remember such a meeting. Later in the film, as Roy sleeps, Memo touches the scar from the gunshot wound inflicted by Harriet Bird. His body jerks with the unconscious shock of recognition, as we see dream images of Harriet Bird crosscut with images of Memo Paris. And finally, toward the end of the film, after the scales have fallen from his eyes, Roy says to Memo, "You were right, Memo, we have met before." Memo represents a reincarnation of Harriet Bird. Roy did not learn his lesson the first time around. He is lucky, like Odysseus with Calypso, to have been given a second chance.

But the greatest trial still lies before Roy. In the hero's journey, as Campbell reminds us, at some point in his quest the hero faces a supreme test. If he is successful he receives a reward. Such a reward may take the form of his sexual union with the "goddess mother of the world" in the sacred marriage. In *The Natural* the audience soon learns that the Knights, despite their late-season slump, still have a chance at the upcoming pennant race. The pennant this year is a true "winner-take-all" event because it offers Pop Fisher a chance to win back the control of his team. Due to personal financial problems in the previous season, Pop was forced to sell 10 percent of his shares in the team to the Judge, a major stockholder, giving the Judge a controlling interest. Pop only agreed to sell with the caveat that if he won the pennant the

following year he could buy back his shares. Helping the team win the pennant, and defeating the Judge's attempts to get the team to lose, will be the ultimate test of Hobbs' hero status.

Just when things look darkest, and the Knights are losing badly in a game in Chicago that could make or break their chances for the playoffs, Iris suddenly appears in the stands. Like an angel dressed in white, she is backlit by the setting sun in such a way that her brimmed hat appears as a halo. Roy is at bat. Iris, intently staring at Hobbs, moves to her feet and seems to will him to connect with the ball. Roy, as if sensing her presence in the stadium and the strength she sends him, searches the bleachers but does not "see" her. Nevertheless he hits a home run that smashes the clock tower in the field and "stops" time. Like "gray-eyed" Athena who is Odysseus' constant helpmate and redeemer, Iris has helped Hobbs to regain his vision, to shake free from the sexual stupor into which Memo Paris has cast him. (Several close-ups of Iris' grey eyes, as well as the choice of the name "Iris," emphasize this Iris/Athena/vision connection.) Roy is now recommitted to his Grail quest to save the team. The blinding lights of the photographers' camera flashes, however, popping at his home-run triumph, prevent him from again seeing Iris in the stands. It is as if he does not yet "recognize" his Penelope, and thus is not

Just when things look darkest, and the Knights are losing badly, Iris (Glenn Close) suddenly appears in the stands in *The Natural*. Like an angel dressed in white, she is backlit by the setting sun in such a way that her brimmed hat appears as a halo. The low angle shot emphasizes her powerful goddess-like presence. In this image, Iris stares intently offscreen at Roy Hobbs (Robert Redford) whom we know is at bat. As she moves to her feet she seems to will him to connect with the ball. After the moment depicted in this image, we see Roy seeming to unconsciously search the bleachers to find her. Although unable to do so, he nevertheless hits a home run that smashes the clock tower in the field and "stops" time. Like Odysseus' constant helpmate and redeemer "gray-eyed" Athena, "Iris" has helped Hobbs to regain his vision and to shake free from the sexual stupor into which Memo Paris (Daryl Hannah) has cast him. Roy is now recommitted to his Grail quest to save the team. Courtesy of the Museum of Modern Art—Film Stills Archives.

ready to make the sacred marriage with her. Although she is back in his life, he in not yet ready to commit to what she represents.

Later that evening, however, when they meet for a soda in a Chicago drugstore, we gain an inkling of their future destiny together and the importance of Hobbs' journey home. Roy asks her if she has sold her farm. "No," she replies, "I'll always have that." "Good," Roy responds, "it's home." Although he doesn't yet realize it, it is his home too, representing the end of his quest, for his boon is worthless unless he returns home to share it with the community.

The Natural also contains elements of the father quest. At this same meeting between Iris and Roy we learn that Iris has a sixteen-year-old son. Not realizing, as the audience does, that the boy is his, Roy asks where the boy's father is. She tells him that he lives in New York (home of the Knights), adding, "I've been thinking he needs his father now. He's at that age." "Sure," replies Roy, "A father makes all the difference." Like Telemachus, waiting at home twenty years for the father he has never met, Roy's son has unknowingly been waiting for his own father to return. By his comment to Iris, Roy indicates the importance of fathers, implicitly refers to his own father's role in shaping his destiny, and possibly acknowledges his own role as a father for a son he has never met.

Despite the clarity of vision that Iris offers him, Hobbs is soon "odyssied" again by Memo/Calypso when she slips a "mickey" into his drink at the victory celebration that night. Doubled over in acute pain, he is taken to an area hospital. It is here that the doctors inform him that the silver bullet left from Harriet's attempted murder sixteen years ago has destroyed the lining of his stomach and that his career in baseball is over. Memo, visiting him in the maternity wing (there were no beds available elsewhere) not surprisingly urges him to walk away from baseball, to skip the final games of the pennant race, and to go away with her. She makes her last attempt, in other words, to drag him into sexual oblivion and to get him to abandon his quest.

Hobbs, like Odysseus tempted by the Sirens' song, is also visited in the hospital by the Judge, the owner of the Knights, who offers him a bribe—$35,000—to abandon his pennant dreams. We learn that the team's former pitcher, Bump, had already sold out to the Judge and that Memo Paris is also the Judge's creature, paid to seduce and destroy Roy's ambitions for the game as she had done to Bump, her old boyfriend.

Iris, his final visitor in the maternity ward, once again saves him from this fate by offering him a vision of what his life has meant. Roy, despairing of the doctor's news, says to her, "I've failed. I could have been so much better." Iris prophetically responds, "I think that we have two lives . . . the life we learn with and the one we live with after that. . . . Think of all the kids you've touched, you've inspired." With these words Iris has captured the essence of Roy's two journeys and has helped him "give birth" to a new insight, here in the maternity ward, this shrine to the great mother. Here in this liminal space of silence and passivity, in this cave/womb, the hero has been granted by the goddess a vision of what his life has meant and will mean to an entire generation of children, including his own. His brief and shining career *has* made a difference; not only to the team and to Pop but also to the many young children he has inspired. His life is not over simply because he can no longer play professional ball. Despite his doctor's warning not to play baseball again, Roy accepts the final challenge of his hero quest, rejects the judge's bribe, and suits up for the last game of the pennant race. For whatever reason, the team is once again doing badly. Although the other team has not scored, neither have the Knights. The score is tied 0–0. Hobbs, sitting in the dugout after a miserable first turn at bat, receives a note from Iris who is in the stands. Desperate to give him something to play for, she writes to tell him that his son is in the stadium watching him play. It is as if all the elements of the sacred marriage and the father quest have come together. Iris is Roy's true mate. The son that they share, who now needs his father, is the product of that sacred union. It is time for Roy to make good on that contract and come home—both around the bases toward home plate and to the farming community where he grew up.

Taking a third swing from home plate, Roy sends a foul pop fly into the stands. "Wonderboy," the magic talisman and father legacy that has helped bring him success, splits in two. There follows a brief moment when the audience is unsure whether Hobbs can continue. He is clearly in pain and is bleeding from his side. It is as if a wounded King Arthur is down on the field of battle without Excalibur to protect him, or a sacrificial Christ is bleeding from his spear-wounded side. Not to be defeated, however, Hobbs turns to the batboy, Bobby Savoy, with whom he has developed a father/son relationship, and says, "Pick me out another winner, Bobby." Bobby immediately searches out "The Savoy Special," a bat that he and Hobbs had fashioned together in the reverential style and strength of "Wonderboy." Hobbs' messianic father legacy has come full circle. Like Christ, who received strength, wisdom, and compassion from his father, and who, in turn, bestowed such gifts on all of humanity with his death on the cross, Hobbs, now bleeding heavily from his side, makes the ultimate sacrifice for his team, his fans, and for his "sons." Despite his intense pain, he hits a magnificent home run that smashes the stadium lights and sends a shower of electrical fireworks raining down. The crowd jumps to their feet as we watch in slow motion as Roy runs the bases and finally comes home. The Knights have won the game, the Judge's takeover plans have been foiled, and Pop can keep his team.

Despite this magnificent pennant victory, however, the quest is not complete until Roy returns home and fulfills the destiny presaged by Iris in the maternity room. The final scene, therefore, is Roy playing catch with his son in the same golden fields in which he had played with his own father so many years ago. Iris, now his wife and the acknowledged mother of his child, looks on. The hero's journey is complete, and although he has had to leave his "magical powers" behind to return to the world of the ordinary—his talisman bat and his tremendous skill at professional ball—what he has gained is much greater then anything he has lost. Odysseus has found his Penelope, made the sacred marriage, dedicated himself to the role of father, and left a legacy of greatness that will inspire children and adults alike who love the game of baseball.

Bull Durham

Bull Durham, released in 1989 and directed by Barry Levinson, tells the story of a North Carolina minor-league baseball team, the Durham Bulls. The film is told, however, from the point of view of Annie Savoy (read "savior," or "savoir" from the French "to know"), a fan who has religiously followed both baseball, and the Durham Bulls in particular, for years. Annie (Susan Sarandon), in a voice-over opening monologue, explains her devout commitment to baseball:

I believe in the Church of Baseball. I've tried all the major religions and most of the minor ones—I've worshipped Buddha, Allah, Brahma, Vishnu, Shiva, trees, mushrooms, and Isadora Duncan. I know things. For instance, there are 108 beads in a Catholic rosary. And there are 108 stitches in a baseball. When I learned that, I gave Jesus a chance. But it just didn't work out between us. The Lord laid too much guilt on me. I prefer metaphysics to theology. You see there's no guilt in baseball. And it's never boring. . . . I've tried them all, I really have, and the only church that truly feeds the soul—day in, day out—is the Church of Baseball.

As devoted a disciple as can be found, Annie is an expert, on every player's hitting, pitching, throwing, and catching record, but also on their potential performance—on the field and in bed. For Annie, sex, like baseball, is also a religious experience. Constantly tending a "shrine" in her bedroom, she frequently speaks in metaphysical terms about both. For example, Annie usually ties up her lover during sexual foreplay and reads to them from the "god" of baseball poetics—Walt Whitman.

Far from being a mere "groupie," however, who cheapens herself by sleeping with any and all players, Annie is instead a goddess/priestess who every season chooses one player with whom to make the sacred marriage. This season, that choice is between Ebby Calvin "Nuke" LaLoosh (Tim Robbins), the rookie with superstar potential, and "Crash" Davis (Kevin Costner), a washed-up player who has been in and out of the minors for years, with a brief stint in the majors in between. The honor of being chosen as Annie's mythical kingly consort for the year ensures that player a chance to learn many lessons about baseball, sexuality, and life. As a result, Nuke LaLoosh and Crash Davis's task is not only to complete a mythic journey, but to be united in sacred marriage with Annie, a goddess/mother figure who reveals secrets to them that aids in the development of their consciousness and allows them to successfully complete their hero quests.

In the beginning of the film, the Durham Bulls resemble the Knights in *The Natural*: they have not won a game all season. Although the team's rookie pitcher, Ebby Calvin LaLoosh, shows promise—his pitch clocks in at 95 m.p.h. and his manager says he has the best arm he's seen in thirty years—in LaLoosh's debut game he walks 18 players, which is the same as the number he struck out. LaLoosh's dilemma as an unseasoned pitcher becomes clear when, Annie, the team's unofficial manager/groupie, asks Millie, her unofficial assistant manager/groupie, about LaLoosh's sexual performance. Replies Millie, "he fucks like he pitches, sort of all over the place." It is clear that LaLoosh has a lot to learn.

As *Bull Durham* begins, Annie's central task is deciding which player will grace her bed for the season and thus will benefit from her wisdom. This season, as mentioned, the field has been narrowed down to LaLoosh, who is desperately in need of her guidance, and Crash Davis, who is more skeptical that she has any lessons for living to offer him. Crash, in fact, is skeptical about everything. Cynical and burned out, he soon discovers to his dismay that he has been hired by the Bulls not to play ball but rather to act as babysitter and nursemaid to "The Arm," Nuke LaLoosh. Not just a babysitter, however — although his job will indeed entail some of this — he, along with Annie, will play an important role in helping Nuke to mature and centering and tempering Nuke's will and ability as a pitcher.

Annie invites both Crash and Nuke back to her house to more formally "interview" them for the job of lover. She ultimately chooses Nuke, both because he is clearly in more desperate need of her attention and because Crash, offended to be considered in competition with Nuke for Annie's attentions, walks out before her final decision is made.

It is clear from the start, however, that although Annie chooses Nuke for the season, the man she really wants, perhaps for the remaining seasons of her life, is Crash Davis. This desire is apparent in the vaguely sexual explanation she offers of her double entendre requirements in choosing her seasonal consort:

I'd never sleep with a player hitting under .250 unless he had a lot of RBIs or was a great glove man up the middle. A woman's got to have standards. The young players start off full of enthusiasm and energy but they don't realize that come July and August when the weather is hot and it's hard to perform at your peak level. The veterans pace themselves better. They finish stronger. They're great in September. While I don't believe a woman needs a man to be fulfilled, I do confess an interest in finding the ultimate guy — he'd have that youthful exuberance but that veteran's sense of timing.

Although, sexually, she may be looking for someone like Crash, as the double entendre of this monologue implies — and indeed Crash frequently encourages her to leave Nuke and go with him — as she explains to Crash, "Despite my love of goofy metaphysics and my rejection of most Judeo-Christian ethics, I am, within the framework of the baseball season, monogamous." Despite

Crash's urging to Annie to dump Nuke, and despite the fact that Annie, lost in a passionate embrace with Nuke, calls out Crash's name instead, it will be some time—an entire season in fact—before she and Crash are truly ready to make that commitment.

Like Roy Hobbs in *The Natural*, Nuke has an innate talent for baseball. As Crash says to him at one point, "You got a gift. When you were a baby the gods reached down and turned your right arm into a thunderbolt." But also like Roy Hobbs, Nuke is warned by both Crash and Annie that raw talent is not enough, that what he needs is discipline, perseverance, and, in Annie's view, an ability to get in touch with his body, his feminine side, and his unconscious. As she says to him at one point in the film, "When you know how to make love then you'll know how to pitch." During pitching practice, for example, she sends him notes giving him pointers such as he is not bending his back on his follow-through. At another point, when his pitching is really in a slump, she sends him on the team's road trip with a black garter belt, instructing him to wear it under his uniform when he pitches. Explaining the garters' powers to Nuke, she says, "It'll fit snugly against your waist and dangle off your thighs and buns in such a wonderful way that you'll start seeing things differently. Plus they'll remind you of me which is better than thinking about those nasty hitters. . . . You've been pitching out of the wrong side of your brain. These'll help move things to the right side." These instructions imply that the garter belt will allow him to get in touch with his body, open up his female energy, and balance his yin/yang flow. Like Roy Hobbs' magical father-gift, his bat "Wonderboy," LaLoosh's mother-gift works. Although he initially refuses to wear the belt, when he does eventually try it out of desperation, his pitching improves dramatically and the team begins to win.

In Odysseus' quest, the goddesses Circe and Calypso represent the realm of preconsciousness and the seductive appeal of returning, like the lotus-eaters, to an infantile state of oblivious being. As such they are a danger to civilization's emerging ego-consciousness and to Odysseus' own developing sense of self. Calypso and Circe, however, for Odysseus and for the culture at large, also represent a necessary passage to the realm of untapped archetypal energy essential for self-knowledge and growth. Odysseus' journey home to make the sacred marriage with Penelope, in other words, could not have been possible without the experiences of preconsciousness/unconsciousness with both goddess figures. Such is the case for Nuke in his relationship with Annie.

Opening up alternative channels of energy, such as that found in the unconscious, can be frightening. Annie's problematic impact on Nuke's unconscious, for example, becomes clear when he finds himself having a dream in which he stands naked on the pitcher's mound wearing nothing but his cap, a jock strap, and Annie's black garter belt while hundreds of fans look on from the stands in mocking disbelief.

The double-edged appeal of the unconscious, and the maternal as representative of that unconscious, is also played out in a conversation between Nuke and Annie. Repeating wisdom he has been given by Crash, Nuke explains to Annie why he superstitiously cannot sleep with her in the middle of his winning streak. After comparing a "woman's pussy" to the Bermuda triangle, he explains that "a man can get lost in there and never be heard from again." Annie replies, "What a nasty thing to say." Nuke explains, "[Crash] didn't mean it nasty. He said that gettin' lost and disappearing from the face of the earth was sometimes a good thing to do—especially like that. But he also said there is a time for discipline, and I think this is one of those." Both Crash and Nuke realize, in other words, that making the sacred marriage with a goddess figure requires an ability to explore the realm of the unconscious and the chthonic without remaining there indefinitely. Like Odysseus who cannot stay for an eternity with Circe or Calypso if he is to complete his hero quest, or Roy Hobbs, who risks oblivion because of Harriet Bird's silver bullet and Memo Paris' overpowering sexual draw, Nuke and Crash understand that the sacred marriage involves a balancing of yin and yang energies, not the dissolution of the one into the other. This, in part, is one of the lessons to be learned.

The baseball season is almost over, however, and so Annie's work with Nuke also comes to a close, hastened only slightly, perhaps, by the much coveted but rarely occurring invitation Nuke receives for a major-league try-out. And just as Roy Hobbs in The Natural no longer needs the magical bat "Wonderboy" to complete his hero quest, Nuke no longer needs Annie's goddess-gift of the black garter belt. He returns this talisman to her, saying, "I think I'm ready for the show."

Nuke *is* ready for "the show" and Annie is ready for Crash. Nuke's departure paves the way for their inevitable sexual and spiritual union, a union that we realize will last much longer than one season. (As if to acknowledge this change Annie explains to Crash that "I'm quitting too. Boys, not baseball.") It is clear from their sacred marriage that Annie has as much to learn from Crash as Crash does from her. He represents the seasoned veteran—just as solid in September as he was in May—a player who can go the distance and still take his time. She represents the Bermuda triangle, the dark secrets of unfathomable places, the mystery of all women in whose passion and glory man is willing to lose consciousness to learn the lessons that only she can teach. But most of all their union represents a meeting of equals, a kingly consort fit for a queen, a balancing of the yin/yang energies of which Annie always speaks, a testimony to the need for all heroes to return home and to make the sacred marriage if they are truly to become whole. Although Crash does not return to some childhood home, as does Roy Hobbs in *The Natural*, we get the sense that his wanderings from small town to small town in the minors are finally over. He is ready to settle down, not only in a relationship with Annie, but in one place. After briefly leaving town on one last journey, to complete a minor-league record of the most RBIs, Crash returns "home" to Annie, his goddess consort, who, metaphorically speaking, represents his home and the end of all his earthly wanderings.

The Piano

The Piano (1993), directed by Jane Campion, earned the prestigious Palme d'Or at the Cannes film festival, and Anna Paquin received an Academy Award for best supporting actress. Not only did the film receive rave reviews; many critics consider it one of Campion's most important films to date.

The Piano, as we will see, tells a masterfully crafted version of the female sacred marriage quest while also providing an extended visual and verbal discussion on the powers of both speech and silence, the conscious and the unconscious — and the "savage" and the "civilized." Issues of consciousness and unconsciousness (and their articulation in this film as a polemic between the "civilized" (conscious) and "uncivilized" (unconsciousness) — are central to the hero's quest not only because they represent the key tension in individual and cultural evolution, but because consciousness has traditionally been associated with the masculine while unconsciousness has traditionally been equated with the feminine (as we saw in both *Bull Durham* and *The Natural*). As such, the analysis that follows focuses not only on the sacred marriage quest, but also on how that quest is bound up with the tensions between consciousness and unconsciousness, the "civilized" and "uncivilized," and, by extension, the feminine and the masculine.

As the film opens, Ada (Holly Hunter), in voice-over, explains, "I have not spoken since I was six years old, Lord knows why, not even me. My father says it is a dark talent and the day I take it into my head to stop breathing will be my last." Thus, from the outset the mystery of the absence of speech is presented as a puzzle for both the protagonist and for the audience. In part, this will be Ada's quest, to discover the roles of silence and speech in her life, to find her "voice," and to commit to the sacred marriage with a man finally deemed to be her equal, a man finally able to hear her voice. This opening line also makes us aware of Ada's extremely strong will. Her defiance of many societal conventions of her age means that she will stop at nothing to achieve happiness and emotional fulfillment, even to the extent of engaging in an illicit affair with her husband's overseer Baines (Harvey Keitel) and to tempting fate by casting herself into a raging sea in order to test her will to live against her will to die.

Ada continues in voice-over, "Today he married me to a man I've not yet met. Soon my daughter and I shall join him in his own country. My husband says my muteness does not bother him. He writes, and hark this: God loves dumb creatures, so why not he!" Ada is being sent to New Zealand to fulfill a contractually arranged marriage. Despite a lack of love for a husband she clearly does not know, we have no sense of her disposition toward this arrangement. Thus, she seems to be stepping to the threshold of adventure willingly as she begins her Odyssean journey into the unknown. We are also getting an inkling of the sort of man she will be marrying, someone who sees nothing wrong with comparing his wife to an animal, who possesses the typically Victorian attitude of the husband as the stronger protector of his weaker wife, and who assumes that because Ada is mute, this means that she has no "voice" and hence nothing to say. This perspective will account for why Ada will never be able to make the sacred marriage with him.

Continuing in voice-over, Ada remarks: "Were good he had God's patience, for silence affects everyone in the end. The strange thing is, I don't think of myself as silent; that's because of my piano. I shall miss it on the journey." Ada's piano is a central metaphor for her voice. As an artist and as a woman, it is the source of her inspiration and creation. Campion will literalize the piano as voice with frequent use of a swelling piano soundtrack that not only provides segues between scenes, but also acts as a narrative voice for scenes with and without dialogue.[28]

Ada's piano, from a mythological perspective, can also be seen as her hero's talisman, the magical instrument that will be both the source of great comfort and the means by which she accomplishes great things. Only through it can she speak, when Stewart (Sam Neill) "takes" it from her she becomes powerless or "mute"; when it is returned to her it becomes central to her

Ada (Holly Hunter), together with her daughter Flora (Anna Paquin) and her piano, stands on a wild and windswept New Zealand beach while waiting for the arrival of her new husband. Both the sea and Ada's piano represent a powerful and relentless presence from this moment of their arrival until their final departure at the end of the film. Both become narrative voices that mediate the tensions between consciousness and unconsciousness. Just prior to the depicted moment, for example, after her boat runs aground in New Zealand, Ada, like some dark angel floating about them all, is carried ashore by a score of sailors while being held aloft to keep her dress from being submerged in the surf. Just after this moment, her husband Stewart refuses to bring her piano from where the sailors have left it on the beach and Ada is forced to abandon it to the elements and an encroaching sea. Courtesy of the Museum of Modern Art—Film Stills Archives.

sacred marriage with Baines. When her hero quest is almost complete, however, she will no longer need it, and thus, as in many hero legends, she will leave it behind as she returns home with Baines to the everyday world of domesticity.

The piano can also be seen as a metaphor that coalesces seemingly opposing visions. On the one hand, mastery of the piano for eighteenth- and nineteenth-century middle- and upper-class women represented the height of refinement. It was expected in English society, for example, that a marriageable young woman would have some training in voice, piano, needlepoint, or some other form of handicraft or art. As such, playing the piano was a mark of meeting conventional societal expectations. It was "civilized." On the other hand, mastery of the piano to the point of virtuosity was *not* expected of women. Such virtuosity could be seen as a potential career, and as such, would pose a challenge to a woman's only acceptable career, that of wife and mother. Ada's skill with the piano, in particular, can also be see as a vehicle for the release of unbridled passion and sexual energy, and thus in clear defiance of eighteenth- and nineteenth-century societal expectations about acceptable demeanor for young women. Ada's piano playing, in other words, is "uncivilized." Therefore, on the one hand the piano represents the realm of the super-ego, or the rational domain of consciousness. On the other, it represents the id, the deep well of unconsciousness and the possibility for unlimited vision and passion. As the film progress, however, the piano invites even more complex interpretations. Her piano, as the voice that Ada thought she could not do without, by the end of the film, as we will see, becomes the potential instrument of her demise in an ocean grave.

The sea, like Ada's piano, also plays an important role in the film and, like her piano, becomes an additional narrative voice mediating the tensions between consciousness and unconsciousness. The sea is a powerful and relentless presence from the moment of Ada's arrival on the island with her daughter Flora (Anna Paquin) until their final departure at the end of the film. At the beginning of the film, for example, after her boat grounds on the beach in New Zealand, like some dark angel floating about them all, Ada is carried ashore by a score of sailors, held aloft to keep her dress from being submerged in the surf. When her husband Stewart refuses to bring her piano from where the sailors have left it on the beach and she is forced to abandon it to the elements, an encroaching sea threatens to carry it away while a relentless downpour offers a warping hazard to its wooden frame.

Thus the sea represents, as it does for Odysseus, unconsciousness. On the one hand it presents a threat—the fear of drowning and the erasure of identity/voice. If the piano represents Ada's voice, or her identity as an artist, and the sea represents silence or the lack of voice and identity, the sea taking Ada or taking her piano/voice represents the possibility of her loss of identity, her submersion in oblivion. At the same time, however, the sea also represents the allure of the irrational and the appeal of dissolving one's ego-consciousness into unconsciousness. Just as Odysseus is fearful of drowning at sea, he is also drawn to its power and is lured by the appeal of losing himself to the rational and everyday realm of consciousness. Tensions in the interpretation of the sea as threat versus sea as lure are illustrated, for example, in the realization that the sea can either be as gentle as a mother rocking her baby to sleep or as fierce as a mother lion demanding blood and cold death.

The Piano also provides a meditation on the "savage" and the "civilized," and, rather than simply valorizing one over the other, likewise presents complex interpretations of both while demonstrating Western culture's ambivalence toward both. Ada's new home in New Zealand, for example, is presented as an outpost of civilization in the midst of a muddy and stifling uncivilized jungle. Her new husband is a colonist, trying to carve a profitable estate from this ever-encroaching and all-devouring wilderness. Stewart's Aunt Morag lives and works at a nearby mission house, dedicated to educating and "civilizing" the "savage" Maori Indians. Ada's piano, like Ada's arrival as wife and homemaker, likewise provides an image of civilization or refinement in this sweaty male wilderness. For example, just before Stewart, her husband-to-be, emerges out of the dense primeval forest to meet his wife for the first time, he becomes self-consciously aware of his "savage" male looks. Pausing to look at Ada's refined and feminine portrait, he sheepishly takes out a pocket comb and mirror as if to civilize his unruly male presence before meeting his lady wife. The film also contrasts the life of the white colonists with the indigenous Maoris who often work for and trade with the white settlers. Although the Maori people have a civil relationship with the whites, we often see scenes where they make fun of the whites and their "civilized" ways of life.

The sacred marriage quest itself can be seen as an attempt to balance and unite diverse energies—such as the savage and the civilized, the conscious and the unconscious, the male and the female, the mundane and the divine—without the dissolution of the one into the other. As such, a marriage that does not balance these energies is a failure, a sham, or an incomplete marriage. It is not surprising, therefore, that Ada's marriage with Stewart will never survive—based, as it is at times, solely on the civilized and Christian propriety without love or passion, or at other times, solely on the savage (as when he tries to rape her). Thus, it is not long before we realize that Ada's marriage with Stewart, her legal husband, is a sham. It is an arranged marriage. She is a mail-order bride. No formal marriage ceremony, exchange of vows, or sexual union takes place between the two.

Since it is important to keep up social conventions, however, a wedding photograph is created as proof of their union. As Stewart's Aunt Morag says to Ada, "If you cannot have a ceremony together you have at least a photograph." On the day of the photograph, Aunt Morag and the women of the mission put on Ada's wedding gown, like a stage costume, over her regular clothes. Like a stick-figure doll, she is maneuvered outside to a facade set up by the photographer as background for the photo. Standing stone-faced next to her husband, the photographer snaps pictures in a drenching downpour that threatens to engulf them all in a mudslide. The marriage, like the wedding photo and the wedding costume, is itself a facade, a puppet play, a mockery of the sacred marriage. It is not surprising, therefore, that except for her husband's inappropriate and clumsy attempts at passionate embraces, their marriage remains unconsummated. It is also not surprising that on their "wedding day" all Ada can think of is her abandoned piano, vulnerable to the whim of the elements and the pouring rain.

Ada cannot make the sacred marriage with Stewart because he does not see her as an equal and does not hear her voice. He thinks that his wife's muteness is good and that women are better seen than heard. This is illustrated, for example, when Stewart seems to agree with his aunt's demeaning assessment of Ada's muteness when she says, "Certainly there's nothing so easy to like as a pet, and they're silent." Stewart also does not share Ada's passion for the piano and has no respect for Ada's playing or the piano's importance as her voice. Stewart may even be fearful of the piano as a representation of unbridled passion and the unconscious. This is illustrated, for example, by his decision to leave the piano behind on the beach and the ease with which he later gives the piano to Baines in exchange for some of Baines' land.

As the film progresses, Baines, by contrast, becomes deeply interested in hearing Ada's voice. It is Baines, not her husband, whom Ada ultimately convinces to take her to the beach so that she can visit with and play her stranded piano. In one of the most visually stunning scenes of the film, shot on the wild and storm-swept New Zealand coast, we see the passionate release of Ada's voice as she plays with abandon to an audience of Baines, Flora, and the vast and turbulent ocean. Baines, a silent witness, seems deeply moved by her passion and the beauty of her music/voice as it seems to merge with the natural elements and the endless vista.

The film's visual style is an important contributor to its dreamlike and mythic quality. Possibly, in part, as a result of Ada's muteness, dialogue in the film is minimal. The musical soundtrack and the visual style instead tell a great deal of the story. Campion's camera captures scenes with the detail of the painter's eye, as a result, multiple mise-en-scènes often linger in the film-viewer's mind long after the last words have been spoken. For me, such images include a submerged Ada, her voluminous dress swirling around her, gleaming bubbles of silvery air escaping from her lips at the moment of decision between life and death in the depths of a gray-blue sea; or a frozen Ada, framed against a background of silver-gray trees, just after Stewart has chopped off her finger and just before she sinks like a balloon run out of air into an all-consuming sea of mud; or an ecstatic Ada, passionately weaving a musical spell at her piano, and framed against a blue-gray vista of the wild New Zealand coast. Such ghostly images take on an ethereal, dreamlike quality for the viewer and seem, alternately, to be both the stuff of our worst nightmares and of our deepest desires.

Baines, Stewart's overseer, perhaps best represents the strange tension or balancing act the film achieves between the "uncivilized" and the "civilized." In doing so, we soon realize that he will be the perfect mate to consummate a sacred marriage with Ada. As an overseer who works with Stewart and the natives, he has one foot in both the native and non-native worlds. Although he is a white man, he has adopted Maori ways, even to the extent of wearing native body tattoos and taking a native woman as his bedfellow. Although he cannot read well, he speaks the Maori language as fluently as he does English. His dress, in fact, combines elements of both native and western fashion. His response to music, specifically Ada's piano playing, represents both his appreciation of the "finer arts" of civilization and his connection with the deeper "uncivilized" impulses of unbridled passion that Ada's piano playing represents.

It is not long after the visit to the beach and the piano that Baines devises a plan to see Ada more often and to hear her play. To do so he strikes a deal with Stewart: he will trade some of his acreage in exchange for the piano and piano lessons from Ada. Stewart, foolishly believing that he has gotten the best of the bargain, enthusiastically agrees. Once Baines brings the piano from the beach and pays to get it tuned professionally, the "piano lessons" begin. It quickly becomes apparent, however, that Baines is not interested in playing the piano. What he wants is to see and hear Ada play. Even this is not enough when his overwhelming sexual desire for her results in their strange bargain: Ada can earn her piano back by allowing Baines to do whatever he wants while she plays—one black piano key for each honored request. Ada, at first unwillingly, agrees to this arrangement.

In perhaps the strangest and most haunting seduction scene in cinema history, we watch the slow opening up of their passions for each other, laced through with some of the most passionate and reflective piano playing in the film. Baines, over the course of his "piano lessons," slowly seduces Ada into making the sacred marriage with him by helping her seduce herself with her own voice. Through Baines, she will learn to be more fully open to the realm of the unconscious. Like any mythic hero, she must descend to this world and be prepared to learn the lessons she will encounter there. As Ada speaks to Baines through the piano she is opened, once again, to the possibilities of sexuality and abiding love. Lying on the floor at her feet as she plays, he explores the sensuality of a hole in her black wool stockings as her feet vigorously pump the piano's foot pedals. Standing over her shoulder, he tenderly dwells on the paleness, softness, and strength of her forearms. As she caresses the keys of the piano, he caresses the arms that bring those keys to life.

As is often the case in the sacred marriage of the female hero with her godly consort, she is often unwilling to make the match and must be wooed and seduced. But, as Campbell notes, "the heavenly husband descends to her and conducts her to his bed, whether she will or no [and] the scales fall from her eyes [as] her desire finds its peace." [29] Such is the case for Ada. Initially cold and unyielding to Baines' caresses, Ada continually attempts to increase the number of piano keys she wins from him for each request in order to hasten the return of her piano and the end of their bargain. As reluctant hero, in other words, she is fearful of letting go or "taking the plunge." Finally, despondent over his role as sexual aggressor and Ada's unwillingness to yield to his passion—or even to her own for that matter—he calls the bargain off saying, "the arrangement is making you a whore and me wretched. I want you to care for me but you can't." Baines returns her piano.

Although Ada has now reclaimed what she thinks is her heart's desire, she can no longer play it. It is as if she now longs to hear her other voice—the voice she was beginning to rediscover with Baines, or that speaking with her piano's voice has become meaningless to her since there is no one to hear and understand its meaning. Passionately angry, perhaps more so at herself than at Baines, she bursts into his hut. "What brings you here?" he demands. "Did you lose something? I'd not found anything." These are prophetic words since Ada has indeed lost something, the beginnings of her reawakened sensuality, and the possibility to find a mate that will offer the appropriate balancing of male and female, conscious and unconscious, savage and civilized energies. She begins pounding on his chest as tears well up in her eyes. She beats him both because he has opened her again to her sensuality and because he has taken it away. They kiss passionately as Baines carries her to his bed.

Unlike Baines, who has patiently waited for Ada to decide whether to join him in the sacred marriage, her husband Stewart continues to do violence to Ada's body and soul in order to make her love him. Tipped off by Flora about the true nature of Ada's piano lessons with Baines, Stewart follows Ada to Baines' hut one day and secretly spies on their lovemaking through a chink in the hut's floorboards. He becomes voyeuristically inflamed by their passion. Rather than immediately confronting the two with his discovery, however, he prefers to vicariously revel in a sexual passion and sensuality he has never known. Stewart therefore bides his time until one day, unable to contain his jealousy, he confronts Ada and tries to force her to yield to him the passion she has given to Baines. We witness a "lyrical" rape scene in which his brutish attempts as sexual intimacy are rebuffed to the swelling chords of an angry piano sonata. Unsuccessful, he boards up all of the windows of the house and double-locks the doors with Ada inside. If he cannot have her, then no one else will. She is a caged bird, another one of his possessions, like the land around which he has put fences in order to declare his ownership and to ensure that any "wilderness" does not encroach upon it.

Despite his demeaning attempts to control her, Ada still attempts to make the sacred marriage with him. Stealing into his room one night, she begins to tentatively caress him, running her hands up and down the curves and hollows of his body. Stewart awakens and jumps with fear. Possibly afraid of his own sensuality and his body's response to her caresses, or confused about how to handle sexual intimacy that is not brutish or controlling, he pushes her away.

Desperate to experience once again the relationship she had with Baines, Ada removes a white key from her piano, inscribes it with the message, "Dear George, you have my heart," and instructs Flora to take it to Baines.

Throughout the film we witness an interesting bright angel/dark angel contrast between Flora and Ada. Although Flora clearly loves her mother, over the course of the film she becomes seduced by the appeals of "civilization" and, as a result, becomes the pupil of her Aunt Morag in learning proper Christian ways. For the morality pageant that the pastor and the female workers in the mission stage for the community, Flora plays the role of an angel. She becomes so enamored of her white and silver stage wings fashioned for her by her Aunt Morag, however, that she wears them continually throughout the film. Thus she becomes a symbol of Christianity, rationality, and the realm of consciousness that directly contrasts with her mother's dark garb, hair, and demeanor, which more closely symbolizes the realm of the chthonic, the nonrational, the passionate, and the unconscious.

It is not surprising, therefore, that Flora, acting as a good "Christian" daughter, betrays her mother's passion and reports on Ada to her stepfather Stewart. Instead of taking the piano key to Baines, Flora brings it to Stewart, who is out on his property mending fences in his attempt to once again keep certain things out and keep other things in. Such a revelation, however, brings with it havoc and a punishment that even Flora could not have anticipated.

Enraged beyond all sense, Stewart breaks down the door of the house and uses an ax to gouge a hole in the piano. He pulls Ada outside to the woodshed chopping block and chops off one of her fingers. Stewart's acts represent a double mutilation; not only does he attempt to destroy the instrument of her voice, but also her ability to make that voice come to life with her playing. Later, as Ada lies in bed, sleeping off her pain and the shock of what has occurred, Stewart silently enters her room and attempts to rape her. As she awakens, he pleads with her, saying, "I meant to love you. I clipped your wings, that's all." When he is in control and she is powerless, even to the point of being mutilated, then he desires her. It is clear that they will never meet as equals, and, as such, a sacred marriage that balances yin and yang is impossible.

Stewart chopping off Ada's finger is actually foreshadowed in the mission's morality play about Bluebeard the pirate and his decapitation of his eight wives. The drama is acted out as a shadow play in which a bright light, focused on the action occurring behind a sheet, casts a shadow on a sheet visible to the audience. In rehearsal for the play, the mission's pastor demonstrates how the special effect of the shadow play will work. Instructing a young woman to hold out her arm and watch carefully, he takes an ax and "cuts off" her hand in an effect that appears so real that the young girl jerks back her arm with a scream. Later that night, during the actual staging of the drama, the Maori tribesman, thinking that the decapitations they are witnessing on stage are real, jump up from their seats in order to save Bluebeard's eighth wife from her fate. Although such an action disrupts the drama and becomes a source of amusement to the white colonists who laugh at the "primitive" Indians' ignorance of the convention of drama, the Maoris' actions imply a type of nobleness not possessed by these "civilized" men and women who take pleasure in acting out bloody morality plays as warnings to "bad" wives. Ada, of course, is the "bad" wife who will experience this same punishment for real when Stewart—the film's representative of civilization and Christian values—savagely chops off her finger. Patriarchy, as the rule of male energies that worships consciousness and the Cartesian "sovereign rational subject," will never allow for the balancing of the male and female, and the conscious and unconscious energies that makes the sacred marriage possible. Unholy matrimonies, such as Bluebeard's and Stewart's can only be based on savagery and silence.

By the film's conclusion, possibly ashamed of his actions and his attempts to own and control Ada like a possession or a slave, or possibly awakened to the realization that she can never make the sacred marriage with him, Stewart agrees to let her leave with Baines. In the second to the last scene in the film, as the Maoris deftly row the large canoe, holding Baines, Flora, Ada, and all of Ada's possessions, including her piano, it soon become apparent that the ungainly weight and size of the piano may capsize the boat. The Maoris urge Baines to throw the piano overboard. He refuses, explaining that Ada needs her piano. Ada, experiencing a change of heart, tells Baines that she wants the piano dropped overboard. In the meantime Ada has secretly slipped her foot into the center of the coil of rope that holds the piano lashed to the boat. Baines, in disbelief at Ada's request, refuses to jettison the piano. Once she insists, however, he complies. Loosening the ropes that holds it immediately causes the piano to plunge overboard, taking Ada with it. We are witnessing Ada's choice of suicide by drowning in the great motherly sea of unconsciousness. At the last minute, however, she changes her mind. Kicking off the shoe that holds her tied to her piano/anchor, she immediately begins to rise to the surface. As she says in voice-over:

At night I think of my piano in its ocean grave, and sometimes myself floating above it. Down there everything is so still and silent that it lulls me to sleep. It is a weird lullaby and so it is; it is mine. There is a silence where hath been no sound. There is a silence where no sound may be. In the cold grave, under the deep deep sea.

In this, the film's climax, when Ada's will chooses life over death, the piano and the sea merge as metaphors in such a way that they starkly illustrate the complex interpretative possibilities of the sea as metaphor as well as the protagonist's and the dominant Western culture's ambivalent relationship to consciousness and unconsciousness. It is clear that, for Ada, such an identity-death in the sea is not necessarily bad; there is clearly an appeal to the unconscious or the realm of oblivion. Such a place "lulls [Ada] to sleep." Like a maternal lullaby it is a source of comfort rather than fear. Although Ada chose not to be submerged with her piano in the silent watery deep, and thus, like Odysseus, chooses life and identity over death and oblivion, death and oblivion are not to be feared, just as the realm of the unconscious or maternal preconscious is not to be feared or reviled. The film also leaves the viewer with inklings that Ada's decision to have the Maori sailors toss her piano overboard was made because she no longer needs the piano to find or express her voice. In her choice of life over death (consciousness over unconsciousness), Ada completes her hero quest, makes the sacred marriage with a true mate, and begins the process of finding her voice. Ada's sacred marriage with Baines, himself a representative of both the civilized and the savage, the refined and the natural, and her discovery of love and sexual passion in a union of equals, has itself become a source for self-expression, a different type of voice with which to speak. The piano, as magical talisman, also belongs to the extraordinary realm of questing. The hero, now returning to the everyday world, no longer needs such a talisman and thus leaves it behind. Her hero's boon, in the world of the film, is a private boon, possibly best shared with her daughter Flora and her husband Baines. The boon that she provides the film-viewing audience, however, is the ability to better grapple with our own balancing acts—between silence and sound, male and female, the "savage"

and the "civilized," and the unconscious and the conscious—as we try to find our own voices and complete our own hero quests for home.

Thelma and Louise

Thelma and Louise provides a modern twist on the sacred marriage quest for both heroines; instead of making a marriage with an appropriate male consort, both women, in their rejection of the patriarchal institutions that constantly control them, make the sacred marriage with each other and with all women.

The film's provocative conclusion, as well as its cultural timeliness, placed it in the middle of academic and popular media debate about contemporary feminism, the choices women make or are compelled to make, and the future of the women's movement in general. The film basically divided feminists and non-feminists into two opposing camps: those that saw it as a liberating portrayal of the plight facing contemporary women—misogyny, discrimination, prejudice, and sexual violence—and those that felt the film exaggerated women's predicament, polarized male/female relationship, engaged in reverse-sexism in its depiction of men, and generally offered sui-

Thelma (Geena Davis) and Louise (Susan Sarandon) in *Thelma and Louise*. The film provides a modern twist on the sacred marriage quest for both heroines; instead of making a marriage with an appropriate male consort, both women, in their rejection of the patriarchal institutions that constantly control them, make the sacred marriage with each other and with all women. Courtesy of the Museum of Modern Art—Film Stills Archives.

cide—a defeatist choice for women living under patriarchy—as a solution to the problem.

Although not directly engaging this debate, this reading of the film views the protagonists' choice of death rather than surrender as embracing the challenges of ego death and unconsciousness by making the sacred marriage with the Great Mother. Viewing the film as entirely metaphorical, such a reading does not, by any means, champion suicide for women as a viable response to living under patriarchy. It instead highlights the dilemma that all heroes and heroines of the quest myth face: completing the journey and finding a boon to share with the culture requires a submission of will and ego-identity rather than willful self-aggrandizement. In order to "live" for others the hero must first "die" to self, like Ada in a stormy sea or like Roy Hobbs from a silver bullet. In order to be apotheosized by the culture the hero must be free of any desire for such apotheosis, like Roy Hobbs when he returns home to the simple life of father and husband, or like Crash Davis when he completes his minor-league record in anonymity and dedicates his life to coaching, or like Thelma and Louise when they go sailing off the side of a cliff into the Grand Canyon and eternity. The question that remains, however, is whether the protagonists' choice of death over life (or the extinction of self for Self) represents a surrender to unconsciousness/oblivion and thus a failure to complete the hero's quest by not returning to consciousness and community, or rather represents an evolution beyond the imperfect realm of (male) consciousness to be unified in an enlightened state of being or consciousness.

What is particularly interesting about *Thelma and Louise*, and here I acknowledge stretching the hero quest a bit, is that although there is no hint that either heroine is apotheosized by a fictional community in the film, the overwhelming popularity of the film and the debate it spawned among feminists point to the heroines' Odyssean trajectory as providing a profound boon to a nonfictional community challenged by its messages about women and men and the choices they make in relationships and in life.

Thelma and Louise, from the opening sequence, establishes the state of both heroines' relationships with the men in their lives. Planning a weekend getaway, it becomes apparent that Thelma (Geena Davis) needs her husband's permission to go and that she is so certain he will not give it that she leaves without telling him. Despite his critical and hot-tempered demeanor toward her, she acts loving and understanding and even prepares him dinners for all the nights she will be away. This is clearly a marriage based upon inequality and lacking in mutual love and respect. Meanwhile, Louise (Susan Sarandon), busy finishing up her last shift in the diner, admonishes two teenage girls not to smoke because it will "ruin [their] sex life." In the very next shot, Louise lights up a cigarette, the film's clear comment on the state of her own "ruined" sex life.

Both women, possibly because of dissatisfaction in their relationships with men, move gleefully and willingly to the threshold of adventure, Louise packing methodically and soberly for the weekend with all her shoes neatly encased in plastic bags, Thelma dumping the entire contents of her lingerie drawer into her suitcase.

Initially, Louise will play the sober adult or mother figure to Thelma's irrepressible child. Louise, for example, must tell Thelma what to pack, must remind her what to tell her husband Daryl about the trip, and only reluctantly agrees to stop at a roadside bar when Thelma, the winsome child, begs and pleads. Once inside the bar, Louise, the responsible adult, warns Thelma, the errant child, not to drink too much or to get romantically involved with a stranger. Thelma, who doesn't smoke, like an adolescent teenager playing at being an adult, imitates Louise by theatrically lighting a cigarette and vamping it up. Later in the film, the height of Thelma's childishness occurs when she engages in an affair with J.D. (Brad Pitt), a hitchhiker who steals all of their getaway money. Their roles soon switch, however, as Louise falls apart over their outlaw status and the theft of all their money. Thelma, like a child whose time to grow up has come, soon takes over, not only driving the car, but also robbing a convenience store for travel money. It is clear, in other words, that both women have a great deal to learn from each other as the teacher/student relationship continually shifts back and forth between the two of them.

The central event in the first half of the film, of course, and the catalyst for the heroes' journey, occurs in the roadside bar parking lot where Thelma is almost raped by Harlan, a loud-mouthed, redneck drunk. Louise, protecting her friend as well as possibly reliving her own traumatic experience with rape years earlier in Texas (although the audience does not know this at the time), pulls out Thelma's gun and shoots Harlan point blank in the chest, saying, "In the future, when a women's crying like that, she ain't having any fun." Although Thelma asks Louise, "Shouldn't we go to the cops, tell them what happened?" Louise explains to Thelma the rape dilemma—faced by many women—that Thelma now faces. The fact that Thelma had been dancing cheek-to-cheek with Harlan all night and acting very friendly with him would be interpreted by the police or by a jury as Thelma "asking" to be raped. Trapped in what seems a no-win situation, the women decide to leave the scene of the crime. What began as a weekend getaway for two friends has now turned into a desperate flight from the law. A serious and difficult journey toward self-discovery awaits both women. It will be a trip fraught with difficult choices and many lessons about men, relationships, and life.

Mirrors, a recurring motif in the film, are directly related to this process of self-discovery. Originally an object of objectification and the male gaze, they become a window into the souls of both women, particularly Louise, while offering them both a chance to reassess themselves as women on their own terms and in relation to men.

A mirror image first appears in the roadside bar, prior to the attempted rape. Louise stops in the bar's crowded women's room to relieve herself before they continue on their road trip. In a conventional portrayal of the role of mirrors in many women's lives, Louise stands with a dozen or more women, crowding each other out for a view of themselves in the sweaty bathroom mirror. The camera takes the point of view of the mirror so that the women, Louise included, are staring directly at us as they reapply lipstick, brush their hair, or powder their faces. We, the audience, are in the position of male surveyor, assessing the women assessing themselves through the eyes of male society's assessment of them. The central question they implicitly ask themselves as they primp and preen is how they look to the other (male). As typical, this mirror scene does not call attention to itself. When linked with the many mirror images in the film that will follow, however, it takes on added significance.

Louise's second mirror encounter occurs shortly after she has shot Harlan, Thelma's attempted rapist. Staring reflectively into a mirror, ostensibly to check her criminal appearance (that is, for any blood on her cheeks, and so on), it seems as if she is also asking herself if she looks like a murderer, or rather, deciding if this is what a murderer looks like.

Thelma's first mirror encounter occurs later in the film when, at a roadside stop, she applies lip gloss and eyeliner while looking in the car's rearview mirror. Suddenly, an image of J.D. the hitchhiker appears in her mirror. This is another example of the male gaze in cinema. We are watching a female adorn herself while watching her being watched by an assessing male character. It is obvious that he, like we, find her desirable. Her concern about her appearance, through the application of makeup, indicates her complicit role in this "attraction game." This initial "mirror play" eventually leads to Thelma's one-night stand with J.D. where, for the first time in her life, despite years of marriage, Thelma experiences sexual satisfaction. Such an encounter, however, simply turns out to be another "rape," as J.D. steals the $6500 getaway money that Louise had her boyfriend Jimmy wire them.

A scene between Louise and her boyfriend Jimmy (Michael Madsen), who accompanies the money he was supposed to have wired, while not involving a mirror per se, is also directly related to the gaze, or the role of seeing oneself and seeing the other. It begins as Louise refuses to tell Jimmy why she asked him for the money and why she and Thelma are on the run. Angry at her refusal, he starts to smash up the room. Shouts Louise, "You start this shit and I'm out of here." It is clear that this is not the first time she has seen this behavior from him, and it hints at the possibility of a history of anger and violence in their relationship. The mood shifts dramatically, however, as he quietly hands her an engagement ring. Seemingly at a loss for words, she says, "Why now?" Jimmy replies sarcastically, "Try not to get too excited. I just flew across two states with that ring in my fucking hand . . . I thought you wanted to get married?" "I do," Louise replies, "but not like this." It is clear that he wants to marry her at this moment because he is afraid of losing her. Possibly for the first time in their relationship he realizes that he cannot take her for granted, and that something has changed, that Louise has changed. She replies, "I do love you, but I think it's time to let go of old mistakes, just chalk it up to bad timing." Louise then shifts the direction of the conversation to bring him, and the audience, back into the history of their relationship. She asks him if he remembers when they first met, and what happened. "I said you had a nice pair of eyes," he replies. Louise shuts her eyes, just as she had apparently done when they first met. She reminds him that he had had no idea what color those "nice" eyes were. She then asks, "Do you know what color are my eyes?" "They're brown," he replies without hesitation. "Damn, Jimmy," she says, "what did you do? Take a pill that makes you say all the right stuff?" Whereas earlier in their relationship he had "seen" her, possibly as attractive or sexually provocative or available, he did not really "see" her. As a male, he objectified her as desirable woman, with a gaze that assessed but did not truly "see." Now, by telling her the color of her eyes, he acknowledges that his gaze no longer sees her as object but as subject, as a person, with feelings, needs, fears, and desires. Although Louise cannot make the sacred marriage with Jimmy, despite the promise of growth that his comments now demonstrate, she keeps the ring and promises to think it over.

The shift from woman as object to woman as subject is perhaps best demonstrated in the next mirror sequence occurring in the film. While Louise waits in the parking lot of a convenience store, unaware that Thelma is inside robbing the store, she notices a number of older women watching her with disapproval. Immediately self-conscious about her appearance, she looks in the car's rear-view mirror and starts to apply lipstick to her naked lips. Half-way through the gesture she changes her mind. Rather than simply putting the lipstick away, she throws it out the window. The older woman's gaze represents the conventional dictates of a patriarchal society regarding a woman's demeanor and appearance. Women, in such a conventional world, are often stronger adherents to the "rules" of appropriate femininity than are the men for whom such rules, at least in theory, are fashioned. Louise's immediate response of shame acknowledges the power of such an objective assessment to put a woman in her place and to make her feel inferior about her possible inability to measure up to such standards of female beauty. Most significantly, however, Louise jettisons these requirements with the toss of a lipstick. No longer willing to live the "inauthentic" life of being "seen" without truly being seen, she abandons the trappings of conventional female oppression, possibly even knowing the exacting price that such a decision will later require of her.

A scene that shortly follows reinforces Louise's rejection of these patriarchal norms of beauty. Stopping at a dusty roadside motel and gas station, and without a word being spoken between the two of them, Louise trades all of her jewelry, possibly including Jimmy's ring, for an old man's cowboy hat. Her jewelry represents vestiges of her commitment to attractive female appearance; shedding it means finally letting go of such an obligation. The cowboy hat, by contrast, represents something practical; possessing a deep brim of shade it will help her stay cool and will keep the sun out of her eyes. If her jewelry represents female passivity (with the exception of a watch, there is nothing that women's jewelry "does" except adorn), her new hat represents "male" activity (although a hat may be an adornment or a fashion statement, it "does" a number of practical things, as indicated, for its active wearer).

In sum, the film's mirror motif demonstrates Louise's opening up to the process of self-discovery. Originally an object of objectification and the male gaze, mirrors become a window into the souls of both women, particularly Louise, and offer them a chance to "grow up" while reassessing themselves as women on their own terms and in relationship to men.

Such a transformation, occurring in both women, is demonstrated in numerous other ways in the film as well. The first inkling of a shift, for example, occurs after Louise murders Harlan in the parking lot. After Louise pulls herself together from such an emotionally devastating experience, she tells Thelma, "I'm going to Mexico. Are you up to this? It isn't a game. I'm in deep shit and I gotta know what you're gonna do. This time things have changed, everything's changed, but I'm going to Mexico. I'm going." Although Thelma says nothing in reply, it is not long before she signs on for the ride. After a particularly painful phone conversation with her husband Daryl, we see Thelma reject her marriage with him entirely by her comment to Louise, "So how long until we get to goddamn Mexico?" After Thelma robs the convenience store, Louise comments that Thelma may have found her calling, to which Thelma replies, "Maybe—the call of the wild," at which point Thelma stands straight up in her seat as they drive along and whoops out loud.

Louise, in particular, gains insight into her connection with all things and the importance of giving up ego-identity in order to grow when their travels take them to a breathtakingly beautiful spot in the desert. By this point in the film their situation is exceedingly grim. The police are quickly closing in on them as their choices narrow considerably. After a frenetic car chase in which the women barely escape, the mood of the film shifts dramatically as they find themselves in this barren wilderness. Representing the hero's time spent in liminal passivity, this moment offers Louise a brief time-out from active questing in order to gain insights that will carry her through the rest of her journey and to her ultimate decision. Like Christ spending forty days in the desert and receiving a vision of his mission and ultimate death on the cross, we sense that Louise may also see her own demise, but also its representation of something larger than herself: that by dying to "self," like Christ she is opened to "Self." As the sky moves from sunset into night, we watch her become lost in quiet contemplation of the awesome beauty of the night and the vast anonymity of the stark desert plain.

Evidence for Louise's and Thelma's transformation is provided in the very next scene when Thelma says to Louise, "Something's crossed over in me and I can't go back. I mean, I just couldn't live." "I know what you mean," Louise replies. "They're charging us with murder. He said we got to figure out whether we want to come in dead or alive." Coming in "alive" would of course be the rational choice, involving surrender, acknowledgment of their guilt, and possibly either a life sentence in jail or capital punishment, particularly for Louise as the gunman. Coming in "dead" implies not surrendering, not compromising the feelings that their new sense of clarity and liberation have brought them, and not being subjected to a legal system that, at least traditionally, has prosecuted victims of rape more harshly than perpetrators. Paradoxically then, coming in alive is really coming in dead, while coming in dead, or "dying on their own terms," is really coming in alive. Thelma seems to implicitly acknowledge this paradox of terminology when she replies, "I feel awake, wide awake. I don't think I ever remember feeling this way. Everything seems different."

In the final chase scene, as they attempt to allude the dozen or more squad cars chasing them, Louise inadvertently almost drives over a cliff. At the last minute she brings the car to a screeching halt. The women, paralyzed with fear, peer over the edge of the canyon that almost claimed their lives. Their fear of death at this moment is palpable. And yet, this moment is also a crossroads for them. Notes Thelma of the vast beauty and power of the canyon arrayed below them, "Isn't it beautiful?" "Yeah," agrees Louise, "It's something else alright." It is not too much of a stretch to view this moment as one of transcendent awareness for both women as they connect with the vast natural (maternal) world, shed their fear over the loss of ego-identity, and acknowledge having found their "home" in the universe. All fear gone, all that remains is to make the final "leap of faith" into the womb/tomb of the Grand Canyon.

This action occurs as we get a point-of-view shot from the perspective of the lawmen in their squad cars. A dozen or more sharp shooters have their rifle sights trained on the backs of the two women's heads. We see the woman through the rifle scopes' crosshairs. With this "voyeuristic" point-of-view shot we are once again made aware of the "seeing and being seen" male gaze motif, except this time the true seriousness of this fetishized game is strikingly apparent. Louise, as if realizing this deadly inevitability, says to Thelma, "I'm not giving up." Replies Thelma, "OK, listen. Then let's not get caught. Let's just keep going." "You sure?" asks Louise. "Yeah," affirms Thelma. They kiss in passionate embrace and grab hands. Louise floors the gas pedal. Their car becomes airborne, sailing off the side of the canyon wall and into eternity. The final image is a freeze-frame of the car caught in mid-air, which then dissolves to a bright white screen.

In one interpretation, by choosing death over life the women have chosen not to compromise their vision, the boon that they share. They have also chosen to make the sacred marriage with each other, evidenced by their passionate kiss, their hand-clasp, and their commitment to this choice, rather than with men who require them to live on terms that compromise their soul and their vision. In choosing death they have chosen to surrender ego-identity, or modern consciousness, to be reunited with the Great Goddess in order to make the final journey home. In another interpretation, however, they have failed at the hero's task, having refused the call to return to the world of the everyday and the ordinary. By rejecting such a realm, they indicate that the community is beyond redemption, and thus, a rejection of patriarchy becomes a rejection of all possible visions in which men and women can live and love together and fashion a transcendent home on earth.

Perhaps, in the typical paradox of mythology, there are elements of "truth" to both interpretations of the protagonists' return to the Goddess/ Great Mother. For, as Campbell reminds us:

> She is the world creatrix, ever mother, ever virgin. She encompasses the encompassing, nourishes the nourishing, and is the life of everything that lives.
>
> She is also the death of everything that dies. The whole round of existence is accomplished within her sway, from birth, through adolescence, maturity, and senescence, to the grave. She is the womb and the tomb: the sow that eats her farrow. Thus she unites the "good" and the "bad," exhibiting the two modes of the remembered mother, not as personal only, but as universal. The devotee is expected to contemplate the two with equal equanimity. Through this exercise his spirit is purged of its infantile, inappropriate sentimentalities and resentments, and his mind is opened to the inscrutable presence which exists, not primarily as "good" or "bad" with respect to his childlike human convenience, his weal and woe, but as the law and image of the nature of being.[30]

Problematizing Gender and Sexual Orientation in the Sacred Marriage Quest Film

Despite the fact that both heroes and heroines can make the sacred marriage in mythology, it is often the case that the hero is male and thus his consort is the goddess. As a result, a great deal more has been written about the hero's sacred marriage with the goddess than the heroine's marriage with the god. When the goddess figure is depicted in Judeo-Christian myth, as we have seen, she is often split into the "good" goddess/mother and the "evil" goddess/mother;

similar to the Madonna/whore dichotomy that has evolved in Western literature and has been noted by critics of Western culture. Such a bifurcation can be viewed as the failure on Western culture's part to embrace the whole of the goddess and what she represents in terms of both spirit and flesh, good and evil.

This pattern of purely good versus purely evil goddess figures is evident, for example, in the film *The Natural*. Iris, Roy Hobbs' childhood sweetheart and the woman with whom he ultimately completes the sacred marriage, is depicted as the embodiment of angelic goodness. Thus by being continually dressed in white while being rendered relatively asexual by the film, she hardly embodies the ideal sacred marriage mate who exhibits a balancing of darkness and light, the civilized and the savage, the sexual and the virginal. Harriet Bird and Memo Paris, by contrast, as the "bad" women or sexual temptresses in Roy's life, are reduced solely to their physical natures and their evil intentions toward him when it could be argued that both women, and Bird in particular, have important lessons to teach Hobbs, and, as goddess/mother figures, possess both "good" and "evil" natures.

Not only has the role of the goddess in Western myth been overly simplified, but female heroes have themselves received little treatment both in scholarly writing on myth and in Western mythology. Speaking to both the diminishing of women as goddess and as hero, Campbell notes:

The function of the female [in patriarchal mythology] has been systematically devalued, not only in a symbolical cosmological sense, but also in a personal, psychological. Just as her role is cut down, or even out, in myths of the origin of the universe, so also in hero legends. It is, in fact, amazing to what extent the female figures of epic, drama, and romance have been reduced to the status of mere objects; or, when functioning as subjects, initiating action of their own, have been depicted either as incarnate demons or as mere allies of the masculine will.[31]

In those rare cases when women are depicted as active and willful heroes of the story, as in *Thelma and Louise* and *The Piano*, they are still presented with a dilemma. If the goddess and Great Mother are collapsed into one figure, as they are implicitly in Campbell's discussion of the Oedipal quality of the sacred marriage, then desiring a return to the impersonal mother of preconsciousness requires female heroes to make the sacred marriage with a female consort rather than a male. This may account, in part, for the lesbian undertones in *Thelma and Louise*. While not in themselves problematic, since such an interpretation at least presents these women with an alternative definition of sexual orientation, it circumscribes this as the only choice, thereby excluding heterosexuality.

Possibly most disturbing in *The Piano* is Ada's decision to give up her piano for a life of blissful domesticity with Baines. Her decision to throw her piano overboard on her journey to Nelson with Baines, in one interpretation, signifies her choice of the voice she has discovered through loving Baines over the voice she has constructed for herself through her piano. Although she resumes piano playing and gives piano lessons in Nelson, we sense that she will never again open herself to the wild flights of fancy she experienced in some of her earlier passionate playing. Her sacred marriage, in other words, as the culmination of her search for home, has dimmed her artistic or creative energy. Significantly, the film never presents this as a compromise or a limitation.[32]

In sum, although *The Natural* and *Bull Durham* provide mythic admonitions about the importance of making the sacred marriage, both portraits remain flawed—in *The Natural*, in its attempt to separate the goddess figure into "good" and "bad" goddesses, and in *Bull Durham*, in its inability to portray the goddess figure in a way that does not draw on the traditional stereotype that a woman's main goal in life is finding and keeping a man. While men "act" in the realm of action and events, women, like Annie, traditionally "are." [33] embodying the virtues of waiting patiently at home for their man to finally realize that home is where he needs to be. Ultimately, however (except in unusual turns of events, such as occurs in the conclusion of *Thelma and Louise*), the sacred marriage quest may be ideologically limiting by possibly excluding all definitions of sexual orientation other than heterosexuality. Women make the sacred marriage with men and vice versa.

Although the sacred marriage quest for female heroes has received a good deal less treatment in film and literature, both of the female quest films discussed in this chapter, *The Piano* and *Thelma and Louise*, offer powerful, if sometimes paradoxical examples of such a quest. Both films articulate what is at stake for both women and men as they seek to come together as equals in an age that has not worked out liberating definitions of what it means to be male and female and appropriate articulations for coming of age through the union of the sacred marriage.

5 The Father Quest in American Film

Simba: Who are you?
Rafiki: The question is who are *you*?

—*The Lion King*

I'm thirty-six years old. I have a wife, a child and a mortgage, and I'm scared to death I'm turning into my father.

—Ray Kinsella, *Field of Dreams*

Campbell explains that "There is a little motif that occurs in many narratives, related to a hero's life, where the boy says, 'Mother, who is my father?' She will say, 'Well, your father is in such and such a place' and then he goes on the father quest." [1]

Finding the father is finding the self. As Campbell explains, "there's a notion that the character is inherited from the father, and the body and very often the mind from the mother. But it's your character that is the mystery, and your character is your destiny. So it is the discovery of your destiny that is symbolized by the father quest." [2] This coming of age for the hero requires moving from the realm of the mother into the realm of the father, "who becomes, for his son, the sign of the future task, and for his daughter, of the future husband. Whether he knows it or not, and no matter what his position in society, the father is the initiating priest through whom the young being passes on into the larger world." [3]

In the *Odyssey*, for example, Telemachus sets out on the father quest to find Odysseus. Since he was a baby when Odysseus left for the Trojan War, Telemachus has never really met him. His task, therefore, is not only to bring his father home, but also to find out who is father is, and, by extension, to find out who he is as well. The legend of King Arthur provides another example of the father quest in mythic literature. Arthur, as a boy, is raised in obscurity and is unaware of his royal lineage. Part of his quest, under the guidance of Merlin, a shaman/father figure himself, is to learn who his royal father is and to accept the destiny that this knowledge brings with it.

Elements of the father quest exist in the Christ story as well. Often referred to by Campbell as "father atonement," the father quest not only means finding the father, but also being "atoned" or "at one" with the father.[4] Jesus Christ, for example, came from the Father, and after his questing to bring enlightenment or knowledge of the transcendent to humanity, he returns to the Father. During his time on Earth he has numerous conversations with the Father, many of which are designed to help him reconcile his will with his Father's and to better understand his Father's will and his own quest on Earth.

Although the version of the father quest appears in a number of the films discussed in this book, this motif is central to the viewer's experience of *The Lion King* and *Field of Dreams*. This chapter, therefore, is devoted to an analysis of the father quest in these two films and concludes with a discussion of the problematic portrayal of class, race, sexual orientation, and gender in both father quest films.

The Lion King

The Lion King, an animated feature-length film released by Disney Enterprises in 1994, has become one of the biggest commercial and popular successes of all time. Grossing more than $300 million at the box office, the film has the distinction of being the most successful animated feature in history. It is also the top-selling home video, having sold more than 30 million copies. The film spawned a sequel, *The Lion King II: Simba's Pride*, released to video in 1998, and a Broadway musical that, as of 2001, continues to play to sold out houses and critical acclaim.

The film, perhaps best of those to be discussed in this chapter, depicts the father quest as the search for one's destiny. The film is a coming-of-age quest for Simba, the lion cub whose hero tasks will be to face his own shadow—his guilt over his father's death—to find the father inside of him, and to accept his destiny as the future king. The film's power and beauty is generated not only by the elegant manner in which it tells the father quest, but also by the ease with which it combines a version of the creation myth (the circle of life), the sacred marriage quest (Simba and Nala), and the grail quest (restoring the Pride Lands from the wasteland it has become). As such, like George Lucas' Star Wars trilogy, it comes closest to encapsulating the various permutations of quest mythology inside of one story. In telling its story, however, as we will see, *The Lion King* reinforces traditional understandings of class and gender and "naturalizes" the idea of a benevolent monarchy.

The film's opening montage, a visual and musical tour de force, works successfully to frame this coming-of-age story in the larger context of creation/re-creation mythology. As we watch the rapid and purposeful movement of numerous African animals surging across the vast savanna, we hear strains of Elton John's song "Circle of Life" combined with African tribal music. It feels like the first day, of creation. All is in balance and harmony. The power of new life surges in every beast of the earth and every fowl of the air. God, implicitly present in his magnificent creatures, sees that his creation is good. The animals, as if mysteriously summoned by a will greater than their own, move toward Pride Rock, where Mustafa, a male lion and the king of the beasts, stands proudly surveying his kingdom—the gathered animals and the vast plains that stretch before him. This is a very special gathering. The wise old baboon Rafiki, the king's shaman/wizard, embraces Mustafa, who in turn embraces his mate Sarabi. For the first time we see the small lion cub that Sarabi has nestled in her arms. Rafiki, cracking open an egg or fruit, anoints the newborn cub with the egg/fruit by making a sign on his forehead, blows the dust of the earth onto the wet egg/fruit, and then holds up the cub for all to see. In choreographic unison, the animals bow to the chosen one, the future king of Pride Rock, as the music swells and the title credits appear.

Simba's birth is a celebration of the continuity of life. His baptism with a "sign" demonstrates fulfillment of the "covenant" God has with his creatures, that he would always send them a king/prophet to protect and guide them and bring them wisdom, just as God, in the Christian tradition, sent his son to the people to guide them and bring them enlightenment. The egg or fruit, traditional symbols of new life, reinforces this interpretation. Its mandala shape reinforces the "circle of life" theme. Rafiki's blowing dust unto the wet egg/fruit brings to mind the dust of the earth and the symbolic meaning of "ashes to ashes, dust to dust," or that in this case it is death that makes new life possible. In the Christian symbology of Ash Wednesday, it is specifically Christ's death—the perfect sacrifice—that makes new life with God possible.

The wise old baboon Rafiki, the king's shaman/wizard holds up Simba, Mustafa's and Sarabi's newborn cub, for all the animals at Pride Rock to witness and celebrate in *The Lion King*. Just prior to the moment depicted, Rafiki, cracks open an egg/fruit(?) anoints the newborn cub with it by making a sign on his forehead, and blows the dust of the earth onto the wet egg/fruit. After the moment depicted in the above image, we see all the animals of the Savannah, in choreographed unison, bow to the future king of Pride Rock, as the music swells and the title credits appear. Simba's birth is a celebration of the continuity of life, represented by his baptism with the egg or fruit, traditional symbols of new life. Courtesy of the Museum of Modern Art—Film Stills Archives.

Rafiki anointing Simba's forehead with ashes is also a reminder that even from the moment of birth we begin a journey toward death. Thus a celebration of the continuity of life also implies an acknowledgment of the continuity of death, since life springs from death and death concludes life.

In the very next scene we witness a heart-to-heart talk between Mustafa and Simba that characterizes the full nature of this circle of life. Mustafa and Simba, standing on the very pinnacle of Pride Rock, survey the vast savanna below:

Mustafa: Everything the light touches is our kingdom. A king's time as ruler rises and falls like the sun. One day, Simba, the sun will set on my time here and will rise with you as the new king.

Simba: And this will all be mine?

Mustafa: Everything.

Simba: Everything the light touches. What about that shadowy place?

Mustafa: That's beyond our borders. You must never go there, Simba.

Simba: But I thought a king can do whatever he wants?

Mustafa: Oh, there's more to being king that getting your way all the time.

Simba: There's more?

Mustafa: Simba, everything you see exists in a delicate balance. As king you need to understand that balance and respect all the creatures, from the crawling ant to the leaping antelope.

Simba: But Dad, don't we eat the antelope?

Mustafa: Yes, Simba, but let me explain. When we die our bodies become the grass and the antelope eat the grass, and so we are all connected in the great circle of life.

Just as the king's body becomes grass for the antelope, all things must die, but in dying, live. Such an interpretation, for example, can be given to the standard Western response to the death of a monarch, "The king is dead. Long live the king." Such an image also reinforces the Christian imagery of Christ the king dying for his people in order to provide them "sustenance" for a new life. Campbell, in fact, asserts that "The Christ story involves the sublimation of what originally was a very solid vegetal image. Jesus is the Holy Rood, the tree, and he is himself the fruit of the tree. Jesus is the fruit of eternal life, what was on the second forbidden tree in the Garden of Eden." [5] This image of Christ as a source of spiritual sustenance, or rebirth out of death, is echoed in the Holy Communion where communicants eat of the body and blood of Christ for spiritual survival—an echo of physical survival.

Campbell elaborates on this visceral quality to the savior/king in his discussion of the death and resurrection of a savior figure in many creation/re-creation legends:

For example, in the story of the origin of maize, you have this benign figure who appears to the young boy in a vision, and gives him maize and dies. The plant come from his body. Somebody has to die in order for life to emerge. . . . [an] incredible pattern of death giving rise to birth and birth giving rise to death. Every generation had to die in order that the next generation can come.[6]

This lesson regarding the circle of life is also an important lesson for Simba to learn from his father, for as Campbell explains, in the father quest, the father can only "entrust the symbols of office . . . to a son who has been effectually purged of all inappropriate infantile cathexes—for whom the just, impersonal exercise of the powers will not be rendered impossible by unconscious (or perhaps even conscious and rationalized) motives of self-aggrandizement, personal preference, or resentment."[7] This is echoed in Christ's words to his Father in the Garden of Gesthemene, when he says of his destiny to die on the cross, "Not my will but thy will be done." Simba, like Christ, must learn from his father that he rules only for the good of his subjects, and that as king he must be prepared to sacrifice all ego desires as well as his own life. As Mustafa explains to the young Simba, "there's more to being king that getting your way all the time."

Mustafa's serious philosophical lesson on the nature of life and death is followed by a playful pouncing lesson, however, in which the extent of his love for Simba becomes clear. Even when Mustafa later chastises Simba for journeying to the Elephant Graveyard, the "shadowy place" expressly forbidden him, he is a gentle disciplinarian who finishes his lesson with a playful "nuggie" on Simba's head. In response to this affectionate gesture Simba asks, "Dad, we're pals, right? And we'll always be together." Becoming more serious, his father replies, "Simba, let me tell you something that my father told me. Look at the stars. The great kings of the past look down on us from those stars. So whenever you feel alone just remember that those kings will always be there to guide you. And so will I." Mustafa's words are reminiscent of Christ's words to his disciples when he tells them he will always be with them, even unto the end of time. Death, in other words, will not separate them. All of the lion kings of the past are connected to each other in the great circle of life, as are all living things.

The central event of the film, and the catalyst for Simba's hero adventure of self-discovery and maturation, is the death of his father Mustafa, through the villainy of Mustafa's brother Scar. Scar uses Simba as bait for Mustafa by planting the lion cub in the path of a herd of stampeding wildebeests. Mustafa, alerted by Scar to Simba's predicament, succeeds in rescuing Simba from the stampede but at the forfeit of his own life. The source of Simba's guilt over his father's death and that ultimately accounts for his departure from Pride Rock, is the belief, deceitfully instilled by his Uncle Scar, that Simba is responsible for that death. Although this is literally true, in the sense that Mustafa would not have died if Simba had not been in desperate need of rescue, it is not true in the sense that Simba was unaware that Scar intentionally placed him in harm's way. Simba is also unaware that Scar incited the herd to stampede in order to kill his brother the king.

Coming upon a weeping and remorseful Simba, cradled in his dead father's arms, Scar asks, "Simba, what have you done?" Explains a half-weeping Simba, "The wildebeests. . . . he tried to save me. It was an accident. I didn't mean for it to happen." Scar replies, "Of course, of course you didn't. No one ever means for these things to happen, but the king is dead and if it weren't for you he'd still be alive. What will your mother think?" Pleads Simba, "What will I do?" Replies Scar, "Run away, Simba. Run, run away and never return." And thus begins Simba's hero quest into the heart of darkness to discover who he is and where his destiny lies.

Willing himself to die on the parched and barren plains under a merciless sun, Simba is instead rescued by Poomba and Timone, a wart hog and a meerkat, who soon teach him to forget his past by adopting the motto, "Hakuna Mattata," which means, as the animals break into song to explain, "no worries for the rest of your day. It's our problem-free philosophy, Hakuna Mattata." As Timone explains to Simba, "You've gotta put your past behind you . . . bad things happen and you can't do anything about it, right? When the world turns its back on you, you turn your back on the world." Simba protests, "Well, that's not what I was taught." Explains Timone, "Well, then maybe you need a new lesson."

Simba's time spent learning this "new lesson" is equivalent to the time Odysseus spends with Circe and Calypso in oblivion after having abandoned his homeward quest. Simba's self-exile in obscurity, however, like Odysseus' time with Circe and Calypso, will ultimately allow him to grow in body and spirit in a way that prepares him for completing his father quest—the journey homeward and the challenges that will await him there.

Meanwhile, back in the Pride Lands, Simba's uncle Scar, who has taken over as king of the beasts, has made a wasteland of the kingdom. Possessing no respect for the balance of nature nor the circle of life, Scar has allowed the lands to be overgrazed, making them prone to the fires and droughts that have devastated the herds. It is time for Simba to come home and assume his rightful place as king of the Pride Lands.

Nala, Simba's former playmate and betrothed, is sent on a journey in order to find help. She finds Simba. The joy at their reacquaintance, however, is overshadowed by Nala's shock at finding Simba alive, as she says, "Everyone thinks you're dead. . . . It's like you're back from the dead. You don't know what this will mean to everyone. What it means to me." Simba, to Nala, if not yet to himself, is a resurrected savior. The old Simba, the childlike naive and ego-driven Simba, is dead; the newly consecrated Simba is about to take his place. It is clear, for example, that Nala expects Simba to return with her to take his rightful place as king and to restore the Pride Lands from the wasteland that Scar has created. Simba, however, is a reluctant hero unwilling to face his destiny, recognize his father-potential, and complete his hero's quest by returning home and bestowing his boon—the salvation of Pride Rock—on the community at large. As he explains to Nala, "I'm not the king. Maybe I was gonna be, but that's a long time ago." When Nala protests, "we've really needed you at home," he retorts, "No one needs me. . . . I can't go back, you wouldn't understand." In exasperation at his unwillingness to accept his destiny, she cries, "What's happened to you? you're not the Simba I remember." "You're right, I'm not," agrees Simba, "Now are you satisfied." "No, just disappointed," she responds. "You know," accuses Simba," You're starting to sound like my father." Nala retorts, "Good, at least one of us is." By her words Nala reminds him of the father-potential existing inside of him and that growing up and facing his responsibility toward the community is the same as finding and realizing his father-potential. She can see it inside of him, even if he cannot. Simba, in fear, runs from Nala and from his fate.

Looking up at the stars in the night sky and crying out in anger, Simba finally remembers his father's words to him on that starry night so long ago: "You said you'd always be there for me, but you're not and its because of me. It's my fault. It's my fault." In despair at the loss of his father, and thus himself, he settles on a log overlooking a stream and stares down in silence at his reflection. It is not long, however, before he is wakened from his reverie by the chattering of the seemingly foolish baboon Rafiki, Mustafa's old adviser/holy man. Calling him a "creepy little monkey," Simba asks that he stop following him. When Rafiki refuses to leave, Simba, in exasperation, demands, "Who are you?" Replies Rafiki, "The question is, who are you?" "I thought I knew," whispers Simba sadly, "Now I'm not so sure." As a shaman/mentor figure for the hero, Rafiki states the central question of the film, which happens to be the central question for the hero on a father quest: "Who are you?" Simba's departure from Pride Rock, his time spent in exile, his journey of self-discovery, and his immanent journey home have been about answering that question.

When Simba replies that he does not know who he is, Rafiki retorts that *he* knows who Simba is, adding, "You're Mustafa's boy." Surprised that someone here in exile would know his father, Simba pursues the questioning saying, "You knew my father?" "Correction," says Rafiki, "I *know* your father." Explains a literally minded Simba, "I hate to tell you this, but he died a long time ago." "Nope, wrong again," corrects Rafiki. He's alive and I'll show him to you." Intrigued by these comments, Simba follows Rafiki on a dark and wild chase through deep underbrush to a silvery star-lit pool of water. "Look down there," commands Rafiki. In awe and anticipation, Simba bends down over the still pool only to be greeted by his own reflection. Instantly disappointed, he complains, "That's not my father; it's just my reflection." "No," corrects Rafiki, "Look harder. You see, he lives in you." With these words, Simba's reflection slowly transforms into his father's face. Looking up into the star-filled sky, he hears his father's voice calling, "Simba, have you forgotten me?" A shadowy image of Mustafa emerges from a bank of clouds as Simba replies, "No, how could I?" Retorts his father, "You have forgotten who you are and so have forgotten me. Look inside yourself. You are more than what you have become. You must take your place in the circle of life."

Campbell explains that in the father quest, "Ideally, the invested one has been divested of his mere humanity and is representative of an impersonal cosmic force. He is the twice born: he has become himself the father." [8] When Simba complains, "How can I go back? I'm not what I used to be," Mustafa explains, "Remember who you are. You are my son, and the one true king; remember who you are." Simba is correct, as Nala was, in saying that he is no longer the lion cub he used to be. The new Simba has known sadness, guilt, death, and separation. This knowledge, however, does not make him less; indeed, it makes him more than he was before. If anything, it makes him ready to become his father. He is now twice-born. As Campbell explains:

The problem of the hero going to meet his father is to open his soul beyond terror to such a degree that he will be ripe to understand how the sickening and insane tragedies of this vast and ruthless cosmos are completely validated in the majesty of Being. The hero transcends life with its peculiar blind spot and for a moment rises to a glimpse of the source. He beholds the face of the father, understands—and the two are atoned.[9]

Ready, for the first time, to realize his father-potential and accept this destiny, fraught as it is with memories of his father's death, his guilt over that death, and his fears over his own inability to take his father's place, Simba returns home.

Just as Odysseus is greeted by the wasteland created of his hearth and home by the ill-mannered suitors for his wife's hand, Simba returns to a community deeply scarred by the ravages inflicted by his uncle Scar. And, like Odysseus, Simba's homecoming requires him to win back his rightful place as ruler and as Nala's true mate. Part of this battle involves facing guilt over having caused his father's death. Such guilt represents the Shadow-self from which Simba had fled so many years ago. Simba can only come of age and fulfill his potential as an adult and as a hero figure, however, by facing his shadow—neither running from it nor being consumed by it, but rather acknowledging it as something that will always be a part of him. His shadow, thus acknowledged, will no longer have the power to control his life. He does this when he confronts Scar in battle for the position of king.

The battle won, all that remains is for Simba to make the sacred marriage with Nala, his true mate. That union not only represents a boon for the hero—a reward for accomplishing his hero's journey—it also signifies the continuance of the circle of life. As the film draws to a conclusion, the animals once again converge on Pride Rock, in the "new" morning, after the Fall, when balance and harmony have once again been restored by the hero's return. Simba, standing in the place once occupied by his father, is joined by Nala, his betrothed, as Rafiki, the shaman/counselor to the new king, holds up their newborn cub, a young lioness. Once again, out of death—the Pride Lands, Scar's, Mustafa's, Simba's old nature—comes life. Such a life, lived in balance and harmony with the universe, once again assures the covenant of eternal life for all creation.

Problematizing Class, Race, Sexual Orientation, and Gender in *The Lion King*

The Lion King provides an example of a mythic story that turns the circle of life, specifically, and creation mythology, generally, into a justification for hierarchy. Although Mustafa's and Simba's dominion over the beasts of the jungle and birds of the air offers a benevolent monarchy—in contrast to Scar's corrupt version of leadership—it is a monarchy nevertheless. This monarchy is epitomized, for example, in the film's opening and closing sequences.

As the opening music swells and all the birds of the air and beasts of the field gather to witness the baptism of King Mustafa's new lion cub, Simba, we realize that these animals are being called by the obligations of monarchy. As subjects, literally "subject" to the will of their king, they must obey such a summons and thus, by their appearance, assert their fealty as vassals to their lord. This opening sequence climaxes with each animal bowing head and knee in reverential respect and celebration of the continuance of the "royal" family in the form of the birth of its newest member, their future king. The idea that attendance at the ceremony is mandatory is emphasized in the next scene when King Mustafa chastises his brother Scar for failing to come to his nephew's christening ceremony.

The film's closing sequence also echoes this monarchy mandate with the summons, once again, of all of the animals to witness the birth of King Simba's own lion cub. Thus, in its conclusion, the film reassures us of the monarchy's continuance. Although individual monarchs can be tyrants—as we are reminded by the devastating reign of King Scar, who usurps the throne through fratricide and destroys the Pride Lands through neglect and overgrazing—it is the future king, young Simba, who as Grail king, restores the land and assumes the throne as benevolent steward. Thus the message is that although there may be bad kings—rotten apples in the barrel—the institution of the monarchy—the apple barrel itself—is good and should be preserved and cherished.

The film's anthropomorphic interpretation of the animal kingdom, based as it is on assumptions about the natural order of things, invites problematic application to the human world. These animals, in other words, walk and talk the language of hierarchy and privilege, implying that if it works for the animals, then why not for their human counterpart as well? Although it may be, as Campbell asserts, that life lives by the killing and eating of life in the "great circle of life," this should not be seen, I believe, as a justification for determining who gets eaten and who gets to do the eating. So, for example, contemporary exegesis of Christ's words to his disciples that "the poor you will always have with you" [10] is often used to rationalize the existence of the homelessness problem in America or the persistence of the caste system in India. In such an interpretation, a failure of social policy in the first instance and a socially sanctioned system of repression in the second are ordained by social Darwinism as part of the natural order of things. Such thinking is, at the very least, conservative and, at the very most, fascistic.

The Lion King not only celebrates monarchy; it also champions patriarchy as well. Western culture's anthropomorphic interpretation of the male lion of the herd as the "king of the beasts" easily translates as a justification for male rule in human society. Mustafa is a male king. At his death, Mustafa's brother Scar assumes his place rather than Mustafa's royal mate Sarabi. Simba, Mustafa's son, once he returns to Pride Rock, is almost solely responsible for wresting the throne away from his tyrant uncle. Although the film concludes with the birth of Simba's daughter, rather than a son, there is no clear indication that she will be the future ruler of Pride Rock. Presumably that role will be reserved for an as-yet-to-be-born male heir.

Sexual orientation and race are also presented in a stereotypical and often demeaning fashion in The Lion King. Simba's evil uncle Scar is not only a darker lion than Simba and Mustafa; he is also a more effeminate or less brawny lion than either of them. Although equating masculinity with heterosexuality is itself a stereotype, certainly Zazu's comment about Scar that "There's always one in every family. Two in mine actually," can easily be read as a comment on everyone having a gay relative or two. Zazu's comment also implies that gay relatives are always something of an annoyance to the "normal" functioning of happy families. This interpretation of Scar's sexual orientation is reinforced by our awareness that he does not have a lioness as a mate. In sum, Scar, the central villain in the film, suggests a dark (read, African-American) and effeminate (read, gay) character as well, thereby offering a portrayal that may be perceived as racial and sexually demeaning.

Racial stereotyping also occurs in the characters of Rafiki, the shaman/wiseman, and the lead hyena, whose voice is provided by Whoopi Goldberg. Although Rafiki is a powerful figure and a positive force in the life of the pride, he is portrayed with a black African accent and takes the form of a monkey, which may reinforce a particularly demeaning stereotype about African Americans. Our awareness that Whoopi Goldberg is a black woman may also shade our interpretation of the evil hyena character she plays in the film.

Thus, although *The Lion King* offers a powerful and moving portrait of "the circle of life," the grail quest, the sacred marriage quest, and, most significantly, the father quest, it does so in a fashion that raises many troubling questions about privilege and hierarchy, gender roles, racial identity, and sexual orientation.

Field of Dreams

Perhaps no recent American film has evoked as tangible a response from film-viewing audiences as *Field of Dreams* (1990) has. The site where the movie was filmed has become a virtual American mecca, resulting in thousands of tourists each year fulfilling the film's prophecy, "if you build it [they] will come." Roger Aden, writing in 1994, notes that "two years after the film's release, over 25,000 people visited the Iowa cornfield/ballpark that served as the site of the film. Now, five years after the film's release, thousands of people still visit the field each year." [11] The film itself did well in box-office and video release, earning a respectable $62 million in theaters [12] and more than $30 million in its first year on video.[13]

Aden goes on to argue that the film's primary appeal rests in the "field of dreams" site's ability to act as a "therapeutic place metaphor," which allows "the dead to return, the old to be young, and the confused to be directed by a disembodied voice." Aden continues, explaining, "All of the major characters troubled by some event in their past, use the field to atone for their actions and to find a heaven on earth." [14] This "heaven on earth" theme is demonstrated, for example, in two different scenes from the film in which long-dead ballplayers ask Ray (Kevin Costner) if his ballpark/cornfield is heaven. "No," replies Ray both times, "It's Iowa." The second time, talking with the ghost of his dead father on the ballfield at dusk, Ray, in turn, asks, "Is there a heaven?" "Oh yeah," replies his father, "It's the place where dreams come true." With a backward glance at his warmly lit farmhouse in the distance from which we hear his daughter's faint laughter, Ray responds, "Maybe this *is* heaven."

Thus the journey home—to heaven, the place where dreams come true—in *Field of Dreams* is visually literalized on the baseball field—since the ultimate purpose of every ballplayer at bat is to run the bases and go home—it is geographically realized by Iowa—the American heartland, a paradisiacal place to which weary urbanites "return home" in order to invoke the simpler life of the American garden before the industrial Fall—and it is metaphorically represented in Ray's quest to be "at home" in the universe by resolving his contentious relationship with his long-dead father. Ray's hero quest not only involves reconciling his relationship with his father and thus discovering his father-potential; it also involves helping others reconcile their relationships with their past—from Shoeless Joe Jackson (Ray Liotta), to Archie "Moonlight" Graham (Burt Lancaster) to Terence Mann (James Earl Jones). Thus, *Field of Dreams* also replicates the hero quest home for a number of the film's supporting characters. Ultimately, each one is a restless soul seeking a place in the universe, and thus is trying to go home.

Ray's field of dreams, however, is exclusively a male questing ground, opening the film to gender critique. Although Ray's wife Annie (Amy Madigan) has a personal quest of her own, to find a way to reconcile her 1960s values and lifestyle with a 1990s world and thus feel "at home" in such a world, significantly, her completion of this quest, as we will see, does not require Ray's baseball field. Ultimately, however, Ray's hero quest provides the field of dreams to the community at large. In the film's conclusion, this is represented by the headlights of hundreds of cars making their way to this newfound Eden.

The remainder of the chapter details the various versions of the hero's quest for home in *Field of Dreams*, with an emphasis on Ray Kinsella's father quest. It concludes with a discussion of the film's problematic portrayal of gender and ideology.

The Literal Journey Home on the "Field of Dreams"

In *Field of Dreams*, the importance of the baseball field itself is evident not only in the film's title, but also in the amount of film time spent on or near the field. We witness numerous scenes, for example, of Ray constructing the field, the major-league players playing on the field, Ray and other spectators either watching the events on the field from the sidelines or joining in the game itself. The goal of baseball, of course, is to come home. The team with the most players who come home in a given game wins. Baseball, according to Grella, is "the one arena of American life where you can go home again." [15] Angelaccio, in his extended analysis of the mythic qualities of baseball, expands on this notion, noting:

For A. Bartlett Giamatti, home plate is the "center of all the universes, the *omphalos*, the navel of the world," organizing the "field as it energizes the odd patterns of squares tipped and circles incomplete." More importantly, home is the goal of both teams on the field. It is the ego-locus, where every individual in the field wants to eventually arrive. Not surprisingly, it is also the same place he or she starts. It is literally "home." In mythic terms, home plate as the center of the mandala, as well as the mandala-field itself, represents an inner balance and harmony which every person tries to find. The field becomes the sacred place, the garden, in which to find oneself, in which to "come home." [16]

That Ray has turned his family home—the place where he makes a living—into a ballfield emphasizes the field's representation of the possibilities of coming home.

But the field is more than a static representation of home; it instead represents a dynamic journey, a battle in which the batter faces numerous obstacles on his quest to round the bases and return home. He can be struck out, called out by a pop fly caught by the other team, tagged out, or even sacrificed on an out for another runner. If he makes it around the bases and reaches home, it is because he is often aided by others along the way, team members who either advance him around the bases or make sacrifices for him to be able to advance. And if he reaches home, he does so not for his individual glory but for the team's win and for the fans' pleasure. In sum, the batter engages in a hero's journey outward and homeward in which he faces many obstacles, but also encounters many helpers along the way. If he succeeds, it is for the good of the community at large rather than his personal aggrandizement.

That a baseball field is the centerpiece of this film, that Ray and many of the film's characters play baseball on this field, that the baseball field is the place where "dreams come true," represents the hero's journey home (to home base) on the most literal of levels.

The Geographical Journey Home to the "Field of Dreams"

The journey home in *Field of Dreams* is more than a literal trip around the bases, however; it is also a geographical journey home to the garden—represented as a return to the Midwest, America's "heartland."

In the early days of colonization, many immigrants viewed America as an earthly Eden. As Conrad Ostwalt explains:

The governing literary image of American space [during the first 100 years of colo-
nization] revolved around the understanding of America as a sacred garden; it was a
garden because America was the land that God had created and challenged with a special purpose; America was sacred because the New World was the meeting place of
God and human beings.[17]

American Puritans, as Sanford points out, believed that

America had been singled out, from all the nations of the earth, as the site of the Second Coming; and that the millennium of the saints, while essentially spiritual in nature,
would be accompanied by a paradisiacal transformation of the earth as the outward
symbol of their inward state.[18]

America not only represented a spiritual world to early colonists, however;
it also symbolized the possibility of a "a sacred social world where people
could aspire to live without sin and in total harmony with one another." [19]

As America, particularly the Northeast, became more and more indus-
trialized, the idea of an earthly Eden was displaced to the West. According
to Henry Nash Smith, "The master symbol of the garden embraced a cluster
of metaphors expressing fecundity, growth, increase, and blissful labor in the
earth, all centering about the heroic figure of the idealized frontier farmer." [20]
This image of an agrarian Western Eden was frequently contrasted, in literature and culture, with urban areas, which by the mid-1800s came to be viewed,
according to James B. Lanman, as "the sores of the political body." [21]

Although despised by many in the mid-nineteenth century, by the turn
of the twentieth century, with the dawn of industrialization, urban areas became centers of economic and social life. As a result, as Ostwalt explains,
"Americans lost all expectations of a sacred land that promised possibility for
all; both the garden myth that promised the beauty of an unspoiled nature and
vision of a perfect society disintegrated." [22]

Despite this "loss of Eden," there are some contemporary indicators,
Aden argues, that "Americans are seeking to move back into the garden, using
it as a place of refuge and spiritual rejuvenation" with an increasing "emphasis
on production rather than consumption as well as [a] valuing of the spiritual
over the secular." [23]

Perhaps with the settling of California as the last Western frontier, the
one remaining location for an Eden on earth is the sparsely populated Midwest, America's heartland. "The obvious [remaining] model for this mono-
mythic Eden," Jewett and Lawrence assert, is "the Midwestern small town." [24]

It is not surprising, therefore, that as part of the wave of urbanites trading the city for the country, Ray and Annie, in *Field of Dreams*, leave Berkeley, California, to buy a family farm in Iowa, Annie's home state.

But even this Eden has felt the encroaching impact of modern development and the erosion of traditional values. The movement of the machine into this last garden, for example, became starkly apparent during the 1980s as family farm after family farm, facing bank foreclosures for defaulted mortgages, disappeared from the American Midwest, swallowed up by larger and larger farm conglomerates. The 1980s demise of the family farm appeared to be a repeat of the dust-bowl days of the 1930s, when frequent crop failures, fluctuations in populations, and the displacement of the tenant farmer also marked the demise of the promised agrarian Eden as dramatized in John Steinbeck's *Grapes of Wrath*. Farm Aid, the charity benefit concerts organized by singer-songwriter Willie Nelson and other pop and country singers, illustrates the plight of these farmers in concerts designed to raise money to help subsidize small farms and keep them afloat. This gloomy atmosphere also provides the backdrop for *Field of Dreams* as Ray and Annie, finding themselves behind in their mortgage payments, are faced with the possibility of selling their farm to Ray's brother-in-law, Mark, a representative for a large, anonymous farming corporation.

The loss of Eden in the twentieth century, however, is represented more broadly in the commercialization of baseball. The seven White Sox players who threw the 1919 World Series for money became iconic of the steadily increasing emphasis in baseball and in all professional sports on profit over allegiance to the fans and the sport. In *Field of Dreams* this is represented by the loss of the Brooklyn Dodgers to Los Angeles and the subsequent bulldozing of Ebbets Field.

The loss of Eden is also represented in *Field of Dreams* as the demise of 1960s American activism and idealism. In the film, Terence Mann, the 1960s writer and activist, by the 1990s, has become a cynic and a hermit. We discover, for example, that he has opted out of public life and is more interested in designing video games for profit than novels for political comment. The loss of 1960s idealism is also illustrated by Ray's wife Annie's quest to keep the local school board from banning a number of important novels from the school library, deeming them pornographic. That both Ray and Annie leave Berkeley, a West Coast mecca for activists and political idealists during the 1960s, also implies that this Eden, by the 1990s, had lost its power to sustain a community of believers. It's not surprising, therefore, that the 1919 White Sox baseball team, Terence Mann and Ray and Annie come "home" to the heartland, for it is here that they can finally find healing in this, the last hope for an American Eden on earth.

The Metaphoric Journey Home on the "Field of Dreams"

Field of Dreams not only presents the hero's quest as a geographical journey home to the garden; it also tells a version of the father quest—Ray Kinsella's quest to "find" or understand his father and thereby understand himself is a metaphorical journey to finally feel "at home" in the world.

All three quests, the literal journey home in baseball, the geographic journey home to America's heartland, and Ray's personal father quest to be atoned with his father and at home with himself, are illustrated in the film's opening montage with accompanying voice-over. The film's opening image is a sepia-toned photograph of Ray's father, John Kinsella, as a young boy, wearing overalls and sitting in a vast field of corn. Ray, in voice-over, explains:

My father's name was John Kinsella. It's an Irish name. He was born in North Dakota in 1896 and never saw a big city until he came back from France in 1918. He settled in Chicago where he quickly learned to live and die with the White Sox; died a little when they lost the 1919 World Series, died a lot the following summer when eight members of the team were accused of throwing that series. He played in the minors a year or two but nothing ever came of it. Moved to Brooklyn in '35, married Mom in '38, and was already an old man working at the naval yards when I was born in 1952. My name's Ray Kinsella. Mom died when I was three and I supposed Dad did the best he could. Instead of Mother Goose, I was put to bed at night to the stories of Babe Ruth, Lou Gehrig, and the great Shoeless Joe Jackson. Dad was a Yankees' fan so of course I rooted for Brooklyn. But in '58 the Dodgers moved away, so we had to find other things to fight about. We did. And when it came time to go to college I picked the farthest one from home I could find. This, of course, drove him right up a wall, which I suppose was the point. Officially my major was English, but really it was the Sixties. I marched, I smoked some grass, tried to like sitar music, and I met Annie. The only thing we had in common was that she came from Iowa and I had once heard of Iowa. After graduation we moved to the Midwest and stayed with her family as long as we could—almost a full afternoon. Annie and I got married in June of '74; Dad died that fall. A few years later Karen was born. She smelled weird but we loved her anyway. Then Annie got the crazy idea that she could talk me into buying a farm. I'm thirty-six years old, I love my family, I love baseball, and I'm about to become a farmer. But until I'd heard the voice, I'd never done a crazy thing in my whole life.

This voice-over is accompanied by a literal visualization of the events being narrated, starting with the sepia-toned photo of Ray's dad as a boy. This is followed by a sepia-toned photo of John as a young man in uniform, followed by various shots of Chicago; newspaper headlines of the 1919 World Series scandal; a photo of John Kinsella in his minor-league uniform; shots of Brooklyn; a wedding photo of John and his wife; the naval yards where John worked; a color photo of John, wife, and baby Ray; baseball cards for Babe Ruth, Lou Gehrig, and Shoeless Joe Jackson; black-and-white footage of a wrecking ball in Dodger Stadium; Ray's college yearbook photo; shots of the Berkeley campus; various scenes of 60s activism; Annie's college yearbook photo; a photo of Ray and Annie in graduation robes; home movies of Ray's wedding to Annie; color photos of Ray, Annie, and their new baby Karen; and home movies of Ray and Annie standing in front of their newly purchased Iowa farm while Annie attaches the "sold" sign to the real estate placard.

This opening montage with accompanying voice-over, primarily about Ray's relationship with his father, more specifically establishes a context for the audience's understanding of Ray's ambivalent relationship with baseball, his father, and coming home. Although Ray was born in Brooklyn, his father's birthplace, North Dakota, like Iowa, represents the American heartland. When Ray decides to move to Iowa with Annie, although he doesn't know it at the time, he is returning to his ancestral home. As a city kid Ray, unlike his father, knows nothing about farming. Ray is also ambivalent about this journey "home," as he says to Annie at a point later in the film, "I'm thirty-six years old. I have a wife, a child, and a mortgage, and I'm scared to death I'm turning into my father." Ray is also returning home to America's pastoral Garden of Eden, as represented by the initial shot of John Kinsella as a boy in the cornfields, and the final video footage of Ray and Annie in front of their newly purchased Iowa farm. The locations featured in between these pastoral images are mostly industrial— the streets of a busy Chicago, the Brooklyn Navy Yard, a wrecking ball in Ebbets Field. All of them are images of a bastardized or destroyed Eden, particularly the wrecking ball in Ebbets Field since it is well known that the team left Brooklyn for more money.

Ray's contentious relationship with his father is also quickly established. We sense that, just as in choosing favorite baseball teams, whatever Ray's father liked, Ray would like the opposite. "Already an old man working at the naval yards when [Ray] was born in 1952," Ray and his father are also from radically different generations, his father a product of the Depression and World War I, Ray a product of the Sixties. It is also a relationship marked by

alienation—they always fought—separation—Ray moved as far away from his father as he could—and missed opportunities—Ray's father never got to meet his granddaughter, Karen.

Ray's ambivalent relationship with baseball, only hinted at in the opening sequence, is clearly illustrated later in the film when we find out that John Kinsella tried to live out his major-league baseball dreams through his son Ray. At one point Terence Mann asks Ray what happened to his father. Explains Ray, "He never made it as a ballplayer so he tried to get his son to make it for him. By the time I was ten playing baseball got to be like eating vegetables or taking out the garbage. So when I was fourteen I started to refuse. You believe that? An American boy refusing to have a catch with his father? . . . Anyway, when I was seventeen I packed my things, said something awful, and left. After a while I wanted to come home but I didn't know how. Made it back for the funeral though." Ray's comment establishes both his hero quest and his father quest. Since he was seventeen he has been trying to come home, and when he finally did—for his father's funeral—it was obviously too late for Ray to reconcile his relationship with him. Ray's conversation with Terence Mann continues:

Mann: What was the awful thing you said to your father?
Ray: I said I could never respect a man whose hero was a criminal.

Ray Kinsella (Kevin Costner), his wife Annie (Amy Madigan) and daughter Karin (Gaby Hoffman) are greeted by a youthful John Kinsella (Dwier Brown), Ray's father, in the film *Field of Dreams*. In the film we learn that Ray and his father are from radically different generations—his father a product of the Depression and WWI, Ray a product of the Sixties. All of his life, Ray and his father experienced a relationship marked by alienation—separation—and missed opportunities. Ray's contentious relationship with his father is illustrated in the film when we discover that John Kinsella tried to live out his major league baseball dreams through Ray. Resisting his father's influence, Ray eventually refused to play baseball with his father and left home at seventeen. When Ray finally came home it was for his father's funeral, obviously too late to reconcile his relationship with him. Thus, the magical meeting between Ray and his father, John, made possible by Ray's field of dreams—depicted in this image—represents the culmination of Ray's father quest to find his father and thus, to find himself in order to complete his metaphorical journey "home." Courtesy of the Museum of Modern Art—Film Stills Archives.

Mann:	Who was his hero?
Ray:	Shoeless Joe Jackson.
Mann:	You know he wasn't a criminal.
Ray:	I know.
Mann:	Then why did you say it?
Ray:	I was seventeen. The son-of-a-bitch died before I could take it back, before I could tell him. He never met my wife. He never saw his granddaughter.
Mann:	This is your penance.
Ray:	I know, I can't bring my father back.
Mann:	So the least you can do is bring back his hero.

By the end of the film, of course, as we will see, Ray actually does manage to "bring [his] father back," by building the fantastical field of dreams where anything is possible. Like the unhappy members of the 1919 White Sox team, Ray's father also comes back to life, appears on the magical field, and plays ball with his estranged son Ray.

Ray's "call to adventure" takes the form of a voice and a vision. We see long shots of endless fields of corn, a white farmhouse in the distance, and Ray walking through the corn. Suddenly Ray hears a voice, indistinct at first, but clearer the second time, saying, "If you build it, he will come." Again Ray hears it. His wife Annie says that she did not hear it. Later that night in bed, he hears it for a fourth time. "Build what?" he asks out loud as he moves to the bedroom window and looks out at the cornfield. It is not long before his wife teases him about this voice while local farmers question his sanity. It is not long before Ray questions it as well. In the cornfields the next day, however, he hears the voice again repeating the same command, "If you build it, he will come." Ray, exasperated at this point, cries out, "All right. That's it. Who are you, huh? What do you want from me?" Suddenly, as if in reply, he has a vision of stadium light as a baseball field appears in the distance. "If you build it," says Ray, seeming to understand for the first time, "He will come."

At dinner that night he explains to his wife, "I think I know what 'If you build it he will come' means. I think it means that if I build a baseball field out there that Shoeless Joe Jackson will get to come back and play ball again." In bed that night, we witness the following conversation between the two of them:

Annie: Wait, are you actually thinking of doing this?
Ray: No, I mean, I can't think of one good reason why I should but . . . I'm thirty-six years old, I have a wife, a child, and a mortgage, and I'm scared to death I'm turning into my father.
Annie: What's your father got to do with all of this?
Ray: I never forgave him for getting old. By the time he was as old as I am now, he was ancient. He must have had dreams, but he never did anything about them. For all I know, he may even have heard voices too, but he certainly didn't listen to them. The man never did one spontaneous thing in all the years I knew him. Annie, I'm afraid of that happening to me and something tells me that this may be my last chance to do something about it. I want to build that field. Do you think I'm crazy?
Annie: Yes, but I also think if you really feel you should do it, you should do it.

It is interesting that "the voice" never directly specifies who the "he" is that will come to the field if Ray builds it. Although Ray's interpretation of "he" as Shoeless Joe Jackson turns out to be correct, there are a number of others that must make the journey to the field for healing and transcendence, among them the seven other banned White Sox players, the baseball rookie Doc "Moonlight" Graham, Terence Mann, the American people, Ray's dad John Kinsella, and most important, Ray himself.

Shoeless Joe and the 1919 White Sox Team's Journey Home

As neighbors watch from the road, Ray plows under his livelihood—acres and acres of his cornfield. Riding with his daughter Karin on the tractor, he tells her stories of Shoeless Joe Jackson and the infamous 1919 World Series. The stories continue as he installs stadium lights and lines the baseball field. We then watch as he waits, through summer, fall, and winter, endlessly staring at the field he has built and wondering why he built it. The Kinsella family finances continue to deteriorate. Annie warns him they are in danger of losing their house and farm. But just when things seem darkest, Shoeless Joe appears on Ray's field of dreams.

As Ray starts to pitch balls to Jackson, Jackson recounts his love for the game saying, "Getting out of baseball was like having part of me amputated. . . . Man, I did love this game. I'da played for food money. It was a game—the sounds, the smells. Did you ever hold a ball or a glove to your face? I used to love traveling in the train from town to town—the hotels, brass spittoons in the lobbies, brass beds in the rooms. It was a crowd, rising to their feet when the ball was hit deep. I'da played for nothin." As Jackson waxes nostalgic for the early days of professional baseball in America, we are immediately aware that he is referring to a bygone era, a time before the "fall" when things were good, and baseball, in its infancy, represented the innocence of an Edenic America. All of that changed, however, for Shoeless Joe, the rest of the 1919 World Series White Sox players, and America itself, with the scandal surrounding the "throwing" of the 1919 World Series by eight members of the White Sox team. Ray's field of dreams, in other words, offers Shoeless Joe and the other players redemption, a second chance to make things right—a chance, almost, to rewind to the past in order to rewrite it. This becomes evident in an exchange between Ray and Shoeless Joe after their game of catch:

Shoeless Joe:	Can I come back again?
Ray:	Yeah, I built this for you.
Shoeless Joe:	There are others you know—there were eight of us. It'd really mean a lot to them.
Ray:	Yeah, anytime. They're all welcome here.
Shoeless Joe:	Hey, is this heaven?
Ray:	No, it's Iowa. (Shoeless Joe turns and then disappears into the field of corn.)

The next day all eight of the blacklisted White Sox players appear on the field for practice while Ray and Karin sit in the stands to watch them play. For Shoeless Joe Jackson and the seven other White Sox players banned from the game for life, playing on Ray's field of dreams allows them to return home to the game they loved and maybe even release their souls from a purgatory-like limbo of regrets and unfulfilled desires in order to reach "heaven."

Annie Kinsella's Journey Home

Things are not over, however, as Ray hears the voice once again, this time telling him to "Ease his pain." Ray doesn't understand what the voice wants. Later that night he and Annie go to a town meeting where the school board is debating whether to ban certain books from the high-school library. As a child of the 60s this issue is of deep concern to Annie, particularly when she discovers that one of the writers whose books they want to ban is Terence Mann, one of her favorite authors. At the meeting, a Phyllis Schlafly look-alike stands up and explains:

The so-called novels of Terence Mann endorse promiscuity, godlessness, the mongrel-ization of the races, and disrespect to high-ranking officers of the United States Army. And that is why right-thinking school boards all across the country have been banning this man's s-h-i-t since 1960. You know why he stopped writing books? Because he masturbates.

Unable to stand for this reactionary rhetoric, Annie jumps to her feet and ex-claims, "Terence Mann was a warm and gentle voice of reason during a time of great madness. He coined the phrase 'Make love, not war.' While other people were chanting, 'burn, baby burn,' he was talking about love and peace and understanding. I cherish every one of his books and I dearly wish he had written more, and I think if you had experienced even a little bit of the Sixties you might feel the same way too." Due to the power of her eloquence, Annie succeeds in rallying other townspeople and defeats the conservative backlash against banning the books of certain writers like Terence Mann. The film im-plies that activism is not dead and that Annie, through this win, has managed to revive her 1960s idealism in order to fight for 1990s causes.

Terence Mann's Journey Home

Annie's triumphal breakthrough at the school's PTA meeting is cut short, however, as Ray tells her, "I think I know whose pain I've got to ease. Terence Mann's." Annie then asks the question that is on the film-viewer's mind when she retorts, "Look, he's my favorite writer too, but what's Terence Mann got to do with baseball?" Explains Ray:

Mann wrote a story twenty-six years ago whose main character was named John Kinsella. Terence Mann's dream was to play baseball on Ebbets Field. The last interview he gave was in 1973. . . . Honey, the guy was a baseball fanatic; listen to this, "As a child my earliest reoccurring dream was to play at Ebbets Field with Jackie Robinson and the Brooklyn Dodgers. Of course it never happened and the Dodgers left Brooklyn and they tore down Ebbets Field, but even now I still dream that dream." The man wrote the best books of his generation. He was a pioneer in the civil rights and anti-war movement. I mean, he made the cover of *Newsweek*. He knew everybody. He did everything. He helped shape his time. I mean the guy hung out with the Beatles. But in the end it wasn't enough and in the end what he missed was baseball. Honey, the guy hasn't been to a live baseball game since 1958.

The middle section of the film details Ray's trip to New York and his attempts to get Terence Mann to join him to watch a baseball game. Ultimately, however, his trip to meet Mann is about getting Mann to reconnect with himself and his 1960s idealism. Ray is successful not only in taking Mann to a baseball game, but also in getting Mann to return with him to Iowa and to the field of dreams. For Terence Mann the field of dreams allows him to regain his purpose, his love of writing, and possibly gain a fuller understanding of humanity. In the film's final scene, for example, as we watch Mann walk across the baseball field and disappear into the cornfield (like the White Sox players when they dematerialize), we sense that he is going on a journey of spiritual self-enlightenment that will ultimately take him to "heaven," or toward a transcendent home.

Doc "Moonlight" Graham's Journey Home

Ray's hero quest for enlightenment not only requires "easing the pain" of Terence Mann, but also that of rookie baseball player Doc "Moonlight" Graham, a one-season baseball player in the major leagues who went on to become a town doctor. Realizing that he would probably be sent down to the minors, Graham left baseball for a career in medicine. The puzzle for both Ray and Terence Mann is discovering why Doc Graham needed him. Although Doc Graham died in 1972, twenty-odd years before the film takes place, Ray is suddenly transported back to 1972 where he bumps into Doc, out for a late night walk. After they walk back to Doc Graham's office, Ray asks him what it was like giving up a career in baseball. Explains Doc Graham, "It was like coming this close to your dreams and then watch them brush pass you in, like a stranger in a crowd. At the time you didn't think much of it. You know, we just don't recognize the most significant moments of our lives while they're happening. Back then I thought, well, they'll be other days. I didn't realize that that was the only day."

Ray: If you could do anything you want. If you could have a wish?
Doc: And you're the kind of man who could grant me that wish?
Ray: I don't know, I'm just asking.
Doc: You know I never got to bat in the majors. I kind of liked to have that chance, just once. To stare down a big league pitcher. To stare him down just as he goes into his wind up. Like make him think you know something he doesn't. That's what I'd wish for. The chance to squint at a sky so blue it hurts your eyes. To feel the tingle in your arms as you connect with the ball. To run the bases, to stretch a double into the triple, and to flop face first into third, wrap your arms around the bag. That's my wish, Ray. That's my wish. And is there enough magic out there in the moonlight to make this dream come true?
Ray: What would you say if I said "yes"?
Doc: I think I'd actually believe you.
Ray: Well, sir, there's a place where things like that happen, and if you want to go I can take you there.

Doc Graham decides not to go with him, at which point Ray asks, "But your wish?" "It'll have to stay a wish," explains Doc, "I lived here, I'll die here, but no regrets."

Ray: Fifty years ago for five minutes, you came, you came this close. I mean it would kill some men to get that close to their dream and not touch it. They'd consider it a tragedy.
Doc: Son, if I'd only gotten to be a doctor for five minutes, now that would've been a tragedy.

Although Ray and Terence leave Doc Graham's hometown without him, on their way back to Iowa they stop to pick up a young hitchhiker by the side of the road. Explains the boy, "I'm looking for a place to play. I heard that all through the Midwest they have towns with teams and in some places they'll even find you a day job so you can play ball nights and weekends." Replies Ray, after a look of astonishment at Terence Mann, "This is your lucky day, kid. We're going someplace kinda like that." At this point, if not before, the audience realizes that Ray and Terence, jumping time zones once again, have picked up a young Archie Graham on his way to seek fame and fortune in a career in baseball. Ray will have a chance to help Doc Graham fulfill his major-league dream after all.

After returning to Ray's farm it is not long before Archie Graham plays ball with Shoeless Joe and many other major-league ballplayers and gets his chance to stare down a major-league pitcher. Ray's daughter Karin, however, during a fight between Ray and his brother-in-law Mark, is accidentally thrown from the bleachers. Knocked unconscious, she stops breathing. The baseball rookie Archie Graham steps off of the field of dreams and is transformed into a 1972 Doc Graham. Examining Karin, he discovers that she is choking on a piece of hot dog that has blocked her windpipe. Dislodging it, he saves her life. "Thanks, Doc," says a greatly relieved Ray. "No, son, thank you," says Doc. At this moment Ray realizes that Doc Graham cannot return to the field of dreams, having crossed over the line from the magical realm into the ordinary realm. Doc Graham, however, has fulfilled his dream, both as a doctor and, thanks to Ray, as a major-league baseball player, and as such, he has no regrets. As if to emphasize this, just before Doc Graham disappears into the cornfield Shoeless Joe calls out to him, saying, "Hey, rookie, you were good."

For Doc "Moonlight" Graham, although he never regrets choosing the life of a doctor over that of a professional baseball player, his one regret is never having a chance to "stare down" a major-league pitcher at bat. Ray's field of dreams ultimately gives him this chance, thus allowing his restless soul a chance to return home.

The American Community's Journey Home

The final journey home in *Field of Dreams* is that taken by the American public, standing in for the hero's community as large. We too, the film implies, like

Ray, like Terence Mann, like Shoeless Joe and the other "blacklisted" White Sox players, also have unfulfilled dreams, or rather, deeply felt regrets at the loss of Eden. No longer innocent and young, we have known sin and guilt, and long once again to be connected with the pastoral and the transcendent. Karin, Ray's daughter, senses the mecca-like draw that her father's field of dreams has for people. Still fearful that he will lose his house, despite all of the metaphysical wish fulfillment that the field of dreams has provided, it is Karin who has the answer. As she explains:

Karin: We don't have to sell the farm. People will come from all over. They'll just decide to take a vacation, see. They'll come to Iowa City. They'll think it's really boring. So they'll drive up and wanna pay us—like buying a ticket.
Mark: Why would anyone pay to come here?
Karin: To watch the game. It'll be just like when they were little kids a long time ago. And they'll watch the game and remember what it was like.

Terence Mann emphasizes Karin's point by saying:

People will come, Ray. They'll come to Iowa for reasons they can't even fathom. They'll turn up your driveway not knowing for sure why they're doing it. They'll arrive at your door as innocent as children, longing for their past . . . for it is money they have and peace they lack. And they'll walk out to the bleachers and sit in the bleachers on a perfect afternoon and they'll find they have reserved seats somewhere along the baseline where they sat when they were children and cheered their heroes and they'll watch the game and it will be as if they dipped themselves in magic waters. The memories will be so thick they'll have to brush them away from their faces. . . . People will come, Ray. . . . The one constant through all the years has been baseball. America is ruled by it like an army of steamrollers. It's been erased like a blackboard, rebuilt, and erased again. But baseball has marked the time. This field, this game, it's a part of our past, Ray. It reminds us of all that once was good and could be again. Oh, people will come, Ray, people will most definitely come.

So Ray's field of dreams not only represents the place where he is finally able to resolve his contentious relationship with his father and thus be atoned with him, it also offers second chances to every one it touches, from Doc Graham to Shoeless Joe Jackson to Terence Mann. Ray's most significant hero's boon, however, is providing the field of dreams to a soul-weary community at large, a nation longing for the healing that the field represents. That the film's impact extends to film audience's actually treating the farm in Iowa where the film was shot as a real field of dreams speaks to the enduring power of such a metaphysical journey home, and this film's ability to manifest this journey in a particularly powerful manifestation of the hero's journey home.

Problematizing Gender and Ideology in *Field of Dreams*

Although the film offers Ray's wife Annie a chance to fulfill her own dreams — to revive her 1960s idealism in a fight for a 1990s cause — Annie's "second chance" does not occur on the field of dreams. As previously noted, Annie and her daughter Karin never actually step foot on Ray's field of dreams. More specifically, not a single women steps onto the field over the course of the film. The field's boundary lines — clearly indicated — circumscribe a powerful and sacred place. This demarcation is apparent, for example, when Doc Graham chooses to leave the field in order to become a doctor again to save Karin's life. He is clearly aware that by of stepping off of the field he cannot return to this magical place. This sacred and powerful place of transformation, in other words, as male totem, is taboo to women.

Although *Field of Dreams* asserts the significance of fathers playing catch with their sons, this does not extend to fathers playing catch with their daughters. Ray's father quest, as previously discussed, is centered on reconciling a contentious relationship with his father. We discover that the tension between the two of them was generated, in part, by Ray's rejection of his father's values and career decisions and Ray's refusal to live out his father's dream of becoming a professional baseball player. This rejection is epitomized in Ray, as a fourteen-year-old boy, refusing to play a game of catch with his father. Fathers, the film implies, play baseball with their sons and often live out their career aspirations through them. The final reconciliation between Ray and his father, of course, occurs near the film's ending as the two finally play catch together on Ray's field of dreams. Although the film seems to imply that Ray has no such tensions or issues with his own daughter, Karin, the viewer cannot help but wonder what would have happened if Ray had had a son instead? Since he has a girl, playing baseball with her and living out his dreams through her is not even an issue.

Thus, *Field of Dreams*, while offering transcendence to Ray and a community of believers on a baseball field where "dreams come true," signifies that this sacred space is a male domain — Annie and her daughter never step onto it—and thus, implies that a woman's place is in the home, or at least not on a baseball field either playing the game or playing catch with their father. The film may also be viewed as reactionary by its use of America in the 1960s to portray the disappointments of the "Big Chill" generation. It does so in such a way that the ideals for which that generation fought—world peace, love and understanding, equality and civil rights for women and minorities—are portrayed as unattainable or unrealistic. For example, the 60s writer and activist Terence Mann by the 1990s is living the life of a bitter and disillusioned recluse in New York City. It appears that he has "sold out" in terms of his 1960s idealism, since he makes a living writing software for video games.

In sum, both *Field of Dreams* and *The Lion King*, while providing mythically powerful portrayals of the hero's quest for home as the hero's quest for his father (self), do so in a manner that raises troubling questions about power, hierarchy, gender, and ideology.

II Mythological Criticism in Sociohistorical Context

This section of the book further develops the model of the perennial journey home by focusing on films that address the American character and the American journey home at particular points in time. Chapter 6, for example, explores the nature of the quest for home during the 1930s Depression era as evidenced in such Hollywood blockbusters as *The Wizard of Oz*, *It's a Wonderful Life*, and *Gone with the Wind*. Chapter 7 takes this same sociohistorical approach by looking at a contemporary manifestation of the quest myth—the current era's attempt to reconcile scientific and technological ways of knowing with spiritual/nonrational ways of knowing—in such science-fiction films as *E.T.*, *Close Encounters of the Third Kind*, *2001: A Space Odyssey*, and *Contact*.

Although all versions of the perennial journey home are grounded in the sociohistorical moment of their telling, and, as such, culturally or historically specific concerns will emerge in any version, it is often possible, even desirable to forefront those cultural and historical concerns to see what they tell us, not only about the tale but its teller, its audience, and its time period. Mythic stories that occur at rupture points in a society, such as the shift from one mode of production to another, or the transition from one dominant philosophical/ideological system to another, are often particularly compelling, because they are often replete with self-conscious examinations of those ruptures. As such, these stories offer fascinating windows into the preoccupations, the hopes and dreams, and the deepest fears of a society as they face what may seem unfathomable futures. In the current era, for example, the growing importance of technology in our lives, particularly computer and biotechnology, coupled with increased fears over their economic, ethical, and political usage, has heightened our sensitivity to the potential clash between scientific and spiritual ways of knowing. The current era's "crisis of faith," in other words, has been radically forefronted in film and literature ever since the publication of Mary Shelley's *Frankenstein*. The science-fiction genre, in particular, as we will see in Chapters 7 and 8, has attempted to work out contemporary society's deepest fears and our wildest desires about the exponential growth of and our reliance on these new technologies.

Mythic explanations, not surprisingly, also offer comforting and familiar interpretations of what may be troubling or disconcerting events. These mythic interpretations, however, may offer acceptable, even laudable rationalizations for unacceptable behaviors or attitudes. *Gone with the Wind*, for example, although providing 1930s audiences with an escape from Depression-era realities and consequent anxieties, may also have sublimated those anxieties into another context—namely the dissolution of the Old South after the Civil War. By equating the 1860s breakdown of plantation life and the dissolution of slavery with the 1930s breakdown of financial and social systems, the film may have celebrated status-quo visions of society where women were homemakers and where simple-minded but big-hearted "darkies" "knew their place." It may have been that *Gone with the Wind*, as we will see, through its use of the mythic structure of the perennial journey home, asserted the value of the institution of slavery and the class system that created it and invited audiences to wax nostalgic over its demise.

6 The Search for Home During the 1930s

Home . . . I'll go home . . . and I'll think of some way to get him back. After all, tomorrow is another day.

—Scarlett O'Hara, *Gone with the Wind*

If I ever go looking for my heart's desire again, I won't look any farther than my own backyard, because if it isn't there, I never really lost it to begin with.

—Dorothy, *The Wizard of Oz*

Welcome home, Mr. Bailey. Remember the night we broke the window in this old house? This is what I wished for.

—Mary Bailey, *It's a Wonderful Life*

The universal quest myth not only manifests itself through such permutations as the father quest or the sacred marriage quest; it also emerges in cultural myths—historically and culturally grounded interpretations of archetypic stories. If, as Joseph Campbell notes, the universal myth transcends cultural and historical conditions to speak to the elemental and identical nature of the human condition, the cultural myth relates the individual to his particular society and affirms the individual as a part of the larger whole.[1]

Janice Rushing and Thomas Frentz explain that a cultural myth "is a narrative whole which the critic reconstructs from singular texts often separated in time and genre but tied together by a single, unifying theme."[2] The American myth of "settling the West" or "manifest destiny" is an example of a cultural myth evidenced in everything from the nineteenth-century novels of James Fenimore Cooper to the classic westerns of the 1940s and 1950s such as *High Noon* and *The Searchers* and the revisionist westerns of the 1970s and 1990s such as *McCabe and Mrs. Miller* and *Unforgiven*. Although cultural myths may vary widely from culture to culture, they are usually grounded in a larger or deeper universal mythic structure that informs them and gives them power. So, for example, the Western expansion myth is grounded in and draws upon such myths as the universal hero quest and the Garden of Eden myth.

This chapter explores a particularly powerful articulation of the quest for home myth, the "loss of home" cultural myth, predominant in such 1930s and 1940s films as *Gone with the Wind* (1939), *The Wizard of Oz* (1939), and *It's a Wonderful Life* (1946). I argue that the appeal and lasting impact of all three films is due, in part, to their drawing on the universal quest for home as well as a particularly strong American manifestation of the home quest, "the loss of home," at a time when American home life everywhere was so directly threatened. This American myth of the "loss of home," as we will see, was experientially grounded for 1930s audiences in the demise of the family farm, the loss of family fortunes, and the rampant rise of homelessness.

When we think of great films in the history of the American cinema, or at least films that have touched audiences of all ages and that remain perennial favorites, *Gone with the Wind*, *The Wizard of Oz*, and *It's a Wonderful Life* certainly come to mind. All three films, in fact, appeared on the American Film Institute's much discussed 1998 list of the one hundred greatest American films of all time; *Gone with the Wind* coming in fourth, *The Wizard of Oz* sixth, and *It's a Wonderful Life* not far behind at eleventh place. *Gone with the Wind* and *The Wizard of Oz*, in particular, as Richard Selcer notes, "span the age gap, the gender gap, and every other gap in the American public." [3] He argues that ever since their 1939 release critics have attempted to account for these two films' widespread popularity and staying power and that despite the explanations provided, no one has convincingly explained their perennial fascination for American audiences. The same could be said of *It's a Wonderful Life*. Although released in 1946, the film contains many of the same Depression-era values so central to the messages of both *The Wizard of Oz* and *Gone with the Wind*. All three films, however, develop this cultural myth of the "loss of home" in a way that offers stereotypical and demeaning depictions of women and blacks while justifying hierarchical relationships in society. Thus, after an analysis each of these films in light of the American "loss of home" myth, the chapter concludes with a discussion that problematizes the films in terms of gender, class, and race. Before discussing each of these films, however, it is helpful to look more closely at the "loss of home" myth, the American concept of home in the 1930s, and its impact on audiences' experiences of these three films.

The American "Loss of Home" Myth in the 1930s

"Like so many cherished ideas, there is a mythology that surrounds the concept of home," writes Richard Selcer. "Artistic minds as diverse as Norman Rockwell, Stephen Foster, Frank Capra, and Robert Frost have captured something of the myth in their works." [4] Selcer goes on to assert that the family home has always been central to American life and that this centrality is echoed in the positive feelings evoked by such phrases as "home-grown," "homestead," "home town," "home-owned," and "home team." To that list could be added such sayings as "home is where the heart is," "home sweet home," and "there's no place like home." Such attachment to the home, and particularly its redefinition in feminine terms ("a woman's place is in the home"), helped give rise to the nineteenth-century "cult of domesticity" in which "the self-contained private home, overseen by the wife/mother, represented the highest ideal of American life." [5]

The roots of the family home, however, are even more deeply embedded in the American immigrant experience. Everyone in America is from somewhere else. Even Native Americans, according to a considerable body of research, came to North America across the Bering Strait during the Ice Age. Thus, all American immigrants, or their ancestors, were either forced to leave home—as was the case for African-American slaves, poor Welsh farmers, and English prisoners shipped to the colonies—or chose to leave home in search of a better life. Home, therefore, was not something taken for granted, but was actively sought and often hard won, as was the case, for example, for those who settled the American West. As a result, home—its initial loss as well as the subsequent quest to regain it—are a defining characteristic of the American experience. According to Selcer, home "has become more than a place to Americans; it is an institution. During the good times in our history, it has been a symbol of everything good in American life. During the bad times, its status has been used as a yardstick for the decline of America." [6]

Such a yardstick was most obviously applied during the Depression years of the 1930s. During this decade, for many, family, home, and the American dream were virtually synonymous terms. "When the Great Depression hit in the 1930s, the small family farm (the homestead) was still the basic unit of American society. More than that, it was as much a part of the American Dream as apple pie and motherhood." [7] Historically, the family farm offered shelter from the vagaries of economic misfortunes, political upheavals, and rapid social change. The Depression, however, not only destroyed financial institutions and engulfed family fortunes; it directly threatened the family farm, so much so that it was virtually wiped out as an institution by the close of the decade. By the 1940s, homelessness had become a serious problem. Speaking of this time, Selcer notes that:

Tens of thousands of Americans were already roaming the nation's streets and highways in search of new homes, having been displaced from their former abodes. . . . For the first time in American history, the homeless were a large and visible problem, numbering in the millions before the end of the decade. They included migrant farm families looking for work and city-dwellers forced to live in Hoovervilles on the outskirts of great cites. They were given various labels: hoboes, panhandlers, apple sellers, hitchhikers, and "fruit tramps," among others.[8]

The homeless problem became so rampant, as Selcer points out, that the U.S. government responded in the form of legislation. The creation of the Homeowners' Loan Corporation and the Federal Housing Administration, coupled with additional tax subsidies for homeowners, offered compelling governmental responses to the economic and social conditions created by the depression.

The demise of the family farm/family home quickly became ripe fodder for the Hollywood industry. A number of movies released in the late 1930s and early 1940s either idealized the family farm/home, such as *The Wizard of Oz*, *Gone with the Wind*, and *It's a Wonderful Life*, or they portrayed the plight of those affected by its loss, as in *The Grapes of Wrath* (1940) or *The Searchers* (1956). As we see in *The Grapes of Wrath*, for example, tenant-farmer families, such as the Joads, are torn apart and forced to take up migrant lifestyles, living on the road and looking for any form of available work. And although *The Searchers*, a John Wayne western directed by John Ford, is about an earlier period in American history, the displacement of the family, burned out by Indians, can be seen as a metaphor for the plight of 1930s families forced off their land by absentee landlords in order to make way for mechanized farming and cheap day laborers. *It's Wonderful Life*, although not about a small family farm, is also firmly grounded in Depression-era values and fears, evidenced by the folksy small-town world made possible by the Bailey Savings and Loan, but directly under attack by the gathering forces of corporate capitalism and greed. Even a fantasy film like *The Wizard of Oz*, as we will see in the following discussion, speaks to Depression-era anxieties, even though fear over the loss of the family homestead is implicit rather than explicit as it is in the other films mentioned.

The Wizard of Oz

Aside from being ranked number six on the AFI list of the one hundred greatest American films of all times, *The Wizard of Oz* also appears seven times on the list of the top fifty most popular movies ever broadcast on television.[9] Although the film was not a hit in theatrical release, as Payne notes, its repeated television broadcasts over the last sixty-odd years have made it an American classic.[10] The film is based on the first of the fourteen books of the same name written by L. Frank Baum between 1900 and 1920. Written primarily as "a populist fable for an American torn between old-fashioned, rural and modern urban, industrial values" at the turn of the century, "when MGM took up the book thirty years later, the Great Depression provided an almost identical backdrop for the reincarnated story." [11] Despite the appropriateness of Baum's book for the times, the original story was heavily altered by screenwriters Noel Langley, Florence Ryerson, and Edgar Allen Woolf. The film was particularly altered, according to Selcer, so as to downplay the populist values in favor of a more central emphasis on home and home-life values. *The Wizard of Oz*, like *Gone with the Wind*, is a product of Louis B. Mayer's studio, known, as Carpenter points out, for "mythologizing the American heartland." [12]

The Wizard of Oz has been subjected to extensive critical scrutiny, analyzed as a populist parable,[13] as a psychoanalytical coming-of-age drama,[14] as an adolescent identity search in a media ritual framework,[15] and as an anachronistic female drama.[16] With the exception of Payne's analysis of the film's therapeutic function, various analyses have failed to explore the cultural and rhetorical dimensions that may account for the film's success and longevity. While not employing a mythic or Perennial philosophy framework per se, Payne explores the film's psychological draw as a female coming-of-age drama using Bruno Bettelheim's *Uses of Enchantment*, Walter Ong's theory of the evolution of communication technology and consciousness, and Erik Erikson's theory of identity development. While I find much of merit in Payne's analysis, as well as Selcer's diachronistic analysis of the film,[17] and indeed

I extend some of their ideas in what follows, I pay particular attention to Dorothy's universal hero quest for home and self while placing this quest squarely against a 1930s backdrop of the demise of the family farm.

As *The Wizard of Oz* begins both Dorothy and her dog Toto are running down a Kansas country lane on their way home to the family farm. From this first scene on, Dorothy, like the typical Odyssean hero, will continually and urgently be trying to return home. This time she is desperate to get home in order to tell her Aunt and Uncle about Miss Gulch's plans to take Toto away from her for chasing Miss Gulch's cat. When she finally is able to impart this news, however, both Auntie Em and Uncle Henry are too busy counting chickens and tending to the general upkeep of the farm to pay much attention to her. The expressions on their faces are grim and determined. Every baby chick is precious and keeps the family from the economic malaise sweeping the country. The mood of the scene, in other words, implies the seriousness of efficient animal husbandry, particularly in light of 1930s audiences' understanding that many family farms stood on the brink of financial disaster.

Somewhat put off by this rebuff and her aunt's anger at Dorothy's disregard for her own safety when she falls in the pig pen, Dorothy feels unappreciated and misunderstood. Although she ostensibly runs away from home in order to keep Miss Gulch from taking Toto away from her, her motives run much deeper than this. In her opening song, for example, she makes it clear that Kansas and the family farm are not her heart's desire as she sings, "Somewhere, over the rainbow, way up high, there's a place that I heard of once in a lullaby. Somewhere over the rainbow, skies are blue and the dreams that you dare to dream really do come true." She finishes with the question, "If happy little bluebirds fly beyond the rainbow, why, oh why, can't I?"

The classical call to adventure for the hero often begins with the hero longing for distant lands, or at least a place where the "grass is greener" than the pedestrian world of the family home. *The Wizard of Oz* is no exception. The central lesson of Dorothy's adventure in Oz, however, like George Bailey's in Bedford Falls, will be to correct this perception and come to see home as the source of all being. Her adventures in Oz, in other words, are needed in order to come to this realization. She must first lose home before she can truly "find" it. There can be no pleasure in paradise regained, in other words, until it is lost.

This catalyst for the hero quest is explicitly acknowledged in the scene with Professor Marvel, the traveling soothsayer and prestidigitator. After asking Dorothy why she is running away, Marvel quickly adds, "Don't tell me.

They don't understand you at home, they don't appreciate you. You want to see other lands—big cities, big mountains, big oceans." Marvel's words underscore this hero's dissatisfaction with home life, which seems too ordinary, too pedestrian, or less than it could be for someone who yearns for travel, adventure, and vaster vistas. Despite this, Professor Marvel, adept at reading the hearts of young girls if not crystal balls, tells her that he can "see" that Dorothy's Aunt Em misses her badly. Very emotional at the thought of upsetting her aunt, Dorothy immediately abandons her quest and decides to return home. "Poor kid," prophetically adds Professor Marvel after she leaves, "I hope she gets home alright."

The fragility of the family home and the ease with which it was disappearing in the 1930s is metaphorically emphasized by the tornado that strikes before Dorothy can reach home. Blowing up vast quantities of dust and debris, the windstorm literalizes the forces both natural and human created that were sweeping family farms off of the map in the late 1930s. To 1939 audiences, in other words, these storm images must have acted as sharp reminders of the Depression-era dust bowl that wrecked havoc on Midwestern farms and forced foreclosure after foreclosure as crops failed, farms became consolidated, and tenant farmers went homeless. Although this phenomenon is not the main focus of *The Wizard of Oz*, as an underlying premise it must have made Dorothy's quest for home all the more urgent to 1939 audiences.

This loss of home, in the 1930s, was not due just to the forces of nature, but also to the relentless pursuit of capital, signified by the increasing number of monopolies in business and industry and the consolidation of wealth into fewer and fewer hands. The film, for example, explicitly acknowledges that Miss Almira Gulch, "the meanest woman in the county," actually "owns half the county," and apparently is vying to own the other half as well. Gulch, of course, is Dorothy's central antagonist, both in Kansas and in Oz, where she is transformed into the Wicked Witch of the West and serves primarily to foil Dorothy's attempts to return home to Kansas. *The Wizard of Oz*, in other words, personifies the 1930s financial threat to family home life in the figure of Miss Gulch/the Wicked Witch.

Although Dorothy eventually makes it home—her second journey home in the film—she is essentially "locked out" from the safety that the family home traditionally represents. Everyone she loves has gone to the root cellar for protection. Although she knocks at the cellar door, they do not hear her. Her return to the house, therefore, offers no protection from the savage winds that blow. Like Tom Joad in *The Grapes of Wrath* returning home to the aban-

doned family farm after five years in prison, Dorothy finds no refuge against
the forces of natural and financial disaster in the house.

Once inside the house Dorothy is knocked unconscious by a flying window frame and begins to dream that the entire house has been pulled into the
eye of the cyclone. Once again, this image literalizes the 1930 forces sweeping homes off the map. Eventually, of course, the house is dropped down in
the fantastical land of Oz.

In one of the most famous scenes in Hollywood cinematic history, the
film changes from black and white to Technicolor, the musical score plays the
refrain from "Somewhere over the Rainbow," and we, along with Dorothy,
receive our first glimpse of the vibrant and colorful fantasy world that is Oz.
Reciting one of the most memorable lines from Hollywood cinema, Dorothy,
a master of understatement, exclaims, "Toto, I've a feeling we're not in Kansas
anymore. We must be over the rainbow." She quickly learns that they are in
Munchkin Land and that she is solely responsible for the death of The Wicked
Witch of the East. After being feted with song and dance for her hero's feat
by the Munchkins, Glinda, the Good Witch of the North, materializes from a
gigantic bubble. Despite all of the excitement generated about Dorothy's vic-

Dorothy (Judy Garland) in *The Wizard of Oz*, running frantically to return home to her Kansas farm in the face of an oncoming tornado. Blowing up vast quantities of dust and debris, the approaching tornado literalizes the forces both natural and human-created that were sweeping family farms off of the map during the Great Depression. To 1939 audiences, in other words, these storm images may have acted as sharp reminders of the Depression-era dustbowls which wreaked havoc on Midwestern farms and forced foreclosure after foreclosure as crops failed, farms became consolidated, and tenant farmers went homeless. As an underlying premise, such "dustbowl" imagery must have made Dorothy's quest for home all the more urgent to 1939 audiences. Courtesy of the Museum of Modern Art—Film Stills Archives.

tory over her own and the Munchkins' central nemesis, all Dorothy can think about is returning home. Thus, in response to Dorothy's inquiry about the best way to get back to Kansas, Glinda advises her to follow the yellow-brick road to Emerald City and seek the advice of the Wizard of Oz.

Along the way, of course, Dorothy meets her three trusty companions the Scarecrow, the Tin Man, and the Cowardly Lion, all of whom initially join her in order to ask the wizard for, respectively, a heart, a brain, and courage. Her companions, in other words, are on important quests of their own. Each of them, like Dorothy, will come to learn that the things they seek—courage, intelligence, and compassion—like home, are things they already possessed. But just as important, like Dorothy in her quest for home, they will learn that they could not have truly appreciated or have come to own these qualities until they were tested.

Just when all four companions are in sight of the Emerald City and what they think is the end of their quest, Dorothy and the Cowardly Lion succumb to the poisonous sleep cast over the poppy fields by the Wicked Witch of the West. Poppies are the central component in opium—a drug traditionally smoked to create a state of lethargy, forgetfulness, and psychological numbness. The poppy field thus literalizes the dangers of the unconsciousness for the hero on her quest. The hero, in her attempts to achieve enlightenment, often spends some time in a liminal state of passive receptivity to that enlightenment. Such a liminal state is akin to a trip into the unconsciousness often symbolized by the underworld, a cave, or a dreamlike state. Although the hero is required to take this step, it is important that they not dwell there indefinitely. Like Odysseus, seduced by Calypso or lulled into a state of blissful forgetfulness by the Sirens' song, Dorothy has fallen under the spell of another sorceress and is about to forget her quest. It is only the valiant efforts of her two companions, the Tin Man and the Scarecrow, that save her from such a fate and return her to the purpose of her quest for home.

The Emerald City, however, rather than providing the goals of all of their quests, turns out to offer a world of false promises. A typical "modern" big city, the Emerald City (read "money" or "precious jewel") is all glitz and glamour. Dazzling to the eye, it only offers surface modifications—a new hairdo for Dorothy, a buff and shine for the Tin Man and the Cowardly Lion, a new stuffing of straw for the Scarecrow—rather than transformations of the heart and mind. Like the Wizard of Oz himself, the Emerald City is all smoke and mirrors.

This portrayal of big cities as impersonal places where the hero loses her soul and her goal, is a predominant theme not only in *The Wizard of Oz*, but also in *It's a Wonderful Life* and *Gone with the Wind*. Since the family home in the 1930s was synonymous with the family farm, it is not surprising that agrarian or populist values would come to predominate in popular films of the 1930s and 1940s. The city, in many films, came to represent those forces that potential destroy the family, seduce the hero, and waylay his quest. This pitting of small-town/agrarian values against big city values will be explored at greater length in the following discussion of *It's a Wonderful Life* and *Gone with the Wind*.

Once they reach the Wizard of Oz refuses to see the questing heroes. Dorothy, in despair laments, "And I was so happy, I thought I was on my way home. Auntie Em was so good to me and I never appreciated it—running away, hurting her feelings."

This yearning for home, as glimpsed through Professor Marvel's crystal ball back in Kansas, and as exhibited in Dorothy's comment here in the Emerald City, is echoed in a later scene in the Wicked Witch of the East's castle, when Dorothy is held prisoner. As her aunt's face appears in the witch's crystal ball, Dorothy exclaims, "I'm frightened, Auntie Em. I'm frightened." Replies her aunt, "Dorothy, Dorothy, where are you? It's me, Auntie Em; we're trying to find you. Where are you?" Dorothy cries out, "I'm here in Oz, Auntie Em. I'm locked up in the witch's castle and I'm trying to get home to you."

This scene also represents a second enactment of the hero's imprisonment in a cave or womb-like place of passivity and enlightenment. As the witch's prisoner, Dorothy is powerless to directly affect her fate. Instead, she must wait and watch as the grains of sand in the hourglass, representing the minutes she has left to live, rapidly disappear. In the typical hero quest, the hero, during her imprisonment or time spent in passive receptivity to her fate, is often confronted with her death and thus the meaning of her life. Such is the case, for example, when Odysseus travels to Hades in order to speak with the shade of his dead mother. We also see this when Jesus Christ spends forty days in the desert and is given visions of his quest as well as his death at the hands of Pontius Pilate. It appears in *It's a Wonderful Life* when George Bailey is given visions of life in Bedford Falls without him. Such is the case for Dorothy, who, seeing her Aunt Em despair in the witch's crystal ball, realizes that home is the most important place in the world, and thus is the proper culmination of all heroes' journeys.

It will take the aid of all of Dorothy's trusty companions, however, to release her from the witch's hold. Importantly, the Scarecrow, the Lion, and the Tin Man's rescue of Dorothy will allow them to exhibit the characteristics they thought they lacked—brains, courage, and a heart, respectively. The Scarecrow smartly comes up with the plan to rescue Dorothy, the Lion bravely leads the charge, and the Tin Man cries compassionately at the thought of Dorothy's dilemma. All three, in other words, possessed the necessary traits; it simply took the adversity of the hero's quest to allow them to actualize this potential.

Dorothy does not realize her own hero's potential, however, until the final scene with Glinda, the Good Witch of the North. Since the Wizard of Oz was unable to help Dorothy in her quest for home, she desperately pleads to Glinda, "Oh, will you help me? Can you help me?" Wisely, Glinda replies, "You don't need to be helped any longer. You've always had the power to go back to Kansas." "Then why didn't you tell her before?" demands the Scarecrow. "Because she wouldn't have believed me. She had to learn it for herself," patiently explains Glinda. Here is the heart of the hero quest for "home." Home is often the literal home from which the hero sets out, but more significantly, it is a state of mind or a way of seeing not possible before the hero departs. The hero's quest not only often requires a journey home to the place from whence the hero departed; it also necessitates a journey home to a state of being or consciousness that was within the hero's heart all along. And such a return is never regressive or simply nostalgic, because although home is the place the hero has "always been" it remains a place that she could not have either recognized or attained before her "departure" or journey outward. Dorothy always held the capacity for home in her heart. Her hero quest was to recognize this capacity and embrace it. So when she is asked by Glinda

what she has finally learned, she replies, "Well, I think that it wasn't enough just to want to see Uncle Henry and Auntie Em and if I ever go looking for my heart's desire again, I won't go looking any further than my own back-yard, because if it isn't there I never really lost it to begin with. Is that right?" Glinda replies, "That's all it is."

The idea that the hero's journey outward into the realm of action and events is ultimately a journey inward to a place the hero has always pos-sessed but could not truly recognize until the journey out is literalized in the film's masterful double casting. As mentioned, Margaret Hamilton, who plays Dorothy's nemesis in Kansas, Miss Gulch, is also cast as Dorothy's nemesis in Oz, the Wicked Witch of the East. Professor Marvel in Kansas is played by the same actor who plays the Wizard of Oz, while each of Dorothy's trusted companions, the Lion, the Scarecrow, and the Tin Man, are played by the same actors who play the extended family of farm workers on Dorothy's Kansas farm. The film subtly references this by Dorothy's comments to all three of her companions in Oz when she says, "You're the best friends anybody ever had, and it's funny, but I feel I've known you all the time. But I couldn't have, could I? Still I wish I could remember. But I guess it doesn't matter now any-way." Of course this is also an obvious plot device since Dorothy's trip to Oz

Dorothy's final homecoming in *The Wizard of Oz*, when she finds herself, as if woken from a dream, surrounded by all of the people that she loves. It is interesting that the hero quest takes places during a fantastical dream state, particularly because, once again, the hero's transformation often occurs in a liminal state akin to a state of dreaming, unconsciousness and/or passivity. On a larger level the entire vision quest is a journey into the deep well of the culture's collective unconscious. Dream states, according to Jung, are often the perfect vehicle for tapping into the energy of the collective unconsciousness. "Wake up honey," says Dorothy's Aunt Em, as she puts a cold cloth on Dorothy's forehead in the moment depicted in this image. As all of the significant people in her life appear at her bedside, she tells them about Oz, saying, "All I kept saying to everybody is that I want to go home, and they sent me home. Doesn't anybody believe me? . . . But anyway, Toto we're home, home, and this is my room and you're all here and I'm not gonna leave here ever again because I love you all and oh, Auntie Em, there's no place like home." Courtesy of the Museum of Modern Art— Film Stills Archives.

is portrayed as a dream. It would not be surprising, in other words, for a young girl's fantasies to be populated by the same people she knows in everyday life simply dressed up in fanciful garb. This double casting, however, takes on thematic significance when viewed in light of the requirements of the hero's paradoxical journey toward enlightenment and home.

It is also interesting that the hero quest takes places during a fantastical dream state, particularly because, once again, the hero's transformation often occurs in a liminal state akin to a state of dreaming, unconsciousness, and/or passivity. On a larger level the entire vision quest is a journey into the deep well of the culture's collective unconscious. Dream states, according to Jung, are often the perfect vehicle for tapping into the energy of the collective unconsciousness.

Near the film's conclusion, Dorothy, with Glinda's guidance, clicks her ruby slippers together three times saying, as instructed, "There's no place like home." As this phrase is repeated in mantralike fashion, Dorothy is transported from her dream state back to her own little bedroom in Kansas. "Wake up, honey," says her Aunt Em, as she puts a cold cloth on Dorothy's forehead. All of the significant people in her life appear at her bedside, including Professor Marvel, as she tells them about Oz.

Dorothy: All I kept saying to everybody is that I want to go home, and they sent me home. Doesn't anybody believe me?

Uncle Henry: Of course we believe you, Dorothy.

Dorothy: But anyway, Toto, we're home, home, and this is my room
                  and you're all here and I'm not gonna leave here ever again
                  because I love you all and oh, Auntie Em, there's no place
                  like home!

Problematizing Ideology in The Wizard of Oz

The Wizard of Oz is laudable in a number of significant ways. Its lead character, for example, is an active and smart young woman who relies on her wits, intuition, and general strength of character to get herself home. Although there are a number of "bad" female witches—the Wicked Witches of the East and West being the prime examples—there is also a "good" female witch—Glinda, the Good Witch of the North. The film avoids, in other words, the typical portrayal of nasty witches as exclusively female. Although the Wizard of Oz is male, and Dorothy does appeal to him to take her home, she ultimately manages to do so herself, along with the help of another woman, Glinda, the Good Witch of the North. The film does not fall prey to the conservative stereotype of the passive female, aided primarily by men to achieve her goals. Although Dorothy has three male companions—the Lion, the Scarecrow, and the Tin Man—she exhibits more gumption and insight than all of them, and is as instrumental in helping them as they are in helping her.

Having said all this, however, it is important to note that the film, drawing as it does on 1930s American audiences' fear of the loss of home, takes that fear and diverts it into a fantasy scenario that offers a fantasy solution to the problem. If only all of the 1930s dispossessed tenant farmers and homeless families could simply click their ruby slippers and find themselves home again. Although appealing, and certainly helpful for alleviating anxieties about contemporary social upheavals, such an impossible fantasy solution may have potentially dissipated the need for political action to solve the homelessness problem of the day.

Gone with the Wind

Released in 1939 and produced by David O. Selznick, *Gone with the Wind* won all of the major Academy Awards that year except Best Actor. The film was based on Margaret Mitchell's novel of the same name, itself a best-selling novel during 1936, 1937, and 1939. Although the film, directed by Victor Fleming and starring Vivien Leigh as Scarlett and Clark Gable as Rhett Butler, was clearly loved by audiences, it was greeted much less warmly by critics, who, for the most part, reserved their praise for John Ford's version of John Steinbeck's *Grapes of Wrath*, also released that year. According to Pauly, *Gone with the Wind*

possesses a significant measure of both historical validity and importance. The fact that it was far and away the most successful film of the decade probably has less to do with the glittering surface that so annoyed critics than the common ground it shared with *The Grapes of Wrath*. Though it was less daring and less accomplished that Ford's work as an artistic creation, *Gone with the Wind* was similarly preoccupied with the problem of survival in the face of financial depravation and social upheaval. Both movies also demonstrate a nostalgic longing for the agrarian way of life which is ruthlessly being replaced by the fearful new economic forces of capitalism and industrialization.[18]

The film presents a conservative vision of the hero's quest for home, with Scarlett O'Hara standing in for a 1930s American public who was not only facing the worst depression in American history, but was also confronted with either the possibility or the reality of the loss of homes and family fortunes. Problematically, however, the film's implicit solution to the loss of home, as we will see, is a reassertion of a system of hierarchy and privilege — the plantation system — based on the repression of women and Africans Americans.

In *Gone with the Wind*, Tara's importance, as Scarlett O'Hara's ancestral home, is repeatedly emphasized throughout the film. After Scarlett protests to her father at the film's beginning that "I don't want Tara. Plantations don't mean anything," he replies, "You mean to tell me, Katie Scarlett O'Hara, that land doesn't mean anything to you? Why the land is the only thing in the world worth working for, worth fighting for, worth dying for, because it is the only thing that lasts. . . . But there, there, you're just a child. It will come to you, this love of the land." As he says these lines we see a pastoral vision — an extreme long shot of the two of them silhouetted in a setting sun against the vast fields of the O'Hara plantation. Later, after Tara has been left in ruins by the northern troops, Scarlett begs Ashley to run away with her, proclaiming, "There's nothing left for me. There's nothing to fight for, nothing to live for." Ashley, refusing her request to leave with her, reminds her, "Yes, there is something. Something you love better than me, although you may not know it. (He takes a handful of red dirt and places it in Scarlett's hand.) Tara." Rhett Butler also asserts Tara's importance to Scarlett when he says to her, "You get your strength from this red earth of Tara, Scarlett. You're part of it and it's part

of you." Depression-era audiences could no doubt identify with Scarlett, her plight, and her slowly evolving appreciation for home. Scarlett's hero quest, in part, will be to gain her father's love of the land and to realize the value of home.

David O. Selznick actually acknowledges placing added importance on Tara and on Scarlett's drive to return home. He reports, for example, "that the one thing that was really open to us was to stress the Tara thought more than Miss Mitchell did." [19]

As Selcer notes, the film version's emphasis on Tara draws on the American cultural myth of "the rural home as a source of strength and stability, cities as dens of iniquity, and the home as a woman's refuge from the world." [20] He notes that the point of view in *Gone with the Wind* is "feminine, that of the homemaker, the nurturer. Her proper 'sphere,' and only place that she can truly be happy, is the home or, more precisely, the pastoral home that is contrasted with the evils of the city." [21] And indeed, the evils of city life are clearly delineated in the film, particularly in scenes of the burning and looting of Atlanta.

But more than the evils of the city, *Gone with the Wind* emphasizes the forces threatening to destabilize an entire way of life. The sign hanging at the front gate of Ashley's plantation at the beginning of the film, for example,

One step ahead of the Northern army that would burn Atlanta to the ground, Scarlett O'Hara (Vivien Leigh) desperately flees Atlanta for home in *Gone with the Wind*. *Gone with the Wind*, as its title asserts, plays to 1930s audience's fears about the economic and social threats to a way of life that, like the homes swept up in the 1930s dust bowl, seemed to be "gone with the wind." (For a strikingly similar image from *The Wizard of Oz*, see page 132.) Courtesy of the Museum of Modern Art—Film Stills Archives.

reads, "Twelve Oaks: Anyone disturbing the peace on this plantation will be prosecuted." Later, after the Civil War has been lost to the Yankees, we again see a shot of this same sign, now hanging askew and much the worse for wear. Rather than representing a threat, the sign instead provides an ironic commentary on the passage of an entire way of life. This image is dramatically emphasized in the scene of the burning of Atlanta. Scarlett, "stuck" in Atlanta in order to help Melanie have her baby, wants nothing more than to return to Tara. Finally overwhelmed with this desire, she begs Rhett to bring her home, saying, "I'm going home and you can't stop me. I want my mama. I'm going home to Tara." As she breaks down in tears Rhett agrees to take her. Just before they leave, however, the following exchange occurs:

Scarlett: Oh, wait. I forgot to lock the front door.
Rhett: (Laughing.)
Scarlett: What are you laughing at?
Rhett: At you, locking the Yankees out.

Later, as they watch the last of the Confederate troops leaving the city, Rhett reminds Scarlett, "I wouldn't be in such a hurry to see them go, my dear. With them goes the last semblance of law and order. (As they watch, looters start to roam the streets.) Scavengers do not waste any time." The vivid portrayal of the breakdown of Southern society as a result of the Civil War no doubt reminded 1930s audiences of the dissolution of civil society occurring all around them as a result of the Depression.

　　Indeed, the forces that threaten to destabilize the Old South are presented in the film in a manner that reminds viewers of the forces threatening to destabilize homes all over America during the height of the Depression. For example, at the end of the first act—for indeed the film self-consciously uses a three-act structure—we see a famished Scarlett scratching in the dry earth for a last forgotten turnip, which she quickly devours like a starved animal.

So hungry that she cannot keep the food down, however, she vomits it back onto the scorched and drought-stricken earth. Pulling herself together, she clenches her fist and shouts to the sky, "As God is my witness, as God is my witness, they're not gonna lick me. I'm going to live through this and when it's all over I'll never be hungry again—no, nor any of my fold. If I have to lie, steal, cheat, or kill, as God is my witness, I'll never be hungry again." As the camera dollies back, we see Scarlett silhouetted against a now barren vista at sunset. The contrast between this shot of the plantation, and the earlier one with Scarlett and her father in the "good old days," is striking. It visually speaks to the extent of Civil War's devastation in the South. Scarlett, of course, makes good on her promise, and although she does end up lying, cheating, stealing, and even killing, she is never hungry again, and in fact, become quite wealthy, first by shooting a Yankee deserter who invades Tara, later by stealing and marrying her sister's successful boyfriend Frank Kennedy, and still later by marrying Rhett Butler for money rather than love. Depression-era audiences could most certainly relate to the fear of being unable to feed their family, to the possibility, for example, of being so destitute that they would not know where their next meal would be coming from.

The film, in perhaps one of the most interesting moments of all, provides a commentary on itself and the role it must have served for Depression-era audiences looking for an escape from the harsh reality they saw around them. We witness, near the middle of the film, the following exchange between Scarlett and Ashley. Ashley has been splitting rails in order to mend some of Tara's broken fences:

Scarlett:	Ashley, what's to become of us?
Ashley:	What do you think becomes of people when their civilization breaks up? Those that have brains and courage come out all right; those that haven't are winnowed out.
Scarlett:	For heaven's sake, Ashley Wilkes, don't stand there talking nonsense to me when it's us who are being winnowed out.
Ashley:	You're right, Scarlett, here I am talking tummy rot about civilization when your Tara's in danger. You've come to me for help and I've no help to give you. Oh, Scarlett, I'm a coward.
Scarlett:	You, Ashley? A coward? What are you afraid of?
Ashley:	Oh, mostly of life becoming too real for me, not that I mind splitting rails, but I do mind very much losing the beauty of that life

I loved. If the war hadn't come I'd of spent my happiest years buried at Twelve Oaks, but the war did come. I saw my boyhood friends blown to bits. I saw men crumple up in agony when I shot them. And now I find myself in a world which for me is worse than death. A world in which there is no place for me and I can never make you understand because you don't know the meaning of fear. You never mind facing realities. You never want to escape from them as I do.

Scarlett: Oh, Ashley, you're wrong. I do want to escape too. I'm so very tired of it all. I've struggled for food, for money. I've weeded and hoed and picked cotton until I can't stand it.

American audiences in the 1930s, like Ashley and Scarlett, must have longed for an escape from the incomprehensible, strange new world in which they found themselves. Such an escape, of course, is provided by this film. By allowing audiences to identify with a character who ultimately triumphs over adversity, despite having to lie, cheat, steal, and kill in order to do so, the film implies that all hope is not lost; just look at Scarlett and let this film be your guide and your escape.

Problematizing Race and Class in Gone with the Wind

Gone with the Wind, released at the height of the Hollywood industry's mastery of the studio system, provides a visually stunning and emotionally involving drama that celebrates the institution of slavery. Although the film tells a version of the destruction of this racist system of privilege and hierarchy during the Civil War, because it does so against the backdrop of 1930s instability, it speaks to the audience's desire for conservative or status-quo visions, regardless of the basis of those visions. Better the gracious order of plantation life and the benevolent rule of kind white masters, the film implies, than economic instability and uncertainly, regardless of whether that instability is brought on by a civil war or a stock-market crash. *Gone with the Wind,* in other words, as its title asserts, plays to 1930s audience's fears about the economic and social threats to a way of life, that, like the homes swept up in the 1930s dust bowl, seemed to be "gone with the wind." Pauly asserts something similar about the film when he claims that the film demonstrates an intense concern for the devastating consequences of these conditions [the economic and social upheavals of the Depression] upon self-reliant individualism and family unity, two of America's most cherished beliefs. . . . However, serious concern for these implications is dissipated into indulgent sentimentalism so that the audience's anxieties are alleviated rather than aggravated.[22]

The film, in other words, provided a sentimental escape from the social and economic realities of the day. Pauly goes on to assert that *Gone with the Wind* succeeded as well as it did in large part because it so effectively sublimated the audience's own response to the Depression." [23]

Plantation life, presented as an ideal model of living, is celebrated in an aesthetic fashion verging on the fascistic. We are invited, for example, to dwell at length on the rich fabrics and striking designs of Scarlett O'Hara's gowns. Both the plantations of Tara and Twelve Oaks offer visions of architectural harmony and aesthetic balance. Their framing against nature (particularly Twelve Oaks) heightens our awareness of their "natural" or "blessed" state of being. What this life represents is apparent in an exchange between Ashley and Melanie at the beginning of the film as they stand on a balcony at Ashley's plantation, Twelve Oaks:

Ashley: You seem to belong here, as if it all had been imagined for you.
Melanie: I like to feel that I belonged to the things you love.
Ashley: You love Twelve Oaks as I do.
Melanie: Yes, Ashley. I love is as more than a house; it's a whole world
             that wants only to be graceful and beautiful.
Ashley: And so unaware that it may not last forever.

While they converse, we witness the entire plantation, bustling with life, spread out before them. This message of the sad passing of a "beautiful" institution is first asserted in the film's opening graphics, which read:

There was a land of cavaliers and cotton fields called the Old South. Here in this pretty world, gallantry took its last bow. Here was the last ever to be seen of knights and their maidens fair, of master and of slave. Look for it only in books for it is no more than a dream remembered . . . Gone with the wind.

This graphic invites us to view the film in terms of a mythic framework of knights and ladies and an era of chivalry. It also encourages us to see the passing of this era as grievous.

This "natural" state of being, not surprisingly, extends to the relations between master and slave. Rhett Butler, for example, refers to Scarlett's personal black maid Prissy as "a simple-minded darkie." Scarlett's father reminds her, at one point, that "you must be firm with inferiors, but you must be gentle with them, especially darkies." Angered at Prissy's "dawdling" when Scarlett awaits her return with the doctor to help with the birthing of Melanie's baby, Scarlett exclaims, "If I don't take a strap to that Prissy!" Not only does Prissy take her time returning like a "lazy darkie," we also find out she has lied about knowing how to birth a baby, and is ultimately portrayed as a foolish, simple-minded girl. Such a stereotypical portrait of blacks is not only demeaning, it also asserts their inferior status to whites, thus legitimizing white rule over blacks while assuming the benevolence of slave masters and slavery as an institution.

An additional example of the film's paternalistic treatment of blacks is provided in a scene that occurs between Scarlett and "Big Sam," one of Tara's black field hands. When Scarlett runs into Big Sam in Atlanta, she is quite pleased, and asks for news of Tara. Big Sam obliges, ending with the news that the field hands have been requisitioned by the Southern troops to dig ditches for them to hide from the Yankees. Big Sam explains that Scarlett's father "took a fit," but "your ma says the Confederacy needs it, so we's gonna dig for the South." After they exchange goodbyes, he adds, "Miss Scarlett, don't worry, we stop them Yankees." The film not only goes to great lengths to present the slaves as well contented and cared for under slavery, it also asserts, by this exchange between Scarlett and Big Sam, that they support the Confederacy. Doing so, the film implies, is in the slaves' best interest, despite *our* realization that the Confederacy was primarily responsible for maintaining their status as slaves.

Gone with the Wind also establishes a stark contrast between "good" girls like Melanie and "bad" girls like Belle Wattley, who runs the local brothel and saloon. Scarlett, of course, is caught between these two potential role models. What is most frustrating for her is her inability to get the hang of either role. Belle Wattley, the prostitute, not only serves as an admonishment to women to refrain from sexual pleasure; she also helps to demarcate the lines of class and privilege between "old money" and "new money." Although Belle, like Rhett, is a war profiteer who ultimately becomes very wealthy, she represents "new money" (read "non-slave-based") or uncouth capitalism. She remains an object of disdain, in other words, both as a capitalist and as a loose woman. Although Melanie, a plantation owner from "old money" (read "slave money"), is kind to Belle Wattley on a number of occasions, it is

clear that her kindness deserves the greatest recognition because she crosses class lines to administer it. It takes a "lady" like Melanie to comfort or aid the poor or lower class.

In sum, *Gone with the Wind* may have provided 1930s audiences with an escape from the Depression-era realities they faced on a daily basis. It does so, however, in a manner that may have alleviated some of their anxieties about their society while sublimating those anxieties into another context—namely the dissolution of the Old South after the Civil War. Ultimately, however, by referencing the breakdown of plantation life through a 1930s frame, the film reinforces status-quo visions of society that claim the superiority of the old way of life, when women were homemakers and simple-minded but big-hearted "darkies" "knew their place." *Gone with the Wind*, whether intentionally or not, asserts the value of the institution of slavery and the class system that created it and invites audiences to wax nostalgic over its demise.

It's a Wonderful Life

It's a Wonderful Life (1940), similar to *The Wizard of Oz* and *Gone with the Wind*, deals with the 1930s-era threat to the American home. And, like *The*

This photograph, taken outside of a movie theater somewhere in South Africa—presumably sometime after the 1939 release of *Gone with the Wind*—was most likely intended for use as part of a public relations campaign to promote the film. This image, however, viewed more than sixty years after the film's release, offers a bizarre commentary on the film's racist message about blacks' contentment with slave/master relations. The image suggests that "Everybody wants to see [read: approves of] *Gone with the Wind*," even native black South Africans. South Africa, until the overthrow of apartheid in the late 1980s, remained one of the most racially segregated and racially oppressive countries in the world. *Gone with the Wind*, released at the height of the Hollywood industry's mastery of the studio system, provides a visually stunning and emotionally involving drama that celebrates the institution of slavery. Although the film tells a version of the destruction of this racist system of privilege and hierarchy during the Civil War, because it does so against the backdrop of 1930s instability, it speaks to the audience's desire for conservative or status quo visions, regardless of the basis of those visions. Better the gracious order of plantation life and the benevolent rule of kind white masters, the film implies, than economic instability and uncertainly, regardless of whether that instability is brought on by a civil war or a stock market crash. *Gone with the Wind*, this publicity photograph implies, provides an object lesson to black South Africans (and by extension to all blacks) to be content with their lot. Courtesy of the Museum of Modern Art—Film Stills Archives.

Wizard of Oz, although detailing life in a small town rather than on a family farm, *It's a Wonderful Life* pits agrarian anti-Federalist values against northern urban Federalist values. In true populist fashion, the small town is equated with the family and community and both are seen as the backbone of American society. As in *The Wizard of Oz*, large cities, by contrast, are viewed as impersonal, amoral, and a direct threat to rural life and values. Home, therefore, means not just the family homestead but the populist hometown world.

Like Dorothy in *The Wizard of Oz* and Scarlett in *Gone with the Wind*, George Bailey, although he never leaves home the way Dorothy and Scarlett O'Hara do, yearns to do so. He finds nothing of value in the small and stifling village of Bedford Falls. His earliest dreams, like Dorothy's, involve travel to distant exotic lands like the ones he reads about in his *National Geographic* magazine. His fondest desire is to travel the world before going away to college. Like Dorothy, he believes that the grass must somehow be greener anywhere else than home. But like Dorothy and Scarlett, he learns that home, and what it represents, is where the most important lessons of all, those about love, family, and community responsibility, are learned. Such celebration of the home and home life, although admirable and instructive, however, as we will see, also proves problematic in its reification of hierarchical relationships, particularly those between men and women and between whites and blacks. Before turning to a discussion of the film, however, it is helpful to look at Frank Capra's films and the populist values so central to many of them.

From the American Revolution onward, as Richards points out, historians have noted two distinct strains in American politics: the Federalist and the anti-Federalist, or populist.[24] Federalism, grounded in the ideas of Andrew Jackson, "came to stand for a warlike, industrial, Europe-oriented America, with a strong central government and the New England mercantile-industrial interests dominant." [25] Anti-Federalism, or populism as it was often called, grounded in Thomas Jefferson's idea, was a reaction to Federalism. Populists envisioned a republic of gentlemen farmers "in which the government was honest, frugal, and unobtrusive and where people had equal opportunity to develop, free from external commitments or internal interference." [26] Populists supported an isolationist and laissez-faire approach to government and capital. "To Populists, the enemy was not money itself but the corporate money power, the big business aristocracy, buttressed by a monopoly of privilege and influence." [27]

The 1920s and 1930s saw the Wall Street crash, the Depression, and the triumph of Franklin D. Roosevelt's New Deal policies. In the unstable economic times that resulted from the market crash, Federalists like John Maynard Keynes and Franklin D. Roosevelt felt it was necessary for big government to control and guide the growth of the economy. These policies, however, seemed to declare to Populists that equality of opportunity, decentralized small-town governance, and the era of the individual were over. The Federalists had "won." Populists, however, continued to battle against these ideals throughout the 1930s and 1940s. It is during this time period that Capra's populist vision emerges, embodied in such works as *Mr. Deeds Goes to Town*, *Mr. Smith Goes to Washington*, *It Happened One Night*, and *It's a Wonderful Life*.

According to Richards, "life, liberty, and the pursuit of happiness, the inalienable rights of man, which inspired the Declaration of Independence, have found their fullest and purest cinematic expression in the films of Frank Capra." [28] He argues that Capra's films, more so than the films of his contemporaries, capture the pre-World War II era ideals of the middle class and the American Dream—such as equality of opportunity and self-determination, anti-intellectualism, and the Evangelical tradition, the celebration of good capitalism, the pursuit of individual happiness, the important role of the good neighbor, and a sentimental and nostalgic vision of American society and small-town life.

These populist themes, appearing frequently in Capra's films, are particularly evident in *It's a Wonderful Life*. Themes such as the role of the good neighbor and a sentimental view of small-town life, in particular, seem to support the "loss of home" myth so predominant in films of the 1930s. By the time *It's a Wonderful Life* had been released (1946), World War II had pulled America out of the depression that had threatened its financial and social stability during the previous decade. Despite this, the film, by its nostalgic vision of a pre-industrial society, its setting in a pre–World War II era, and its story of the encroachment of corporate capitalism, seems to evoke much the same feeling as *Gone with the Wind* and *The Wizard of Oz*, both released seven years before it.

The film begins late one Christmas Eve in Bedford Falls. The opening shot is of the snow-covered streets of downtown. A large sign reads, "You are now in Bedford Falls." Just behind the sign a banner strung from a building declares, "Welcome Home Harry Bailey." We learn that at this moment George Bailey (Jimmy Stewart) is in the process of deciding whether to take his life over the loss of $8,000—a loss that will potentially destroy his reputation in the community, cause dozens of homeowners to lose their mortgages, and ultimately result in the closure of the Bailey Savings and Loan, an institution dedicated to ownership of single-family homes by townspeople of modest means. George, visited by an angel, Clarence, like Scrooge in Dickens's *Christmas Carol*, is being given the rare opportunity to see the difference his life has made in the lives of others by peering into a different past in Bedford Falls, one in which George has never been born.

The two signs, "Welcome to Bedford Falls" and "Welcome Home Harry Bailey," immediately situate us in a nostalgic small-town America that for many people already did not exist by the mid-1940s. The signs "welcome" and "home" imply that Bedford Falls is not only a "homey" place; it's also a place you can feel welcome and to which people inevitably come home. Harry Bailey, George Bailey's younger brother, managed to live the life of adventure, travel, and big-city life that George had always wanted. But through various sacrifices for his family, the Bailey Savings and Loan, and the town in general, George, unlike Harry, never managed to leave Bedford Falls. The film is about George coming to realize the importance of home, family, and community. Ultimately, it is the community that comes to George's rescue by the end of the film, chipping in dollars and cents to make up the $8000 deficit and providing George the same type of hero's boon that he is able to provide them—giving them the chance to buy their own homes, and remain a loving and interdependent community.

That the film begins on Christmas Eve also emphasizes the home motif so central to our experience of the film. Christmas, like Thanksgiving, is a time of homecoming when friends and relatives, no matter how widely dispersed, come together to celebrate the holiday and familial love, often in a hometown setting. This holiday-homecoming motif is emphasized by the fact that the film traditionally airs on American television every year during the Christmas season.

Despite the strong pull of home and "hometown" for many of the residents of Bedford Falls, however, George Bailey, from a very young age, rejects the parochial life he feels Bedford Falls represents. We learn this, for example, in an early scene from George's childhood. As he scoops ice cream for Mary—the young girl destined to be his wife, despite the fact that George remains clueless to this fact for years—George asks here if she wants coconut on her chocolate ice cream. When she says "no" he rebukes her, saying, "You don't like coconut? Say, brainless, do you know where coconuts come from? Look at here—from Tahiti, the Fiji Islands, the Coral Sea." Exclaims Mary, "A new magazine, I never saw it before." George breaks in, "Of course you never. Only us explorers can get it. I've been nominated for membership in the National Geographic Society." We are immediately aware of George's penchant for the exotic and the unknown and his impatience for anyone that does not share this love, which Mary clearly does not. At one point she leans over and whispers in his ear while he scoops her ice cream, "Is this the ear you can't hear in? George Bailey, I'll love you 'til the day I die." Mary, by uttering this line, has clearly stated her heart's desire—loving and possibly marrying George Bailey and staying in Bedford Falls. Unknowingly, for he does not hear her words, and in direct contradiction of her desires, George adds, "I'm going out exploring some day. You watch. I'm gonna have a couple of harems and maybe three or four wives. Wait 'n see." George clearly rejects a hometown and a home life destiny in favor of a more exotic quest for the unknown.

George's "selfish" love of travel and exotic adventure, however, is in direct conflict with his selfless and self-sacrificial nature, which we witness again and again as he grows. The first example occurs in a scene where young George Bailey, his brother, and his boyhood friends sled down a snowy hillside on to a frozen pond. Harry inadvertently slides on to a section of the pond where the ice is weak and falls in the frigid water. George immediately jumps in to save him from drowning. As a result, however, George catches a bad case of pneumonia and loses hearing in one ear from a bad ear infection. We see other evidence of George's sacrificial nature when, also as a young boy, he disobeys the orders of his boss, the druggist Mr. Gower, and refuses to deliver capsules mistakenly filled with poison to a family suffering from diphtheria. Mr. Gower, who had just received a telegraph informing him of his son's death, had been drinking and was not paying attention to his work. George braves the punishment he suffers at Mr. Gower's hands for failing to obey him. But, by his actions, George not only saves lives; he also saves Mr. Gower's reputation. George will again exhibit his self-sacrificing nature when he later attempts to save the Bailey Savings and Loan, the family business dedicated solely to the task of helping townspeople afford their own homes. Despite George's "selfish" yearning for travel and adventure, and despite his desire to "shake the dust of this crummy little town off [his] feet," he actually possesses the very hometown values of sacrificing for others and being a good neighbor that he must come to appreciate and own over the course of the film. The boon that the hero seeks, in other words, was within his heart all along. It could not be recognized, however, until the journey "out" into the realm of action and adventure. That journey out, for George at least, will be a virtual journey rather than a literal one, as he is offered an opportunity by the angel Clarence to review the meaning of his life on that fateful Christmas Eve.

The values of home and hometown life are predominantly represented in the film by George's father, by Mary, and by the Bailey Savings and Loan. Each, in their own way, will have important lessons to teach George about home and hometown life. Each of them, as representatives of Populist values, is also pitted against representatives of Federalist values. George's father, and later George himself, for example, is pitted against the corporate boss Mr. Potter, "the meanest and wealthiest man in town." Mary, the domesticated "good girl," is contrasted with Violet, the "bad girl" with a wanderlust, while the Bailey Savings and Loan, dedicated to home ownership, is the populist counterpart to Potter's Federalist bank, designed exclusively to maximize shareholders' profits. [29]

The centrality of the savings and loan to the town, and as a metaphor for home ownership, and the contrast between Mr. Bailey and Mr. Potter, becomes apparent early in the film in a scene between the two of them. Potter, a parody of Federalist values, is the Baileys' "arch enemy" and the biggest threat in the film to home ownership and small-town populist values. At a meeting between Mr. Bailey and Mr. Potter, Mr. Bailey asks Mr. Potter for thirty more days to pay back a $5,000 loan he owes him. We then witness the following exchange:

Mr. Potter: Have you put any real pressure on those people of yours to pay those mortgages?
Mr. Bailey: Times are bad, Mr. Potter. A lot of these people are out of work.
Mr. Potter: Well, then, foreclose.
Mr. Bailey: I can't do that. These families have children.
Mr. Potter: They're not my children.
Mr. Bailey: Well, they're somebody's children, Mr. Potter.
Mr. Potter: Are you running a business or a charity ward? Not with my money.

The values that George must come to learn are further exhibited by his father in a dinner conversation between the two of them on the eve of George's departure for college. George is about to realize his dream of seeing something of the wider world when his father directly challenges this goal:

Mr. Bailey: I suppose you've decided what you want to do when you get out of college?
George: Well, you know what I've always talked about—build things, design new buildings, plan modern cities. . . .
Mr. Bailey: Course it's just a hope, but you wouldn't consider coming back to the building and loan, would you?
George: I couldn't face being cooped up for the rest of my life in a shabby little office. I'm sorry, Pop. I didn't mean that. I . . . It's this business of nickels and dimes and spending all your life trying to figure out how to save three cents and light the pipe. I'd go crazy. I wanna do something big and something important.
Mr. Bailey: You know, George, I feel that in a small way we're doing something important. Satisfying a fundamental urge. It's deep in the race for a man to want his own roof and walls and fireplace and we're helping him get those things in our shabby little office.

George: I know, Pop. I wish I felt it. But I've been hoarding pennies like a miser here. Most of my friends have already finished college. I just feel like if I didn't get away I'd bust.

George's father articulates the populist values so central to Capra's films. His ideals also represent the lesson that his son George must learn if he is to come of age and complete his hero's quest. Like many heroes, however, George misrecognizes the "call to adventure" rather than refusing it. He thinks, for example, that the "call to adventure" is college, or Tahiti, or life in the big city. It takes his father's patient lesson (and sudden death) and Mary's gentle guidance and love to open his eyes to his true hero's calling.

   If George's father represents the "unglamorous" values of "good" capitalism and the populist belief in a community of believers, Mary represents all of the values of home and domesticity and familial love — values that George is also not yet ready to accept as his destiny. This representation becomes particular apparent in the "Buffalo Girls" scene that takes place after the school dance, when George walks Mary home. During the scene it becomes apparent that George, almost against his will, is attracted to Mary. It is against his will because loving her and what she represents flies directly in the face of George's dreams of travel and exotic adventure. This idea is epitomized in the following exchange as George begins to throw a rock to try and break a windowpane in the abandoned Grandville house. Mary stops him, saying:

Mary: Oh no, George. I love that old house.
George: No, you see you make a wish and then try to break some glass in. You gotta be a pretty good shot nowadays, too.
Mary: Oh no, George, don't. It's full of romance, that old place. I'd like to live in it.
George: In that place? I wouldn't live in it as a ghost. (He throws a rock.)
Mary: What did you wish, George?
George: Oh, not just one wish, a whole hatful. Mary, I know what I'm gonna do tomorrow and the next day and the next year and the year after that. I'm shaking the dust of this crummy little town off my feet and I'm gonna see the world — Italy, Greece, the Parthenon, the Coliseum — and then I'm coming back here to go to college and see what they know and then I'm gonna build things. I'm gonna build airfields. I'm gonna build skyscrapers a hundred stories high, I'm gonna build bridges a mile long. What? You

gonna throw a rock? Hey, that's pretty good. What did ya wish, Mary?

Mary, refusing to answer, simply smiles knowingly, turns and continues to walk.

George's act of throwing the rock at the house is a visual metaphor for casting aspersion on domesticity and hometown values. Mary's refusal, at first, to throw a rock represents her respect for home, family, and hometown values. George's wish when he throws his rock, of course, is for travel and adventure and a life without attachments and responsibilities, while Mary's, we later find out, is to marry George, have a family, and someday live in the Grandville house. George's monologue also exhibits typical Federalist values—a love of big cities, modern cityscapes, and European culture, while Mary's wish represents the Populist celebration of small-town, conservative familial values.

George's father's sudden death, however, interrupts George's travel plans. Once again, George exhibits his self-sacrificing nature by giving up his summer trip abroad in order to help manage things at the Bailey Savings and Loan. Finally, ready to go off to college for the fall semester, he is once again

George Bailey (Jimmy Stewart) and co-workers, drink a toast to "moma and papa dollar," the two dollar bills remaining after the Depression-style run on the Bailey Savings and Loan which almost bankrupt it, in *It's a Wonderful Life*. George declares his hope that the two dollars will be fruitful and multiple in order to insure the financial future of the savings and loan, and, more importantly, of all of the town folk who have home mortgages and life savings invested in the bank's financial solvency. Thus, this image celebrates the Populist value of personal, moderate, community-based "good capitalism," which is directly contrasted in the film with Henry Potter's monopolistic, impersonal, and greed-driven "bad capitalism." This image also depicts the importance of home and homeownership by the model home depicted in the lower left corner and the sign "Own your own [home]" depicted in the upper right hand corner. Courtesy of the Museum of Modern Art—Film Stills Archives.

stopped when Mr. Potter, as a bank board of trustee member, makes a motion to dissolve the savings and loan. George, unable to allow such a thing, responds to Potter's motion, saying:

Just a minute. Now you're right when you say my father was no businessman. I know that. Why he ever started this cheap penny-ante savings and loan I'll never know. But neither you nor anybody else can say anything against his character. Because his whole life was . . . Why, in the twenty-five years since he and Uncle Billy started this thing he never once thought of himself. Isn't that right, Uncle Billy? He didn't save enough money to send Harry to school, let alone me. But he did help a few people get out of your slums, Mr. Potter, and what's wrong with that? You're all businessmen here; doesn't it make them better citizens? Doesn't it make them better customers? You said that they . . . what did you say a minute ago? "They had to wait and save their money before they even thought of a decent home." Wait? Wait for what? Until their children grow up and leave them? Until they're so old and broken down that they . . . Do you know how long it takes a working man to save $5,000? Just remember, Mr. Potter, that this rabble you're talking about, they do most of the working and paying and living and dying in this community. Well, is it too much to have them work and pay and live and die in a couple of decent rooms and a bath? Anyway, my father didn't think so. People were human beings to him. But to you, a warped, frustrated old man, they're cattle. Well, in my book he died a much richer man that you'll ever be.

In this monologue, we witness George beginning to champion many of the values that he previously saw as flying in the face of his dream for exotic travel and "greener pastures." Because of George's eloquent speech, the only condition under which the board of trustees will vote to keep the savings and loan in operation is if George agrees to run it. As a result, George once again sacrifices his college education, even giving the money he saved for college to his younger brother Harry so that he can go in George's place. George has finally recognized his "call to adventure," and sets out to be the good citizen and populist that his parents raised him to be. George, however, expects Harry to come back after college and take over the savings and loan so that George can finally have his chance to go. Such expectations are shattered when, upon completing college and returning to Bedford Falls, George finds out that Harry, newly married, has been offered a good job working for his new wife's father in a glass factory in Buffalo. George is once gain "stuck" in Bedford Falls.

George eventually accepts that his fate is Mary and life in Bedford Falls. This acceptance is confirmed when even their honeymoon must be sacrificed to quell the panic surrounding the savings and loan's funds, and to keep the townsfolk from engaging in a Depression-style run on the bank. George, this time at Mary's urging, uses the money earmarked for their trip to Europe and New York to make good on the withdraws requested by the community.

After George successfully keeps the bank solvent and they close their doors that night with two dollars left, the phone rings. It is his new wife, Mary, telling him to "come home." Confused, George asks, "What home? 320 Sycamore? Who's home is that? The Waldorf? Huh?"

The honeymoon house turns out to be the old Grandville house, quickly made livable for one night through the efforts of Mary and various townsfolk who have pitched in, decorating it with exotic travel posters, lighting a fire in the hearth, and sweeping up some of the debris. A dumbfounded George steps in the door and is welcomed by the perfect picture of domesticity—Mary, dressed immaculately, standing by a romantic candlelight dinner for two with a blazing fire in the fireplace. "Welcome home, Mr. Bailey," she says as they embrace. "Remember the night we broke the window in this old house? This is what I wished for." This culmination of the vision of domesticity is made possible not only by Mary's love for George and for Bedford Falls, but also by the kindness of the community volunteers who make a honeymoon in an abandoned broken-down house possible. In the populist world of small-town America, good neighbors take care of each other.

The film ends where it began, on Christmas Eve, with George and Mary surrounded by all of the members of the community whom George has helped for years to buy and keep their own home. Now they are doing the same for him. Chipping in, even with only a dollar or two, they make up the $8,000 lost by Uncle Billy and then found and stolen by Henry Potter. The money they provide will not only help to keep the bank solvent, it will also keep George, his family, and his home intact. George Bailey's life has been a boon to his community. As Clarence the angel has helped him realize, his life has made a difference. Neither rich nor famous, he is still a hero in the eyes of the people of Bedford Falls and in the eyes of the film-viewing audience. His only "journey" away from home may have been when he was given the chance, thanks to Clarence, to see life in Bedford Falls without him. This metaphysical journey, however, ultimately required a journey inward, even to the point of contemplating suicide, for George to truly understand and embrace the "home" that had been waiting for him all along.

Problematizing Race, Class, and Gender in It's a Wonderful Life

Although *It's a Wonderful Life* celebrates the role of the good neighbor, the value of community, and the centrality of love to salvation, it can also be viewed as an indictment of women and minorities who challenge traditional or conservative visions of their "place" in society. Thus the film contains many repressive or ideologically problematic elements. Specifically, due to its nostalgic vision of America and American home life, the film asserts a conservative vision of the role of women and minorities. Two examples that illustrate this vision are particularly problematic. The first illustrates the film's treatment of Annie, the Baileys' black maid, while the second demonstrates the film's comparison of Mary, the "good" girl, and Violet, the "bad" girl.

The humor of the scene at the Bailey dining table when George discusses his future plans with his father stems from the audience's awareness that Annie, their black maid, is acting like an "uppity nigger." When Annie, a plump and homey "Aunt Jemima" character, is caught eavesdropping at the kitchen door, George jokingly says, "Why don't you come out here and pull up a chair so you can hear better." We laugh because we know that Annie would never do so because her "place" is in the kitchen. When she replies to George's offer that she would come out "If I thought I was gonna hear something interesting," we laugh because although she is an "uppity nigger" who challenges her "place," she is an endearing one who is "almost" a member of the family and who only challenges that "place" in a nonthreatening fashion. As if to reinforce this message, the eavesdropping gag is played out further in the scene for additional laughs.

Another example of conservative or reactionary elements from *It's a Wonderful Life* is the film's treatment of Mary and Violet. Mary, of course,

represents domesticity. Her central goal in life is to get George to marry her and for the two of them to live in the Grandville house. All of her efforts are bent toward this end. George, by comparison, wants to travel, explore, go to college, and build things. Marriage is the last thing on his mind. He must learn to value home and domesticity, and indeed, Mary teaches him this lesson and is responsible, in part, for his change of heart.

Mary, however, a "Madonna" or good-girl figure, is contrasted with Vio-

A newly married George Bailey (Jimmy Stewart) and Mary Bailey (Donna Reed) embrace in front of the fireplace of their new home at 320 Sycamore, in *It's a Wonderful Life*. The old "haunted" Grandville house has been turned into a honeymoon house for one magical night. Just prior to this depicted moment, a dumbfounded George steps in the door to be welcomed by this perfect picture of domesticity. "Welcome home, Mr. Bailey," she says as they embrace. "Remember the night we broke the window in this old house? This is what I wished for." The culmination of this vision of domesticity is made possible not only by Mary's love for George and for Bedford Falls, but also by the kindness of the community volunteers who make a honeymoon in an abandoned broken down house possible. In the populist world of small town America, good neighbors take care of each other and home is where the heart is. George Bailey, the wandering hero, is finally "home." Courtesy of the Museum of Modern Art—Film Stills Archives.

let, a "whore" or bad-girl figure. We find that as a child Violet liked all of the boys rather than having a special someone, like Mary. When Violet parades through the street all of the men ogle and stare at her, but then remind themselves that they are married men. Violet goes off to the big city to "find" herself and perhaps start a career. We sense, however, that without George's offered loan, she would have become a prostitute. The film implies, in other words, that career aspirations for women are dangerous and may even lead to their downfall or "deflowering," since a woman's virginity is one of her most important assets.

Thus, *It's a Wonderful Life*, in its telling of the quest for home myth, asserts the conservative message that a woman's place is in the home and a black's place is in the kitchen of that home.

In conclusion, *The Wizard of Oz, Gone with the Wind*, and *It's a Wonderful Life* offer seductive versions of the hero's quest for home, told against the backdrop of the American "loss of home" myth. This myth, dating back to the experiences of the earliest immigrants to settle in America, and elaborated on at length in such genres of American fiction at the "longstocking" tales of James Fenimore Cooper and Western novels and films, carried a particular currency for Americans during the 1930s and 1940s. It was during this time that the collapse of financial institutions, the demise of the family farm, the rapid rise of homelessness, and nostalgic longings for a preindustrial America provided a particularly poignant context for the story of the hero's quest for home—whether the loss of that home was due to a tornado (*The Wizard of Oz*), the collapse of the institution of slavery (*Gone with the Wind*), or corporate capitalism's threat to the local savings and loan (*It's a Wonderful Life*). No myth in American cinema, as Selcer reminds us, "is stronger or more persistent than the myth of home as the best possible place in the world." [30] Films such as *The Wizard of Oz*, *Gone with the Wind*, and *It's a Wonderful Life*, despite their problematic portrayals of ideology, gender, class, and race, bring this lesson home with compelling clarity.

7

Modern Challenges in the Home Quest: Reconciling Science and Technology with Humanity and Spirit

I was given something wonderful. Something that changed me forever, a vision of the universe that tells us undeniably how tiny and insignificant and how rare and precious we all are. A vision that tells us we belong to something greater than ourselves. That we are not, that none of us, are alone. If I could share that—that everyone, if even for one moment, could feel that awe and that humility and that hope. That continues to be my wish.

—Dr. Ellie Arroway, *Contact*

The Science and Technology Versus Humanity and Spirit Myth

The growth of technology, particularly since the development of the atomic bomb, the computer, and the World Wide Web, has been exponential. The Y2K problem, also known as "the millennium bug," served, for many, to illustrate technology's potentially devastating impact on all areas of human life in the year 2000. It also served, interestingly enough, as a dramatic counterpart to the invention of the atomic bomb, whose potentially devastating impact shadowed the second half of the twentieth century and still influences us today. Not surprisingly, therefore, a recent permutation of the quest myth has focused on contemporary society's collective fears about the encroachment of science and technology into all spheres of human activity. Usually the message of this myth is that "technology is not going to save us. Our computers, our tool, our machines are not enough. We have to rely on our intuition, our true being." [1] More specifically, however, versions of this myth usually attempt to reconcile the potentially conflicted relationship between scientific/ rational ways of knowing and spiritual/nonrational ways of knowing.

Of all film genres, the science-fiction genre is most compelled to explore the relationship between scientific/rational ways of knowing and spiritual/nonrational ways of knowing because when humanity seeks answers to questions regarding its future (the "what if" territory of the sci-fi genre) it is inevitably faced with questions regarding its past, or more specifically its genesis. Both inquiries invite exploration of the universe, our place in it, and possibly others' place as well. In answering such queries as Where did we come from? Where are we going? Are we unique in the universe or are there others? physicists and philosophers alike not only face scientific possibilities and technological capabilities; they often confront spiritual inescapabilites as well. Thus the sci-fi genre utopically wonders at the infinity of space and time that is the universe and the unique (divine?) spark of life that created humanity—both of which science and technology reveal—while dystopically warning that science and technology could paradoxically obscure those same spiritual truths. Films that explore this relationship in powerful and interesting ways include *E.T.: The Extra-Terrestrial, 2001: A Space Odyssey, Close Encounters of the Third Kind*, and *Contact*.

It is not surprising that two of these films are directed by Steven Spielberg—*E.T* and *Close Encounters*—simply because such metaphysical questions seem to be at the heart of many of his films.[2] And by the same token, Stanley Kubrick (*2001, Dr. Strangelove, Full Metal Jacket*) is also know for philosophical musings on humanity's origins and destiny, particularly in light of our developing technological capabilities. The fourth film, *Contact*, directed by Robert Zemeckis (*Forrest Gump*), is based on a book by Carl Sagan, who is arguable the central twentieth-century Perennial philosopher of space exploration.

All of these films attempt to reconcile logical/rational ways of knowing with spiritual/nonrational ways of knowing rather than favor one over the other. Although these epistemologies are often in conflict over the course of the film, they are ultimately not portrayed as mutually exclusive. Usually the relationship is resolved by offering a third or transcendent way of knowing that combines the best of both. Specifically, one or more character in each film is a "boundary spanner," someone with their feet planted in both perspectives who refuses to automatically value one over the other. In *E.T.* for example, the boundary spanners are E.T. and Keys, the head scientist who befriends Elliot. In *Close Encounters*, the boundary spanner is the French scientist who heads the team of researchers who have tracked the alien spacecraft to its landing on Devil's Mountain, Wyoming. In *Contact*, the protagonist Ellie becomes a boundary spanner as does her fellow researcher and friend Kent. Although there are no boundary spanners, per se, in Kubrick's *2001* (certainly the most pessimistic of all four films), it is as if technology generally, and shots of the various spaceships specifically, take on an aesthetic and harmonious quality that is close to spiritual perfection.

Films that take up the question of the relationship between science/technology and humanity/spirit, not surprisingly, also take the form of the quest myth for home. This may be because films about space exploration, alien life forms, and the origin of the universe are implicitly about humanity's quest to find our place in the time/space continuum—to feel "at home" in the universe. Thus, the protagonists of the four of the films discussed in this chapter are all on Odyssean quests. Ellic, in *Contact*, after a trip to the planet Vega, completes her Odyssean quest by returning home to Earth and the world of everyday experience. It is on Vega that she is transformed through meeting an alien and realizing that "we are not alone," both in terms of the existence of others and in terms of a universal force that binds us together. *E.T.* is also about a journey home. The film's most memorable line, "E.T. phone home," reminds us of the desperate race against time that E.T., a metaphoric Christ/hero figure, runs in order to defeat death. *2001: A Space Odyssey* self-consciously references the Odyssean quest by its title. Although *2001*'s David Bowman never returns to Earth, his literal home, his arrival on the planet Jupiter, where he possibly meets the creators of the Monolith, in one interpretation, signifies his unification with the universe, his transformation into a "child of the universe," and his "return" to a transcendent home. Roy, in *Close Encounters of the Third Kind*, like David Bowman in *2001*, also does not return to a literal home and family. Instead, by his decision to leave with the aliens at the end of the film, we sense that he has finally found his place in the universe and will be "at home" in outer space in a way that he never was on the Earth.

All four films also evidence a fascination with what Jung refers to as the child archetype. In all four films a specific child, or children in general, symbolizes not only innocence but also receptivity to creative potential, the nonrational possibility of alien life, and the transcendent. Jung asserts that the child archetype, a significant figure in myth and dreams, manifests itself in numerous contexts and invites multiple interpretations. Some of the more predominant are the child archetype as an individuation archetype,[3] as a representation of preconsciousness or the "childhood" aspect of the collective psyche,[4] as a necessary corrective to the "inevitable one-sidedness and extravagances of the conscious mind," [5] as an archetype of the future, or as a metaphor for beginnings and endings or a unification of opposites, hence, a wholeness archetype.[6]

In both *E.T.* and *Close Encounters*, for example, it is a child who first encounters the alien, and significantly, it is a child who becomes the central link between aliens and humans. Although Ellie Arroway in *Contact* is an adult when she encounters the aliens, we first come to know her as a child, and it is as a child that her fascination with extraterrestrial life begins. In *2001*, the final image of the film is of a child in a womb, possibly implying that infinity/eternity, or the final stage in the development of humanity, is the same as the first; or that the first stage of consciousness contains the final stage, which then is both, seemingly paradoxically, a being and a becoming.

This emphasis on a child figure in all four films mirrors the presentation of the aliens in both *E.T.* and *Close Encounters* as childlike. Both E.T. and the aliens in *Close Encounters*, like children, have big heads and eyes and small bodies. Also like young children, their bodies are hairless and soft, and seem vulnerable and androgynous. Thus, the aliens themselves, like the earth children who meet them, speak to the biblical saying that "a child shall lead them." But more than this, they come to represent boundary-spanning figures, possessing as they do the advanced science and technology that allows interplanetary space flight, while maintaining a sense of childlike awe at the mysteries of creation and the wonders of the universe.

Jung notes that as a "symbol which unites the opposites; a mediator, bringer of healing, that is, one who makes whole," the child figure is often "expressed by roundness, the circle or sphere, or else by the quaternity as another form of wholeness." [7] All four films, particularly *E.T.* and *2001*, are replete with mandala symbols. The word "mandala," from the Sanskrit for circle, is also the term used by Indians for the circles drawn in religious contemplation. According to Jung, the most significant mandalas are found in Tibetan Buddhism. For the Tibetan Buddhist the mandala is ritually used as a "yantra," an instrument of contemplation." [8] The goal of such contemplation is for the yogi to "become inwardly aware of the deity. Through contemplation, he recognizes himself as God again, and thus returns from the illusion of individual existence into the universal totality of the divine state." [9]

As symbols of the unconscious, mandalas, similarly to the child archetype, represent transcendence, unity, or centeredness of being. Jung notes that "they express the idea of a safe refuge, of inner reconciliation and wholeness." [10] "Mandalas are birthplaces, vessels of birth in the most literal sense, lotus-flowers in which the Buddha comes to life. Sitting in the lotus seat, the yogi sees himself transfigured into an immortal." [11] Significant mandalas appearing in the natural world and humanity's experience of that world include the sun and moon, the planets and the solar system, the mother's womb, the birth canal, the circularity of the passage of time, of the seasons, and of the ages of consciousness. Mandalas are frequently represented in significant religious rituals, such as the communion host in Catholic worship, the ritual Hogan hut of the Native Americans, and the sand paintings of Tibetan Buddhism.

2001, perhaps best of all the films discussed in this chapter, evidences numerous mandalas. Kubrick's photographic eye self-consciously constructs multiple mise-en-scènes as graphically complex renderings of various mandalas. Kubrick's excruciatingly slow panning and arcing camera and his inclination toward minimal editing invite the viewer to dwell at length on these graphic renderings. Mandalas are also a recurring motif in Spielberg's *E.T.*, represented in everything from the luminous glow of a flashlight or car headlight, to the incandescence of a full moon, to the circular window in E.T.'s "casket." [12] The spacecrafts in *E.T.* as well as in *Close Encounters* all have a circular or rounded shape. In *Contact*, the transporter in which Ellie Arroway is whisked off to the planet Vega is a mandala inside of a mandala. It carries her though "worm holes," circular tubelike constructions in space. In all four films, mandalas become an important visual motif that invites metaphysical interpretations.

In what follows, I discuss each of the four films at greater length, often focusing on the presence of child archetypes, mandala symbols, boundary-spanning characters and motifs, and the journey home narrative structure—all of which work to reveal each film's attempts to reconcile the tensions between scientific/rational ways of knowing and spiritual/nonrational ways of knowing.

Close Encounters of the Third Kind

Close Encounters of the Third Kind, like *Contact* and *E.T.*, focuses on the moment of contact with aliens while exploring questions of our place in the universe. Examining the relationship between science/technology and humanity/ spirit, the film also takes the form of the quest myth for home.

The Journey Home

The film's protagonist Roy (Richard Dreyfuss) is clearly unhappy with his life on earth. His marriage is in trouble, his parenting skills, although loving, are awkward and unsatisfactory. We witness this, for example, when we are introduced to Roy and his family. As Roy unsuccessfully tries to explain fractions to his eldest son through a demonstration involving railroad cars from a train set, we see another child in the background repeatedly smashing a doll to pieces while a third child whines loudly. Over this din, Roy's wife (Teri Garr) angrily complains about all of the "junk" Roy has left on her kitchen table. Roy makes an unpopular decision to take his children to a classic Disney film instead of "Goofy Golf," fails at explaining fractions to his son, and is clearly miserable in his home life. Just like the toy boxcar hit by an oncoming train in Roy's unsuccessful fractions lesson, we sense that Roy's marriage and family life are also a train wreck waiting to happen. Indeed, it is not long before he receives his "call to adventure" in the form of a close encounter with extraterrestrials that will "rescue" him from his domestic nightmare.

From the moment of this first encounter Roy becomes increasingly obsessed with aliens, to the point of losing his job and becoming disconnected from his wife and children. Since he is ill at ease in his home and in his life, we realize that his quest to find the aliens is a quest to find meaning in his life and a quest to be "at home" in the universe. This quest will take him all the way to Devil's Mountain, Wyoming, where he will come face to face with the vision that haunts him for the film's duration, and where he will finally meet the extraterrestrials.

In the course of his travels to Devil's Mountain, like any hero, he encounters a number of obstacles. These take the form of physical obstacles, such as roadblocks, National Guard troops, and helicopters dusting the area with a sleep agent. But Roy also faces powerful psychological and emotional obstacles as well: his wife's disbelief and lack of support regarding his close encounter, his own apprehension about another alien encounter, and his fears for his own sanity. At the film's conclusion, Roy, of course, overcomes all of these obstacles and managed to make it to the landing site on Devil's Mountain where he witnesses the aliens' arrival.

Once there, the aliens choose Roy—over all of the career astronauts and scientists trained for this mission—to join them when they lift off. At the moment of his selection, a group of aliens, less than half Roy's height, surround him; touching and stroking his arms and legs. This selection and treatment signifies his special status as having been touched by his previous encounter and his spiritual or psychic readiness for such a journey now. The film dwells at length on the moment as well as the moment of Roy's entrance into the aliens' spacecraft. As he ascends the ship's ramp, the film's score, by John Williams, swells with a strain of "When You Wish upon a Star." As he enters the ship, a beatific smile appears on his face. We see a series of interior shots of the spacecraft, appearing as abstract compositions of swirling lights in repeated circular patterns, intercut with shots of Roy's awestruck face. It appears as if Roy is witnessing a divine vision and we sense that his hero's journey is finally complete. Roy is at peace, with himself and with the universe. He is "home" on this alien ship in ways he never was in his domestic home.

The Child (Alien) Archetype

Although we come to know Roy as an adult, and it is as an adult that he is drawn to the aliens and the possibilities of transcendence they offer, *Close Encounters*, like the other films discussed in this chapter, draws heavily on the child archetype and what this archetype represents in terms of both individual and cultural individuation.

As an individuation archetype, according to Jung, the child motif signifies "the maturation process of personality induced by the analysis of the unconscious." [13] As a harbinger of preconsciousness, "the child motif is a picture of certain *forgotten* things in our childhood." [14] As an incipient adult, in other words, the child archetype represents an earlier stage of development, not just in the individual but in the culture as a whole. Thus, it represents the preconscious phase of human development.

However, as Jung points out:

The child motif represents not only something that existed in the distant past but also something that exists *now*; that is to say, it is not just a vestige but a system functioning in the present whose purpose it to compensate or correct, in a meaningful manner, the inevitable one-sidedness and extravagances of the conscious mind." [15]

The child archetype, in other words, acts as a necessary corrective to the current age of consciousness' focus on the self and on rational ways of knowing.

It offers, in other words, an intuitive sense of the Self and of unconscious or transcendent ways of knowing.

As a result, the child archetype not only represents an earlier stage of development; it also represents a future stage of development. According to Jung, "The child is potential future. Hence the occurrence of the child motif in the psychology of the individual signifies as a rule an anticipation of future developments, even though at first sight it may seem like a retrospective configuration." [16] This is because "the 'child' paves the way for future change of personality. In the individuation process, it anticipates the figure that comes from the synthesis of conscious and unconscious elements in the personality." Thus the paradox of the child as both preconsciousness and transconsciousness (or individuation) rests in the idea of an "*a priori* existence of potential wholeness." [17] Rather than being a tabula rasa, as the Romantic poet William Wordsworth points out, the child is instead "the father of the man," such that

Our birth is but a sleep and a forgetting
The soul that rises with us, our life's star, hath had elsewhere its setting, and cometh from afar
Not in entire forgetfulness, and not in utter nakedness, but trailing clouds of glory do we come from God, who is our home.[18]

Thus, the child not only reconciles or unites the conscious and the unconscious, as a symbol of both beginnings and endings, "an initial and terminal creature," the child archetype "symbolizes the pre-consciousness and the post-conscious essence of humanity. His preconscious essence is the unconscious state of earliest childhood; his post-conscious essence is an anticipation by analogy of life after death. In this idea the all-embracing nature of psychic wholeness is expressed." [19]

Close Encounters invites these various interpretations of the child archetype. Roy, for example, is not alone in heeding the call of the aliens. A little boy named Barry is also drawn to the aliens and is actually taken from his mother (Melinda Dillon) by them early on in the film. Part of the film's plot is the boy's mother's search to find the aliens and to take her son back. As such, she joins forces with Roy in their journey to Devil's Mountain, Wyoming, for a predestined encounter with the aliens.

That Barry heeds an instinctual call and is drawn to the aliens signifies his openness to what they represent. As a representative of preconsciousness, he has not yet been jaded by the rational or scientific mode of knowing — embraced by most adults — and thus can accept the nonrational possibility of alien life. The aliens' portrayal as childlike, with small, thin bodies and large heads and eyes heightens this psychic connection between them.

The childlike rendering of the aliens in *Close Encounters* is extremely common in culture, where "child" aliens appear not only in numerous films and television shows, but also in art, advertising, literature, and dreams. Aliens, not surprisingly, are always presented as possessing superior intelligence, or at least as having achieved superior technology, since it is this technology that has allowed them to visit the planet Earth. What is most significant, however, from the perspective of Perennial philosophy, is the idea that the alien-as-child archetype represents not only a more advanced stage of technological development, but also a higher or more enlightened stage of consciousness.[20] The aliens in *Close Encounters*, like the aliens in *Contact* and *E.T.*, are rationally and scientifically capable as well as spiritually and emotionally grounded. In sum, the child/alien archetype, like the child archetype as evidenced in *Close Encounters*, portrays a unified or holistic intelligence while offering a glimpse of the potential postconscious evolution of humanity.

Boundary Spanning

Close Encounters also has a boundary-spanning character, someone, like the aliens themselves, with an appreciation for both rational/scientific and non-rational/intuitive ways of knowing. We are introduced to this character, the French leader of the UFO research team, M. Lacombe (François Truffaut), in an isolated desert in Mexico where a UFO sighting has occurred. As the team's leader, we assume he is a man of great scientific and technological knowledge, yet he also exhibits sensitivity to nonrational ways of knowing. For example, he very carefully and respectfully interviews an old man who claims to have seen the aliens. He does not laugh or dismiss him when the peasant, referring to his encounter, says, "The sun came out last night. It sang to me."

The French scientist's openness to nonrational ways of knowing is also demonstrated when he later interrogates Roy about his compulsion to come to Devil's Mountain, Wyoming. Not only interested in Roy, he is also curious about an entire group of people who have made the pilgrimage, despite propagandistic warnings of an unintentional release of nerve gas in the area and the mandatory evacuation of all human beings. We also find out that all of the people Lacombe interviews report visions or dreams that compelled them to make visual renderings of Devil's Mountain. Some painted pictures, others sketched chalk drawings. Roy, of course, constructs a huge three-dimensional version out of clay in his living room. That the aliens' arrival appears to the group in dreams and visions and is expressed visually in graphic renderings of the landing location, emphasizes the realm of the unconscious (the place from which dreams and visions emerge) while celebrating unconscious or nonrational ways of knowing (visual rather than linguistic thinking). That Lacombe is interested, even respectful, of these dreams and visions, signifies his openness to nonrational or intuitive ways of knowing.

Lacombe is not only fascinated by Roy's and the others' intuitive knowledge of the alien landing (he is, after all the quintessential scientist), he is also respectful of their special status as having been touched by an alien encounter. This is particularly evident in a scene in which he pleads with the military commander to let them stay at Devil's Mountain for the anticipated encounter, arguing that they have a right to be there even if he does not understand why:

Lacombe:	I believe for every one of these anxious, anguished people who have come here this evening, there must be hundreds of others also touched by the vision who never made it this far, or never watched the television, or perhaps they watched it and never made the psychic connection.
Major Walsh:	It's a coincidence. It's not scientific.
Lacombe:	Listen to me, Major Walsh. It is an "event sociologic."

Lacombe's respect is also evident when he later makes the case for Ray to join the other scientists as a candidate for space travel with the aliens, despite the fact that Roy has had no training or preparation for the rigors of space or the psychological impact of such a mission. In sum, the French scientist Lacombe, as boundary spanner, highlights the idea that scientific/rational ways of knowing are not necessarily incompatible with spiritual/nonrational ways of knowing.

The film's attempt to reconcile these potentially conflicting paradigms is perhaps best epitomized, however, in the research team's mode of communication with the aliens at Devil's Mountain. Separated not only by language, but also by galaxies of distance and light years of experience, the humans and aliens bridge the gap through music. The famous five-note musical sequence, crafted by John Williams, along with the rest of the film's score, may still be imprinted in the viewer's mind, years after the film's release.

At the moment of contact, a musician repeatedly taps out the musical sequence on a keyboard. The scientists, along with the film audience, hold their breath for a reply. When the alien ship finally responds, it is as if the audiences, both filmic and real, heave a collective sigh of relief. Contact is complete. An increasingly intense musical conversation ensues. The "dialogue," however, begins to move so rapidly that the musician, unable to keep up the pace, is replaced by a computer. We sense that the scientists, possibly through mathematical modeling, will later decode this cacophonous conversation. For the moment, however, the scientists, like the film audience, are caught up in the beauty, the magic, and the awe of this lyrical meeting.

The choice of music as the language of intergalactic communication epitomizes the merging of rational and nonrational ways of knowing. Music is at once extremely logical and mathematical—based as it is on interval relationships—while remaining deeply emotional and nonrational—touching, as it does, deep chords of feeling in the listener. It is not surprising, therefore, that music is used as the primary means to communicate with the aliens since the film itself attempts to reconcile both rational and nonrational ways of knowing. That both a musician and a computer are used to carry on this conversation further supports this interpretation.

It is also worth noting that the moment of contact occurs at a mountain. From a religious or spiritual perspective, enlightenment often occurs on a mountain. In Judeo-Christian tradition, Moses goes to the mountain to receive the Ten Commandments from God. Jesus Christ is taken to the top of a mountain where Satan tempts him to renounce God and worship Satan. In ancient Greece, during bacchanalian celebrations in honor of Dionysius, the god of wine, the women, in an ecstatic frenzy, would run into the mountains. Monasteries, mosques, churches, and various religious sites are often built on mountaintops as if to be nearer to god or spirit. Mountains, therefore, have traditionally been viewed as places of spiritual/religious ecstasy or enlightenment. The aliens' arrival at Devil's Mountain, therefore, is not only a scientific wonder; it is also an event filled with deep religious or spiritual significance. The religious import, in one interpretation, lies in the fact that if aliens exist, then humans are no longer divinely unique. The spiritual importance, in another interpretation, is humanity's connection to others in ways only imagined and our shared destiny with all living beings, both worldly and otherworldly.

The bridging of rational and nonrational ways of knowing is also highlighted by the church service held just prior to the research team's departure with the aliens. Here, in this most techno-scientific of places, with so

many glaring lights, invasive recording devices, and humming mainframe computers, all of the astronaut volunteers gather for a final religious service. During this service, we witness the following call-and-response exchange:

Priest:	May the Lord be praised at all times.
Astronauts:	May God help us and grant us a happy journey.
Priest:	Show us Your ways.
Astronauts:	And lead us along Your paths.
Priest:	God has given you his angel's charge over you. Grant these pilgrims, we pray, a happy journey and peaceful days, so that with your holy angel as a guide they may safely reach their destination.

Both scientific and spiritual ways of knowing are essential components for these intergalactic wayfarers.

In sum, *Close Encounters of the Third Kind* attempts to reconcile logical/rational ways of knowing with spiritual/nonrational ways of knowing. Although these epistemologies are often in conflict over the course of the film, they are ultimately not portrayed as mutually exclusive. Through the use of music, the child archetype, and a boundary-spanning character, Lacombe, the

The arrival of the alien's mothership at Devil's Mountain, just before the moment of contact between the two species in *Close Encounters of the Third Kind*. Backlit by the glow of the emerging spacecraft, the image of the mountain is reminiscent of the black oblong "Religious" monolith in *2001*. It is significant that the moment of contact occurs at a mountain. Mountains have traditionally been viewed as places of spiritual/religious ecstasy or enlightenment. The aliens' arrival at Devil's Mountain, therefore, is not only a scientific wonder; it is also an event filled with deep religious or spiritual significance. Thus the film, through such imagery as that depicted here attempts to reconcile scientific and rational ways of knowing with spiritual and nonrational ways of knowing. Courtesy of the Museum of Modern Art—Film Stills Archives.

film offers a transcendent way of knowing that combines the best impulses of both epistemologies. The film also takes the form of the quest myth for home. Although Roy, at his quest's end, does not return to his wife and family, his decision to leave with the aliens may indicate that he has finally found his place and will be "at home" in the universe in a way he never was on Earth.

E.T.: The Extra-Terrestrial

Steven Spielberg's Academy Award-winning film *E.T.: The Extra-Terrestrial* was not only a phenomenal commercial success, it is ranked number twenty-five on the American Film Institute's list of the greatest one hundred films of all time. The film not only offers a reconciliation of rational/scientific and nonrational/spiritual ways of knowing, it also provides a provocative meditation on psychic wholeness, the undivided nature of being, and the universal appeal of "home." [21]

Boundary Spanning

Like other films in this genre, *E.T.* has boundary-spanning figures who represent a reconciliation between rational/scientific and nonrational/spiritual ways of knowing. E.T. and the head scientist, "Keys," offer the two best examples of this boundary spanning.

E.T. epitomizes the boundary-spanning function both in the opening scene of the film and as his character is revealed to the audience over the course of the film. We are first introduced to E.T. as a scientist. We witness,

for example, the inside of his spaceship as the camera does a slow pan that reveals what appears to be an ongoing science experiment. Outside of the craft,
however, we see a close-up of E.T.'s delicate and slowly probing hand as he
reverentially lifts a tiny giant redwood sapling out of the soil. The next shot is
an extremely low angle long shot of the towering redwood trees, followed by
an eye-level, long shot of E.T. walking through these grand trees. For emphasis, this shot sequence is repeated. Giant redwoods are the tallest and one of
the oldest trees in the world. As such, they both invite awe and suggest eternity. As a sapling they represent incipient possibilities. As a symbol of nature
they are both a source of scientific exploration and spiritual revelation. E.T.'s
harvesting of this tiny sapling symbolizes both ways of knowing. His visual
placement in the forest represents his connection to this natural world.

E.T. is, however, the quintessential scientist. It is advanced technology
that allows him and his kind to travel to the planet Earth. More specifically,
when he is left behind, it is technological know-how that helps E.T. improvise
a radio transmitter from common household items to signal his people. As if
to affirm the importance of scientific ways of knowing, Elliot, attempting to
figure out what type of equipment would best help E.T. build such a device,
comments to his brother, "I wish I would have listened in science."

Although, as an alien, E.T. possesses advanced technological capabili-

Elliot (Henry Thomas) sees the approaching lights of the men looking for E.T. in *E.T.: The Extra-Terrestrial*. As in the depicted image, mandalas are a recurring motif in the film, represented in everything from the luminous glow of a flashlight or car head-light, to the incandescence of a full moon, to the circular window in E.T.'s "casket." The word "mandala," from the Sanskrit for "circle," is the term used by Indians for the circles drawn in religious contemplation. They often symbolize wholeness or the spiritual unity of all being. This image also highlights the apparent opposition between rational/scientific ways of knowing (represented by the faceless line of men with their flashlights bearing down on Elliot) and nonrational/spiritual ways of knowing (repre-sented by Elliot, as the intuitive/spiritual child archetype open to the wonders of the universe). The chain link fence dramatically portrays the faceoff between these two ways of knowing, while the mystical fog adds to our apprehension regarding the reso-lution of this conflict. The camera's position (our position) on Elliot's side of the fence, however, so that we see the faceless men from Elliot's perspective, indicates where our sentiments will most likely lie in this battle. Courtesy of the Museum of Modern Art—Film Stills Archives.

ties, and indeed, succeeds in fashioning his radar device, his emotional/ nonrational side is repeatedly emphasized throughout the film. In the film's opening scene, for example, we realize that E.T. is terrified, having been left behind by his fellow shipmates. He groans in despair like a forgotten child. His heart light beams strongly from his chest. He is so vulnerable—all raw emotion—even to the extent of "wearing his heart on his sleeve," or rather, on the outside of his chest. When his spaceship lifts off without him, his heart light goes out, as if with the departure of his comrades the source of his being extinguishes. As the faceless men with flashlights try to hunt him down, he squeals with fear, and runs for his life. Without yet having seen E.T.'s face, we have experienced with him a wide array of human emotions: awe at the majesty of the redwood forest, curiosity at their growth, fear of the invading humans, terror at being left behind, and love for other beings.

E.T.'s emotional side is further emphasized in a later scene when a scien-tist questions Elliot's older brother, Mike, about E.T.'s relationship with Elliot. "Elliot thinks his [E.T.'s] thoughts?" he asks. "No," replies Mike, "Elliot feels his feelings." Thus, despite his extensive scientific and technological exper-tise, the film repeatedly establishes E.T. as an emotional and intuitive being.

E.T. is not the only boundary-spanner figure in the film. keys, the scien-tist appearing in the initial scene as one of the men hunting E.T. down and who is later revealed as the head of the research team investigating the spaceship landing, also performs such a function. In fact, he is the only scientist given some humanity in the film. This is evidenced when Keys allows Elliot to spend some time with E.T. after he dies. It is also apparent in Keys' conversation with Elliot as Elliot lies near death on a hospital cot:

Keys: Elliot, I've been to the forest. Elliot, that machine, what does it do?
Elliot: Is it still working?
Keys: It's doing something . . .
Elliot: I shouldn't tell you anything. He came to me. He came to me.
Keys: Elliot, he came to me too. I've been wishing for this since I was ten years old. I don't want him to die. What can we do that we're not already doing?
Elliot: He needs to go home. He's calling his people. I don't know where they are, but he needs to go home.
Keys: I don't think that he was left intentionally. But his being here is a miracle, Elliot. It's a miracle and you did the best that anybody could do. I'm glad he met you first.

From this conversation we realize that Keys, as a child, felt the same awe and wonder Elliot experiences upon meeting E.T. Keys' reference to E.T.'s coming as a "miracle" rather than as an important scientific event suggests his sensitivity to the spiritual dimension of the experience. That he looks to Elliot for advice regarding how to help E.T. shows his respect for Elliot's special child wisdom.

Keys also exhibits boundary-spanning qualities in the film's final scene when he joins Elliot's mom in the forest to witnesses E.T.'s rendezvous with his people. Significantly, Keys does not intervene in the good-byes among E.T., Elliot, his brother, and his sister, nor does he try to stop E.T. from leaving. This is the case even though E.T.'s departure would represent the end of Keys scientific investigation of this extraterrestrial phenomenon.

As a boundary spanner, Keys also offers an important corrective to the other scientists in the film, who, for the most part, are portrayed as more alien that the aliens. We witness this, for example, in the scene where the scientists invade Elliot's house to capture E.T. Dressed in spacesuits that obscure their faces, lit in silhouette to emphasize their facelessness, shot from a low angle to emphasize their ominousness, they break down doors and push through curtains with their arms extended in Frankenstein-like fashion. Indeed, Elliot's mother screams when they appear as if to heighten our awareness of their monstrous similarity.

Shot in cold blue light, and continually framed by plastic sheeting, the scientists are portrayed as methodical, sterile, and unfeeling. Separated from E.T. by spacesuits and plastic cages, they are unwilling to touch or be touched by E.T. or, by extension, the transcendent possibilities he represents. They want to dissect E.T. rather than feel his love for them. Drunk with ego-consciousness, as Rushing notes, "these men want to *possess* the cosmos rather than to become one with it. Instead of being one with God, they try to play God." [22] Elliot, for example, intuitively realizes this earlier in the film when, in response to his mother's order that if he sees the "goblin" again he must tell her so that they can call someone to take it away, protests, saying, "They'll give it a lobotomy, or do experiments on it or something." With the wisdom of a child, Elliot knows that rational/scientific ways of knowing are often in conflict with nonrational/spiritual ways of knowing.

We see another example of Elliot grappling with this conflict in a scene during his science class at school. Possibly telepathically influenced by E.T. and the universal love he represents, Elliot frees dozens of the frogs destined for use in a dissection demonstration, thus illustrating his love for all beings, his reverence for life, and his realization that scientific ways of knowing (dissection) often destroy or obscure spiritual ways of knowing (reverential contemplation).

Thus, Keys, the head scientist, E.T., the extraterrestrial, and Elliot as an extension of E.T., represent boundary-spanning figures able to rise above the perceived conflict between rational and nonrational ways of knowing and, in the case of E.T. (as we will see), offer a possible synthesis of these epistemologies.

The Child (Alien) Archetype

E.T., like Yoda in the "Star Wars" trilogy, is a particularly compelling mythic character in that he combines the child archetype with the archetype of the old man and the elf/dwarf. According to Jung, the old-man archetype "represents knowledge, reflection, insight, wisdom, cleverness, and intuition on the one hand, and on the other, moral qualities such as goodwill and readiness to help, which make his 'spiritual' character sufficiently plain." [23] "In folklore the child motif appears in the guise of the dwarf or the elf as personification of the hidden forces of nature." [24] E.T. looks like an old man, a dwarf, and a child while also epitomizing the qualities ascribed to these figures in myth and

folklore. E.T.'s physical appearance is compellingly childlike. He is short, and appears soft and vulnerable, with a large head, like a newborn baby. The transcendent implications of E.T.'s childlike qualities are pointed out by Rushing, who notes that:

Childhood is . . . "the treasure hard to attain" of the modern age. E.T. (and by extension Elliot, who is now indelibly linked to him) is its representative here. E.T. is both a hero and a treasure in the same way that other truly transcendent figures have been both. E.T., that is, has found the treasure of transconciousness, becoming one with it, and now *is* that treasure for others. As hero, he simultaneously *shows* the way and *is* the way. He demonstrates how to *become* what we can *be*.[25]

Yet E.T. also looks old and wise, like a twisted and gnarled tree root.[26] Being short, E.T. is also close to the earth. Brownish-gray, he is the color of the soil. His appearance, therefore, heightens our awareness of E.T.'s chthonic demeanor and his debt to nature.[27] Thus, innocent and childlike, yet wise beyond counting, intuitive, and connected to nature, the child/old man/dwarf represents beginning, preconsciousness, and incipient possibilities as well as endings, postconsciousness, and psychic individuation.

Elliot (Henry Thomas) and his friends desperately try to outrun the authorities as they race against time to save E.T.'s life by returning him home to his people in *E.T.: The Extra-Terrestrial*. E.T., like Yoda in the "Star Wars" trilogy, is a particularly compelling mythic character in that he combines the child archetype with the archetype of the old man and the elf/dwarf. Innocent and childlike, yet wise beyond counting, intuitive and connected to nature, the child/old man/dwarf represents beginning, pre-consciousness, incipient possibilities, and well as endings, "post-consciousness," and psychic individuation. This image also reminds us that E.T.'s literal and spiritual quest is to go home. It is such an urgent quest that he grows more and more homesick, even unto death, for each hour he is away. E.T.'s sickness can be interpreted, on the one hand, as a hypersensitive response to earth's environment. Like the canary in the coal mine, he warns of the increasing toxicity of our world, both in terms of the destruction of our biosphere and in terms of our spiritual sickness—our disassociation with all things spiritual and nonrational. Our failure, in other words, to move beyond the realm of ego-consciousness, has mired us in a state of "soul-sickness," which E.T., and perhaps only a few other hero-visionaries of our age, can sense. Thus, E.T.'s sickness is a response to being cut off from the divine unity of all things, signified by his separation from his people and his home. Courtesy of the Museum of Modern Art—Film Stills Archives.

The Forest

The forest, like the child archetype, also becomes a significant symbol in the film, representing both a place of deep mystery and refuge as well as a place of natural/spiritual connection. Jung asserts that the realm of the unconscious is "frequently expressed through the symbols of wood and water." [28] For Elliot, the forest represents a child's secret and magical place where we sense that he spends a good deal of time. In a version of Hansel and Gretel, in which the two children leave a trail of bread crumbs in order to find their way home from the forest, Elliot leaves a trail of Reese's Pieces candy in the forest in order to lure E.T. home to his house.

As a liminal space of transformations, the forest is also where contact occurs between the two worlds, extraterrestrial and human. The film begins in the forest with the landing of E.T.'s craft, E.T. builds his transmitter on the "bald spot" in the forest in order to contact his people, and the film ends in the forest when E.T.'s people come to take him home. Keys' first words to Elliot are "Elliot, I've been to the forest," as if to imply a special magical relationship between the two of them (they share the secret of the forest), and between the two of them and the forest (they know what the forest represents).

The Journey Home

E.T.'s literal quest, of course, is to go home. It is such an urgent quest that he grows more and more homesick for each hour he is away, even to the point of death. E.T.'s sickness can be interpreted, on the one hand, as a hypersensitive response to earth's environment. Like the canary in the coal mine, he warns of the increasing toxicity of our world, both in terms of the destruction of our biosphere and in terms of our spiritual sickness—our dissociation with all things spiritual and nonrational. Our failure, in other words, to move beyond the realm of ego-consciousness, has mired us in a state of "soul-sickness," which E.T., and perhaps only a few other hero-visionaries of our age, can sense. As Rushing expresses it, "In dream and myth, home usually symbolizes the whole self. E.T. simply cannot feel at home here, where technology-on-the-loose is so marring our fragile planet. He is sick because he is divided from himself." [29] Thus, in a related interpretation, E.T.'s sickness is a response to being cut off from the divine unity of all things, signified by his separation from his people and his home.

E.T.'s spiritual quest, of course, is to offer a vision of the universe and of universal love heretofore unavailable to Elliot, and perhaps to others on planet Earth as well. The theme of universal love is epitomized in E.T.'s relationship with Elliot. E.T. and Elliot, telepathically connected, feel each other's feelings. When E.T. drinks one of Elliot's mother's beers, Elliot becomes vicariously drunk. When E.T. watches a love scene on the family television at home, Elliot impulsively kisses a girl at school. When E.T. starts to sicken and die because of homesickness, Elliot falls ill as well. The first and last letters of Elliot's name are *E* and *T*. It is as if the two are physically and emotionally connected.[30] E.T.'s connection with Elliot mirrors our own connection with each other in the divine unity of being, asserting, by extension, that without the other we would die. More important, however, it is Elliot's love for E.T. that ultimately resurrects him, implying that love is stronger than death.

This theme of the victory of love over death is also echoed in the presentation of E.T. as a metaphorical Christ figure. During the chase scene, just before Elliot and his friends carry E.T. to the forest, we see a low angle shot of E.T., taken from the perspective of the neighborhood kids on their bikes. Standing in the back of the van, draped in a white sheet, E.T. suddenly materializes, like a resurrected Christ, before his "disciples," the children who are most receptive to his message of universal love. Like Christ, E.T. has indeed died and been resurrected; more important, however, like Christ, it is love (Elliot's and the children's) that resurrects him.

In another interpretation, E.T. dies so that Elliot may live, since E.T.'s lingering homesickness makes Elliot dangerously ill as well. Only in death do Elliot's and E.T.'s vital signs separate. Thus, E.T., a sacrificial Christ, gives his life so that Elliot might live, or rather, through his death and resurrection, all believers of E.T. are offered a vision of universal love, just as Christ offers Christians the possibility of eternal life. At the end of the film, as a reborn E.T. says good-bye to Elliot, he points to Elliot's head and says, "I'll be right here," as if echoing a resurrected Christ's commission to his disciples just before he returns to the Father: "I am with you always, even unto the ends of the world." [31] This eternal presence is further emphasized when Elliot's sister Gert, speaking to E.T. upon his departure, explains, "I just wanted to say good-bye." Her older brother Mike, speaking literally, reminds her that E.T. "doesn't know good-bye." The audience, of course, is invited to interpret this response metaphorically, sensing that E.T., like all such visionaries of the transcendent, does not "know good-bye" because he will be "with [us] always," both in light of his legacy, and in light of our nonrational awareness of the eternal nowness of being and the all-encompassing unity of Self. As E.T.'s rocket vanishes into the blue sky a rainbow appears in its wake, reminding us of Jehovah's promise to his people that they would remember his Covenant with them when they saw a rainbow in the sky, and thus, by extension, reminding us of E.T.'s promise of transcendent love for Elliot and for all earthlings.

Contact

Contact (1998), based on Carl Sagan's book of the same name, was directed by Robert Zemeckis and had great box-office expectations. Although the film was not the run-away success that *Forrest Gump* had been for Zemeckis, it did respectably well at the box office. Like *E.T.* and *Close Encounters of a Third Kind*, the film emphasizes the moment of contact between earthlings and aliens. And like both these films, it asserts that aliens are both benign and helpful mentors of humanity. Of the three films, however, *Contact* most clearly explores the science/religion debate related to space exploration and speculates about intelligent life in the universe. As we will see, Ellie Arroway's most difficult hero's task is to reconcile scientific/rational ways of knowing with spiritual/nonrational ways of knowing. This larger metaphysical quest is also grounded in an emotional quest to "find" her father, to reconcile her relationship with him, and to become individuated in order to make the sacred marriage with Joss Palmer (Matthew McConaughey). Although like most heroes she embarks on an Odyssean quest, in this case to the solar system Vega and back again, her real quest is inward.

The Journey Home

Ellie Arroway (Jodie Foster) follows the typical hero quest in that her journey outward into space is not only echoed by the journey inward to the self; it also culminates in the journey homeward. As such, Ellie not only returns home to planet Earth; as a result of her trip to the planet Vega she is finally "at home" in the universe. Early in the film, for example, we are introduced to the idea that Ellie, as a little girl, is not happy or complete on planet Earth. Her hobby of listening to the short-wave radio in order to contact other radio buffs from around the world is more than just a child's game. She listens almost incessantly in the hopes of making "contact" with her mother, who died when Ellie was a child. Later in the film, when her father dies of a heart attack, Ellie continues her search of the heavens, now trying to "contact" her father as well. Ill at ease in a world that does not hold her mother or her father, it is not surprising that Ellie, both as a child and then as a grown woman, looks to other worlds for comfort and companionship.

Dr. Ellie Arroway, as an adult, is a member of the SETI (Search for Extra-Terrestrial Intelligence) project. Her particular project, however, in support of which she constantly tracks down grant money, is the systematic scanning of space for radio signals manufactured by intelligent life. The film not only details the fantastical moment when such contact is achieved; it also plays out an adventure that results in Ellie being sent to the planet Vega is a spacecraft constructed from the blueprints transmitted via radio waves from the Vegans. Thus, Ellie's hero quest is to leave the ordinary world of planet Earth, to venture into the magical world of space to contact the aliens, and to return home with the scientific knowledge of her journey.

Her hero's quest is more than just a physical quest, however; it is an emotional and a metaphysical journey as well. It involves coming to terms with her limiting presuppositions about scientific discovery and the search for truth, and her incomplete sense of self, due to the early death of her parents. In this sense, Ellie's journey to Vega both attunes her to alternative (i.e., religious or spiritual) ways of knowing and allows her to resolve her relationship with her parents, particularly her father, so that she can truly be at home with herself and "at home" in the universe.

As such, *Contact* also provides a version of the father quest. Ellie's major relationship obstacle is her inability to become emotionally intimate with Joss Palmer. The film goes to great pains to set up the similarity between Joss Palmer and Ellie's father. For example, when Ellie as a child asks here father if we are alone in the universe, he replies, "if we are, it's an awful waste of space." Later, when an adult Ellie begins a relationship with Joss, she over-hears Joss use this identical phrase in response to a reporter's inquiry about his opinion regarding extraterrestrial life. As a result, when Ellie is unable to turn her one-night stand with Joss into something more permanent, we real-ize that her emotional intimacy problems with Joss stem from her fear of his leaving, just as her father "left" her by dying when she was ten years old. It is only when she can reconcile her relationship with her father that she can emo-tional mature, become individuated, and begin an adult relationship with Joss. We see this, for example, when Ellie meets the alien on Vega who appears in the form of her father:

Father/Alien:	You're an interesting species, an interesting mix. You're capable of such beautiful dreams and such horrible night-mares. You feel so lost, so cut off, so alone, only you're not. You see, in all of our searching the only thing we found that makes the emptiness bearable is each other.
Ellie:	What happens now?
Father/Alien:	Now? You go home.
Ellie:	Home? But I've so many questions. Do we get to come back?
Father/Alien:	This was just a first step. In time, you'll take another.

Although the scientist in her quickly realizes that the alien "downloaded" her memory to take a familiar form, and hence, is not really her father, the alien's message to her that "we are not alone" and that the most important thing we have is "each other" has double import for Ellie coming as it does from her "father." On a personal level, it means that her father has not left her, she is not alone—having the memory of her father inside of her—and thus, she need not fear being left by the men she loves. On a spiritual level, it means that we are cosmically connected with others and also with something much greater than ourselves. As a result, upon her return from Vega, and thanks to help from her father/the alien, Ellie is able to restart a relationship with Joss because she has worked through her fear of emotional intimacy.

Also as a result of this meeting, Ellie becomes a prophet/teacher of the people regarding this very important spiritual lesson when she shares her boon—her Vegan experience—with the culture at large. This sharing occurs in her presentation before the presidential commission charged with investigating her claims of alien contact on Vega. Although the commission ultimately dismisses her experiences, as she departs from the Senate chambers and walks down the steps of the U.S. capitol building, we witness a vast crowd of onlookers and well-wishers, representing the large number of believers that her testimony has created.

Later, in the film's final scene, Ellie mentors a class of children about the wonders of space and the possibilities of alien life. Pointing to the vast array of radio telescopes behind her, she explains, "See over there. We're building forty-five brand new dishes, and that means when you put them all together with all the different radio telescopes all over the world, then we get to hear farther into space than anyone's ever heard before." The following exchange then occurs:

Child: Are there other people out there in the universe?
Ellie: That's a good question. What do you think?
Child: I don't know.
Ellie: That's a good answer. Skeptic, huh? The most important thing is that you all keep searching for your own answers. I'll tell you one thing about the universe, though; the universe is a pretty big place. It's bigger that anyone has ever dreamed of before. So if it's just us, it seems like an awful waste of space.

This scene not only evidences Ellie's hero boon, her mentoring gift to the culture at large; it also points to the importance of the child archetype in the film. Not only does the film begin with a child—when we meet Ellie she is a young girl searching the heavens for radio signals from her dead mother—it also ends with a group of children being introduced to the wonders and mysteries of the universe. Thus, once again, the child represents openness to the nonrational as well as the possibility of a transcendent way of knowing in the world. Ellie's final comment also echoes her father's words to her as a young girl. As such, by completing her father quest to Vega, Ellie not only discovers her father-potential; she is also able to pass on this legacy of wonder and awe to other children, some of whom may become future visionaries of this message.

Boundary Spanning

Like *E.T.* and *Close Encounters*, various characters in *Contact* represent either the scientific/rational worldview or the spiritual/nonrational worldview. Ellie's friend Kent, however, spans both. Because Kent is blind and cannot see, he "sees" or rather senses what others cannot. Although he is Ellie's coworker at the radio telescope in Arecibo, Puerto Rico, and thus is a scientist in his own right, he intuits or senses what others cannot. Kent is the one who discovers the interlaced screens in the aliens' radio transmission that provide directions for building the space transporter to Vega. Kent is the scientist Ellie is happiest to see when she is about to be launched in the space transporter for the planet Vega. And finally, Kent is the one who hears Ellie's "good to go" signal in the midst of the static from her headset when no one else can hear her voice. Hearing the "good to go" signal allows mission control to continue launch procedures for the space transporter, sending Ellie to Vega.

Ellie Arroway herself, however, is the film's best example of a boundary spanner, caught, as she is, between two seemingly opposing ways of knowing, one represented by Joss Palmer, her sometimes boyfriend, and the other by Dr. David Drumlin (Tom Skerritt), her professor and mentor. Joss Palmer epitomizes the spiritual or nonrational way of knowing. We learn, for example, that he was a candidate for the priesthood and has a master's in divinity. Later in the film he becomes President Bill Clinton's primary spiritual adviser. At one point, when he is asked by reporters if he believes Ellie when she claims, despite a lack of evidence, that she actually went to Vega, he replies, "As a person of faith I am bound by a different covenant than Dr. Arroway, but our goal is one and the same: the pursuit of truth. I, for one, believe her." In contrast to Joss Palmer, Dr. Drumlin, Ellie's former professor, represents the scientific/rational way of knowing. Drumlin is a major figure in the scientific community and is the president's central scientific advisor. Ellie, caught between these two men, begins the film as a champion of the scientific/rational worldview. Over the course of the film, however, she becomes a boundary spanner who learns to appreciate rather than constantly analyze the awe and mystery of the universe. Such a journey of edification, as previously discussed, becomes her hero quest.

This transformation of Ellie's character is best demonstrated in three different scenes. In the first, she is interrogated by a special commission appointed by the president of the United States to determine the best candidate to send in the space transporter to Vega. Asked by Joss Palmer if she "considers herself a spiritual person," Ellie balks, replying, "I don't really understand the point of the question. I consider myself a moral person." When asked more pointedly by Joss if she believes in God, she offers, "As a scientist I rely on empirical evidence and in this matter I don't believe that there's data either way." By her testimony Ellie demonstrates her adherence to scientific/rational ways of knowing in the world. And, as a result, she "fails" this test and is not selected for the trip to Vega. The setback is only temporary, however, as she is later selected for a second mission to Vega, after the first transporter is blown-up by a religious fanatic.

In a second scene, in which Ellie is in the space transporter heading for Vega, we witness the moment at which she realizes the inadequacy of the scientific paradigm to account for or explain all experiences. During her rapid journey through space, she diligently tries to offer a running "objective" or scientific commentary of what she witnesses for the recording video camera. Finally at loss for words to describe the beauty of the Vegan solar system laid out in front of her, all she can say is "They should have sent a poet. It's so beautiful. So beautiful." Ellie, despite all of her scientific training, feels the need to call on the language of the poet when faced with the inexplicable beauty of the universe.

Finally, in a third scene, Ellie faces the presidential commission established to determine the truth regarding her claim that she visited the planet Vega. Ellie is forced to defend her report because the video-camera headset she had worn during the trip showed no recorded images of her journey, and videotaped records of the launch indicate that the space transporter was only out of contact for less than a second. A committee member asks her, "You come to us with no evidence, no record, no artifacts, only a story that, to put it mildly, strains credibility. Over half a trillion was spent; dozens of lives were lost. Are you really just going to sit there and tell us all we should take this all on faith?" Ellie responds, "It is possible that it didn't happen, yes, as a scientist I must concede that." Later, however, when pressed further by her interrogators, she fervently responds:

I had an experience. I can't prove it. I can't even explain it, but everything that I know as a human being, everything that I am tells me that it was real. I was given something wonderful. Something that changed me forever, a vision of the universe that tells us undeniably how tiny and insignificant and how rare and precious we all are. A vision that tells us we belong to something greater than ourselves. That we are not, that none of us, are alone. If I could share that—that everyone, if even for one moment, could feel that awe and that humility and that hope. That continues to be my wish.

In this scene we witness the transformation of Ellie's character as she reconciles the scientific/rational way of knowing with the spiritual/nonrational way of knowing. Ellie's evolution as a boundary spanner is complete. In addition, as a mythic hero, she has not only completed her journey outward and homeward; she has gone inward to recognize spiritual truths of a transcendent nature.

Mandala Symbols

Like both *Close Encounters of the Third Kind* and *E.T.*, *Contact* is replete with circular or mandala symbols. As mentioned at the outset, the space transporter in which she makes the journey to the planet Vega is a large sphere. At the moment of transport, it is suspended inside of a series of metal hoops that spin around it in rapidly revolving concentric circles. From a distance, the entire configuration looks like a rapidly revolving atom, itself a building block of all life. As a symbol of wholeness or unity, it is not surprising that the spacecraft is a mandala, since this intergalactic ship is designed from blueprints transmitted by some higher intelligence to allow humans to be united with other beings. This mandalic spacecraft also brings Ellie to Vega where she is united with spirit/god and realizes that "we are not alone," but rather are connected to something "greater than ourselves."

The radio telescope at Arecibo, Puerto Rico, through which Ellie continually listens for radio waves from outer space is also a large mandala. This circular or disk-like quality to radio telescopes is emphasized when we see a long shot of a dozen or more telescope dishes in the New Mexico desert, lined up in an identical direction, and "listening" for signs of intelligent life.

Perhaps the film's most significant mandala symbol is the "universe in an eye" motif which occurs both at the film's beginning and again at its end (thus structurally conveying a sense of circularity or completeness). As the film begins, the camera moves forward through what seems like endless layers of cosmic dust in outer space. The colors swirl and collide as we accelerate at the speed of light through galaxy after galaxy. The shot ends with an extreme close-up of ten-year-old Ellie Arroway's eye. This rapid journey through the vastness of the universe concludes in the minuteness of a child's eye. A similar sequence occurs at the end of the film, except that this time we move in reverse, from Ellie Arroway's adult eye out into the limitlessness of the time/space continuum.

This "universe in an eye" motif supports the notion that a journey into space is ultimately a journey into ourselves, or, more specifically, a journey to make sense of ourselves. We go outward into space in order to go inward into self. On another level, this motif highlights the idea that Ellie expresses to the presidential commission at the end of the film, when she says that on Vega she had "a vision of the universe that tells us undeniably how tiny and insignificant and how rare and precious we all are. A vision that tells us we belong to something greater than ourselves." The microcosm of the human being, in other words, contains the macrocosm of the universe and vice versa. The Romantic poet William Wordsworth, for example, expresses such sentiment when he writes, "To see the world in a grain of sand, heaven in a wild flower. To hold eternity in the palm of your hand, infinity in an hour." [32] According to Jung, it is also apparent in Hindu exegesis on the nature of the Atman, "which corresponds to the 'smaller than small yet bigger than big' motif. As an individual phenomenon, the self is 'smaller than small'; as the equivalent of the cosmos, it is 'bigger than big.' " [33] The parallel between the individual eye and the vastness of the universe is also echoed in the constant visual depiction of the planet Vega, itself a large mandala.

Finally, the "compass" motif that occurs throughout the film also operates as a mandala symbol as well as a central metaphor for the hero's journey home. This compass is a Cracker-Jack toy given to Ellie by Joss Palmer upon their first meeting. Ellie later returns it to him when she decides not to pursue their relationship. Much later in the film, when Ellie is chosen to represent humanity and pilot the space transporter to the planet Vega, Joss returns the compass to her, saying that he wants to make sure that she "finds her way home." Later, during her intergalactic travels to Vega, the compass saves her life and actually ensures that she does make it home. During the flight her seat vibrates so badly that the compass slips out of her pocket and begins to float away in the weightlessness of the space capsule. It is important that we remember that the seat into which Ellie is so uncomfortably and complicatedly strapped is an addition to the transporter not in the original blueprint sent by the Vegans. Just prior to launch, Ellie complains to the launch director about this inelegant addition, but is told that it is a necessary precaution to ensure her safety. Instinctively, as the compass floats away, Ellie unbuckles herself from her technological nightmare and floats free in pursuit. Just as we witness a close-up of her grabbing the compass, we hear the seat break loose from its moorings. The shot changes to a medium shot of the chair as it slams into the sidewall of the capsule. We are immediately aware that the impact of the collision would have killed Ellie. Following her intuition, or following her heart (since the compass is a gift from Joss, the man of her heart), and breaking free of the constraints of cumbersome technology in order to seize her destiny ensures that she will complete her journey and go home—both to the planet Vega, a universal or transcendent home where she will meet her father, and back to planet Earth, an everyday home where she will be reunited with Joss, her lover, and will share her hero's boon with the culture at large, the message of universal love and the unity of all being.

2001: A Space Odyssey

If an informal poll was taken to determine the most significant science-fiction film in the history of Hollywood cinema, nine of the ten film critics would most likely select *2001: A Space Odyssey*. Such an accolade would certainly be well deserved. And indeed, in the AFI poll of the one hundred most significant films in the history of American cinema, *2001*, is ranked twenty-second, the highest of any science-fiction film on the list. Although *2001*, like all good sci-fi films, speculates about humanity's future, it has just as much to say about humanity's past. As such, the film offers up an interesting version of a creation myth. As previously discussed, creation myths not only explain the origin of the universe or the planet, where the human race came from, and the role of the creator(s) in the lives of his creations; they also deal with the first crime of killing in order to live, what Campbell calls the "brutal precondition of all life, which lives by the killing and eating of lives." [34] This becomes strikingly apparent in *2001*, a film that is as much about the future of humanity and space exploration as it is about the past, our primal origins, and the first acts of killing that makes life possible. Arthur C. Clarke, who wrote the book upon which *2001* is based and who collaborated with director Stanley Kubrick on the screenplay, asserts the film's mythic/religious status: "We set out with the deliberate intention of creating a myth. M-G-M doesn't know it yet, but they've footed the bill for the first $10,500,000.00 religious film." [35]

If we view the film in terms of a classical three-act structure (as, indeed, the film invites us to do through its use of graphics), the first act is about the origin of human life, the development of technology, and our separation from god/spirit and each other—the age, in other words, of preconsciousness. The second act is about the perfection of that technology until it becomes our god or possibly our demon—the age, in other words, of consciousness. Finally, the third act is about the evolution of the species and our technology beyond consciousness in the hopes that we can once again be reunited with god/spirit and each other—the age of transconsciousness. Kubrick himself hints at this evolution when, discussing the theme of *2001*, he notes:

Man must strive to gain some mastery over himself as well as over his machines. Somebody had said that man is the missing link between primitive apes and civilized human beings. You might say that idea is inherent in *2001*. We are semi-civilized, capable of cooperation and affection, but needing some sort of transfiguration into a higher form of life.[36]

This journey toward a higher stage of consciousness, essentially the hero quest writ large, makes Kubrick's *2001*, contrary to many critics' assessments,[37] profoundly optimistic about the future. For example, Kolker argued that "in his films Kubrick's characters have yielded to or become functions of their environment, or do emotional and physical battle with it and are subdued. We, as spectators, are invited to observe the losing and perhaps consider its ramifications, but little more." [38] In *2001*, as I will argue, this is certainly not the case.

As in this image from *2001: A Space Odyssey*, Kubrick's photographic eye self-consciously constructs multiple mise-en-scenes as graphically complex renderings of various mandalas. This is apparent in the circular rings of the doorway, the circles inside of squares on the wall, and the spherically shaped flight attendant's hat. As symbols of the unconscious, mandalas represent transcendence, unity or centeredness of being. Significant mandalas appearing in the natural world and humanity's experience of that world include the sun and moon, the planets and the solar system, the mother's womb, the birth canal, the circularity of the passage of time, the seasons, and the ages of consciousness. Mandalas are frequently represented in significant religious rituals, such as the communion host in Catholic worship, the ritual hogan of the Native Americans, and the sand paintings of Tibetan Buddhism. The camera's almost annoyingly slow movement and Kubrick's inclination toward minimal editing invites the viewer to dwell at length on these mandalas. Thus, although there are no specific boundary spanning characters, in the film, it is as if the camera, as a surrogate character, represents an attempt to reconcile rational/technological ways of knowing with nonrational/spiritual ways of knowing. Courtesy of the Museum of Modern Art—Film Stills Archives.

In what follows I briefly discuss Kubrick's use of mandala symbols in *2001* while devoting the remainder of the chapter to an analysis of the film's three-act structure—which mirrors the cosmogonic cycle—particularly noting the use of the child archetype and the film's reconciliation of science/technology with humanity/spirit.

Mandalas

Kubrick's photographic eye self-consciously constructs graphically complex renderings of various mandalas in *2001*. The camera's almost annoyingly slow movement and Kubrick's inclination toward minimal editing invites the viewer to dwell at length on these mandalas.[39] In reference to Kubrick's attention to cinematography, Kolker notes that "his composition in depth is almost as extreme as his use of the moving camera. Kubrick used the camera to traverse space, to control it and to understand it. He used the camera as a surrogate or parallel for the point of view of a character." [40] Thus, although there are no specific boundary-spanning characters in the film, it is as if the camera, as a surrogate character, represents an attempt to reconcile rational/technological ways of knowing with nonrational/spiritual ways of knowing. We see this, for example, in the film's opening shot of three glowing spheres—the sun, the

Kubrick echoes the naturally mandalic shape of the earth the sun and the moon in his depictions of technology in *2001*. This image of celestial mandalas includes two spacecrafts (the Orion spacecraft and the Space Station V), and the planet Earth, floating and spinning gracefully through the blackness of space. It is as if all these orbs, both natural and human made, are in perfect harmony. The music of a Strauss waltz adds to the impression that they are dancing with each other (the "celestial music of the spheres"). The slow and "graceful" movement of the camera, together with the synchronous editing of the shots with the downbeat of the waltz, adds to the feeling of harmony. God is truly in his heaven and all is right with the world. Technology appears to coexist in peaceful harmony with the natural world that surrounds it. The film's classical score adds to this feeling of rhythm and balance. Courtesy of the Museum of Modern Art—Film Stills Archives.

earth, and the moon—all in perfect alignment. As if to emphasize this harmonious moment, as the earth appears to arch into the sky, the three ascending tones of Richard Strauss's *Thus Spoke Zarathustra* begin. This musical reference to Nietzsche's work of the same name reminds the educated viewer that Nietzsche's work, like *2001*, is also about the evolutionary progress of humanity from ape, to human, to superhuman.[41]

Later in the film this shot of celestial mandalas will include a mandala-like spacecraft, also floating and spinning gracefully through the blackness of space. It is as if all these orbs, both natural and human made, are in perfect harmony. The music of a Strauss waltz adds to the impression that they are dancing with each other (the "celestial music of the spheres"). The slow and "graceful" movement of the camera, together with the synchronous editing of the shots with the downbeat of the waltz, adds to the feeling of harmony. God is truly in his heaven and all is right with the world.

Technological mandalas will continue to appear with great regularity throughout the film. As Heywood Floyd (William Sylvester), in the second act, talks on the video phone to his daughter back on Earth, a giant glowing circle of light revolves on the wall behind him. When David Bowman (Keir Dullea), in the third act, exercises inside of the spacecraft headed for Jupiter, he runs around in a vast and spinning circle with no "up" or "down." Indeed, the film often distorts the viewer's sense of what is up and down in the weightlessness of space by having characters walk into and out of circular doors that at one point appear to open onto the floor, and at another point appear to open into the ceiling. The mandala-like shape of HAL's red glowing eye is echoed in constant shots of an incandescent Jupiter seen through the circular porthole

of the spacecraft. Despite HAL's evil intentions, technology appears to coexist in peaceful harmony with the natural world that surrounds it. The film's
classical score adds to this feeling of rhythm and balance.

In the scene of David Bowman's final descent to Jupiter, we also witness the "universe in an eye motif" discussed earlier in relation to the film
Contact. The human eye, of course, is a significant example of a mandala. As
Bowman's ship descends toward Jupiter, a long tracking shot of colliding and
spinning psychedelic colors merges with the vast beauty and infinity of space
and ultimately resolves itself in a close-up of David Bowman's eye. The individual is submerged in the universal, the ego dissolves into the unconscious,
and all things are connected in the harmonious unity of time, space, and being.

The Journey Home: Preconsciousness

In *2001*'s "first act" we witness the development of technology as apes become human with the discovery of the first tool. More than illustrating the
development of technology, this opening scene is about the development of
the first weapon, since the bone allows the ape to murder members of a rival
gang. This first act of killing is also significant, however, because as creation
myth, it symbolizes death ensuring the continuance of life. Not only do we
witness the apes using their new weapon on each other; we also see them use
it to bring down game in order to feed the entire group. Thus, the first act
of killing binds us to each other for survival at the moment it paradoxically
separates us as well.[42] By the same token, technology allows the dominance
of one group, race, country, or species over another while also reminding us
of our interconnectedness. For example, for many, the most important lesson
to emerge from the cold war, as the United States and the Soviet Union jock-
eyed for the position of top technological dog, is just how fragile life is and
how profoundly connected to and dependent on each other we remain.

The first act from *2001* is also a version of the Cain and Abel myth, itself
a story not too far removed in biblical time from the Garden of Eden. Early
on in the scene, the two groups of apes coexist with each other. Neither group
seems to be afraid of the other. Although there is occasionally pushing and
shoving for natural resources, there is no sense of dominance or the control
of one group over the other. The bone, as the first weapon, destroys this harmony, and by its use, the first act of sin, the murder of one brother by the other

(Cain slays Abel) ushers in discord. Humanity becomes "marked" by this sin and is cast into a state of separation from god/spirit. Awareness of god/spirit is epitomized in this opening act by the appearance of the black monolith. Thus, this first act of *2001* can be read as a story about beginnings, and the emergence of consciousness from preconsciousness.

At the end of this first act, as a transition device to the "second act," Kubrick visually links the ape's tool of destruction/dominance with such later technological developments as the pen and the spacecraft, also technological marvels that have potentially destructive/dominance capabilities as well.

The Journey Home: Consciousness

The film's "second act" is about humanity's perfection of this technology in our exploration of space and our search for god/meaning, represented by the monolith. Here, technological wonders such as the "space phone" and interplanetary commercial space flight are represented as mundane and ordinary. Technology has become so integrated into every aspect of humanity's experience that it is hardly even noticed or commented upon.

The very technology that is humanity's salvation, however, also represents its damnation, epitomized, for example, by the HAL 5000 supercomputer that runs the spaceship carrying David Bowman, Frank Poole, and the other scientists to Jupiter. During this journey, Kubrick constructs the familiar scenario of technology controlling human beings, thus reminding us of the dangers of technological hubris. HAL's disembodied voice, for example, is everywhere and yet nowhere at the same time. He is a technological Big Brother whose "red eye" monitors the crew's every move. Nowhere is there a place on the ship where Bowman and Poole can escape his surveillance. HAL so dominates all aspects of the mission that his human being "colleagues" have become superfluous or redundant. They are seemingly powerless under his control. HAL's emotionless termination of the "life functions" of the scientists placed under his care, now in suspended animation for the duration of the flight, not only epitomizes this lack of power; it also gives a new meaning to the phrase "cold-blooded" murder. The murder of the apes by the rival gang in the first act was at least a hot-blooded crime.

Yet even this passionless technological monster is able to exhibit what passes for human emotions. We hear his "breathing" echo throughout the ship.

We watch his "eye" follow every move Poole and Bowman make. At times he appears proud of his technological accomplishments, or hurt by the distrust of his human colleagues, or angry at their deception. As William notes, in many ways HAL is more human than his human crew, who have lapsed into a technologically induced stupor, and who act in a mundane, mechanized, and emotionless fashion.[43]

As a result, one of the most disturbing scenes in the film occurs when Bowman finally manages to disconnect HAL's memory bank. As Bowman methodically pulls out each of the cartridges that keep HAL running, HAL pleads for his "life." Unable to stop Bowman, and possibly resigned to his fate, HAL breaks out in a mournful rendition of "Daisy, Daisy" — the first song his creator programmed him to sing. HAL goes back to his own creation myth. As his memory disintegrates his voice deepens, slows, and becomes fainter. We are witnessing a murder. Granted, it is a murder of self-defense, as in the first act of the film, but it is a murder nevertheless. Man kills his technological brother. Cain slays Abel all over again. A story about origins is a story about murder, sin, hierarchy, and separation. Just as Adam and Eve are cast out of the Garden by eating from the tree of knowledge, which brings them awareness of difference, and hence guilt and sin, in Kubrick's creation myth it is technological know-how that provides the means of such separation. Or, in another interpretation, it is our inability to effectively integrate technology into our lives that results in our separation from god/spirit and each other. The "Frankenstein" myth, after all, is not so much about technology run amuck or humanity's attempts to play god as it is about humanity's refusal to acknowledge parentage of our technological creations. Victor Frankenstein's fatal flaw is his failure to love his creature.[44] Thus, the lesson learned from Mary Shelley's *Frankenstein*, and from *2001*, is that we must neither run from our technology nor let it consume us; rather, we must learn how to integrate it into our lives, realizing that it offers both shadow and salvation. Not surprisingly, therefore, it is technology that allows for the potential unification of human beings, not only with each other but also with the infinite. Technology, in *2001*, is a double-edged sword. Although, on the one hand, it results in the dominance of one group over another, and thus serves as a source of discord and distrust (again, think of U.S.-Soviet relations during the cold war, the subject of Kubrick's *Dr. Strangelove*), it also offers the possibility of transcendence, the evolution of consciousness to a more enlightened state of being. This idea becomes apparent in the film's final act, entitled "Jupiter and Beyond the Infinite."

The Journey Home: Transconsciousness

The "third act" of *2001*, the landing on Jupiter, is, of course, the scene that invites critics to do interpretive back flips. In one interpretation, Bowman's search for the monolith (i.e., humanity's search for meaning/god) reveals nothing more than himself, since the man he encounters on Jupiter is an incarnation of himself (i.e., we have created god in our own image, or have, through technology, become our own gods—one possible reading of Shelley's *Frankenstein*). In another interpretation, humanity is god, not in a ego-maniacal sense, but rather in the sense that god/spirit is manifest in all of us and in all things—technology included—and thus our transcendent hero's journey, like Bowman's, is to realize this god-potential, possibly symbolized by the film's final image of a child in the womb.

This image of a child in a womb also provides a culmination of both the mandala symbol and the child archetype. Profoundly optimistic, the child archetype points not only to the past and preconsciousness (the "origin of the species" presented in the film's first act); it also references the possibility of a transcendent future that merges the scientific/rational mind of the current technological age with the spiritual/nonrational mind of the postconscious age. In addition, the mandala, as Jung reminds us, expresses "the idea of a safe refuge, of inner reconciliation and wholeness." [45] As such, the film's final image implies that despite technology's potential to divide and destroy, it may ultimately provide the best tools for healing ourselves and for unifying us with each other and with god/spirit. Thus, Bowman's arrival on Jupiter, and his possible meeting with the creator of the Obelisk, in one interpretation signifies his unification with the universe, his transformation into a "child of the universe," and thus his "return" to a transcendent home.

Conclusion

As discussed at the outset, the sci-fi genre, perhaps best of all film genres, wonders at the infinity of space and time that is the universe and the divine spark of life that created humanity—both of which science and technology reveal—while warning that science and technology could paradoxically obscure those same spiritual truths. Four films that explore this relationship in important ways include *E.T.: The Extra-Terrestrial*, *2001: A Space Odyssey*, *Close Encounters of the Third Kind*, and *Contact*. All of these films attempt to reconcile logical/rational ways of knowing with spiritual/nonrational ways of knowing rather than favor one over the other. Usually the relationship is resolved by offering a third or transcendent way of knowing that combines the best impulses of both. Specifically, one or more characters in each film is a "boundary spanner," someone with their feet planted in both perspectives who refuses to automatically value one over the other.

All four films also evidence a fascination with what Jung refers to as the child archetype. In all four films a specific child, or children in general, symbolizes not only innocence but also receptivity to creative potential, the nonrational possibilities of alien life, and the transcendent. Mandalas, like the child archetype, also represent wholeness, unity, or centeredness of being. Possibly due to Kubrick's photographic eye, *2001*, perhaps best of all the films discussed in this chapter, evidences numerous mandalas. Mandalas, however, as we have seen, are also a recurring motif in Spielberg's *E.T.* and *Close Encounters of the Third Kind*. In all four films discussed in this chapter, mandalas are an important visual motif that often invites metaphysical interpretations.

These films not only take up the question of the relationship between science and technology and humanity and spirit; they also take the form of the quest myth for home. This is not surprising since films about space exploration, alien life forms, and the origin of the universe are implicitly about humanity's quest to find our place in the time/space continuum—to feel "at home" in the universe. Thus, all of the protagonists in the four films discussed in this chapter are on Odyssean quests.

Perhaps the epitome of the Odyssean quest for home, however, is George Lucas' Star Wars trilogy. This trilogy is considered the most successful series in the history of Hollywood cinema, and has spawned a prequel trilogy expected to generate as extensive a following. These films' appeal is not surprising, since they not only tell the story of the hero's journey home, but also speak to our universal desire for healing and transcendence in an era of soul-sickness and fragmentation. Accordingly, the next chapter explores the Star Wars trilogy in light of Perennial philosophy, Jungian psychology, and the Odyssean quest for home.

III Synthesis

Part III of the book provides a synthesis of the analytical model developed throughout. Specifically, Chapter 8 examines the universal quest for home in one of the top-grossing quest trilogies of all times, George Lucas' Star Wars films.[1] This analysis not only explores various permutations of the quest myth—specifically the father quest and the Grail quest—it also explores the films' production background in order to provide a context for the analysis. In addition, the chapter grounds the films in their particular sociohistorical moment, viewing them in light of such cultural myths as the western cowboy hero, Arthurian legend, and the contemporary quest to reconcile technology/science with humanity/spirit. By way of conclusion the chapter problematizes the trilogy in light of gender, race, and ideology. As such, Chapter 8 attempts an almost exhaustive synthesis of the analytical model developed sequentially throughout the book.

The final chapter of Part III examines the value of myth and mythic criticism by placing them in the debate over the progressive/regressive role of myth in discourse. As previously mentioned, mythic criticism is frequently criticized for being apolitical in nature. The charges often leveled are that by assuming universal qualities to human experience, mythic criticism risks erasing awareness of difference (i.e., class, race, and gender); by focusing on spiritual transcendence, mythic criticism potentially ignores the impact of material conditions (i.e., wealth and poverty); and by exploring visions of unity, mythic criticism may ignore the existence of power and dominance structures that divide (i.e., political, economic, and religious systems). Accordingly, Chapter 9 addresses these concerns while also confronting ways in which some of the films discussed in the book construct the hero quest in a fashion that reinforces traditional class, gender, and ethnic stereotypes.

As Rushing and Frentz explain, "Narratives may implicitly advocate any number of courses of moral action in relation to the end point of cultural individuation. Those that imply a movement toward individuation would be judged as morally superior to those that imply a movement away from it." [2] Thus with an eye toward "cultural individuation," the chapter concludes with a discussion of the types of myths necessary as we move into the new millennium.

8 The Star Wars Trilogy

The Star Wars trilogy, perhaps more than any films in the history of Hollywood cinema, are the quintessential hero quest films. While offering the most clearly articulated version of the Odyssean hero's journey outward, inward, and homeward, they also draw on such cultural myths as the western cowboy hero and Arthurian legend, and such universal myths as the father quest, the Grail quest, and the quest to reconcile technology/science with humanity/spirit. Most significantly, these films manifest the clearest articulation of Perennial philosophy, Jungian psychology, and Zen Buddhism.

Since George Lucas, the trilogy's creator, writer, and producer, and the director of *Star Wars: A New Hope*, claims to have drawn on myth and fairy tale in his crafting of the films, it is helpful to look at the Star Wars trilogy's production background before turning to an analysis of the films.

Production and Distribution Background

Finished in May 1974, the first draft of the screenplay for the first film in the trilogy, *Star Wars: A New Hope*, took a year to complete. The second draft, done by January 1975, was titled *Adventures of the Starkiller, Episode One of the Star Wars*. George Lucas had enough material in the screenplay for three movies, however, so he cut it in half in order to save the rest for the two sequels that were to follow.[1]

All of the main parts for *Star Wars* were cast from cattle calls (mass auditions common to the film industry). Even the three main characters, Luke Skywalker, Han Solo, and Princess Leia, were played by relative unknowns.[2] Mark Hamill (Luke Skywalker) and Carrie Fisher (Princess Leia), like Harrison Ford (Han Solo), although not without some film and television experience, were both relatively unknown in the movie industry. Better known, of course, were Alec Guinness as Obi-Wan Kenobi and James Earl Jones, who provided the voice of Darth Vader.

Produced by Twentieth Century Fox under the supervision of Gary Kurtz, *Star Wars* began production on March 25, 1976, in Tunisia. Production ran seventy days, from March to July 1976, with the majority of the film shot at Elstree Studios in Britain. The film was released in the summer of 1977. Although George Lucas was paid $150,000 to write and direct *Star Wars*, Star Wars Corporation, Lucas' company, contracted for 40 percent of the net profits. The film's initial budget of $3.5 million increased to $10 million, with the special effects alone costing $3 million.

Star Wars revolutionized the look of contemporary movies with its special effects and with Lucas' insistence that the sound and music (John Williams' score) be recorded in Dolby stereo, which, at the time, was considered an innovation. The film needed to sell $32 million in tickets before Fox would break even—tougher than it sounds since the film only opened in thirty-two theaters across the country. *Star Wars* was apparently not an easy sell to theater owners, who, at the time, were generally leery of sci-fi films. As Pollock explains, "The film industry's confidence in a movie is gauged by the amount of money exhibitors will guarantee for the right to play it. *Star Wars* secured only 1.5 million in guarantees, rather that the ten million expected of big movies." [3] Despite this, at its opening, the film was "making more money per theater than any film in history." [4] Within weeks of its release, *Star Wars*

had become a national phenomenon. There were nightly reports on the network news programs, and newspapers and magazines were filled with stories. *Star Wars* was part of the cultural vocabulary. . . . By the end of August, *Star Wars* had grossed $100 million, faster than any film in Hollywood's eighty-year history. . . . Fox research showed that *Star Wars* had the largest word-of-mouth recommendations ever recorded . . . more than one in twenty filmgoers in 1977 saw *Star Wars* more than once. . . . *Star Wars* was [also] a smash hit in France . . . and was an enormous success throughout the rest of Europe, especially Germany and Italy.[5]

The film was nominated for ten Academy Awards (including best director, best screenplay, and best picture). George Lucas' wife, Martha Lucas, was also nominated for best editing along with Richard Chew and Paul Hirsch. The film ended up winning five Oscars, including editing, art direction (John Barry), costume design (John Mollo), musical score (John Williams), and special effects (John Dykstra, Richard Edlund, Grant McCune, John Sears, and Robert Blalack). A special award was given to Ben Burtt for sound effects.

Fox reissued *Star Wars* in the summer of 1978 (even though it had already been playing in theaters for more than a year) to make an additional $46 million in only five weeks. A three-week reissue in 1979 made $23 million more. As of 1990, *Star Wars* had earned more than $524 million worldwide, not including figures from its most recent 1997 release. ·

Within three months of its release, Alan Dean Foster's ghostwritten novelization of the film was the number one paperback best-seller. John Williams' musical score from the film "became the largest selling film score from a non-musical in Hollywood history," making Fox an additional $16 million. To this day, the tremendous demand for Star Wars memorabilia remains unabated, and the May 1999 release of the first film in the prequel trilogy, *The Phantom Menace,* continues the demand for Star Wars memorabilia.

George Lucas was able to arrange an even better financial deal for his company, Lucasfilms, when it came time to negotiate the rights for *The Empire Strikes Back*, the second film of the Star Wars trilogy. Lucasfilms eventually took 77 percent of the film's gross while Fox paid all distribution costs, only retaining the rights to release the film in theaters for seven years. Since they also only retained first right of refusal on any sequels to *Star Wars*, Fox was forced to take these terms, realizing that if they refused, due to *Star Wars'* phenomenal success, Lucas would take the film elsewhere on the same terms. Lucas also retained the television and merchandizing rights (although Fox later negotiated 10 percent of merchandizing profits from all three Star Wars films when Lucas needed loan guarantees from Fox for an additional $3 million when *Empire* went over budget).

The first draft of *Empire* was written by Lucas over the spring and summer of 1978. Lucas later turned the screenplay over to Lawrence Kasdan who, at the time, had just completed a first draft of *Raiders of the Lost Ark* for Spielberg and Lucas. Irvin Kershner, a veteran Hollywood filmmaker in his late forties, was chosen by Lucas to direct. The film was shot on a Norwegian glacier, at Elstree Studios in England, and at Lucas' ILM (Industrial Light and Magic) in Marin County, California. John Williams was again chosen to write and direct the musical score. All of the main cast members returned. Mark Hamill and Carrie Fisher had, in fact, signed on for all three films from the start, whereas Lucas was able to renegotiate Harrison Ford's contract for about the same pay scale as the first film. It apparently was also not difficult, based on *Star Wars'* success, to convince Alec Guinness and James Earl Jones to continue as Obi-Wan Kenobi and Darth Vader, respectively.

Empire had a four-month, $18.5-million budget with which to shoot 64 sets and 250 scenes (the budget would later balloon to $33 million, almost costing Lucas his entire production). Filming began on March 5, 1979, in the town of Finse, Norway. It was here that Kershner shot all of the scenes representing the ice planet Hoth.

Kershner, a former musician, looked upon *Empire* as the middle movement in a symphony. As he explained, "It has to be slower and more lyrical. The themes have to be more interior, and you don't have a grand climax. That became the challenge." [6] As a vegetarian and a follower of Zen Buddhism, Kershner was also very focused on the philosophical underpinnings of *Empire*. Like Lucas in his preparation for writing *Star Wars*, Kershner, in his preparation for directing *Empire*, studied fairy tales and myths. He reports viewing the film as a vehicle for touching the fantasy life of children. "I wanted them to see the expression of a lot of their anxieties, fears, and nightmares and offer a way to deal with them." [7] Although every scene was carefully storyboarded, Kershner would often have inspirations on the set that caused him to make last minute changes and improvise—changes, no doubt, that added to the film's eventual $33 million budget.

Lucas maintained control over the film's special effects and worked primarily at ILM during the production, although he frequently visited the production set to apply pressure on Kershner to stay on budget. Working in ILM, however, allowed Lucas considerable influence on the film's final visual form since *Empire* has more than 600 special effects shots—twice as many as *Star Wars*. Lucas, along with Paul Hirsch, was also involved in the editing of *Empire*, although Lucas would eventually give all editing credits to Hirsch.

Empire eventually ran $14.5 million over budget, costing Lucas $33 million to complete. At the time, this represented the biggest expenditure ever made by an independent filmmaker. *Empire*, however, unlike *Star Wars*, eventually brought Fox $26 million in theater guarantees. With a May 21, 1980, release date, *Star Wars* fans began lining up three days prior to the film's premiere at the Egyptian Theater in Hollywood, which was planning to show the film for a continuous 24-hour period. In its initial release, *Empire* ended up selling more than $300 million in tickets worldwide, and, in 1990, was the third most successful film in Hollywood history, only trailing behind *Star Wars* and *E.T.* (this record has since been broken).

The first draft of *Return of the Jedi*, originally titled "The Revenge of the Jedi," was written by Lucas in four weeks—a far shorter time span than the two years that *Star Wars* had taken. Lucas hired Richard Marquand to direct, giving him 92 days to shoot the film. All principle actors signed on to complete their roles in the trilogy. Production locations again included Elstree Studios and ILM as well as locations in Arizona and California. Kasdan again worked with Lucas on the script, while John Williams again conducted the London Symphony Orchestra for the musical score. Production began in January 1982 and the film was released in the summer of 1983.

Lucas looked everywhere for ideas for the Star Wars trilogy, which is at the same time derivative and original. The major influence on *Star Wars* is *THX 1138*, Lucas' first big-budget independent film. "Lucas also borrowed liberally from the Flash Gordon serials he had watched as a child, transplanting video screens, medieval costumes, art deco sets and blaster guns to *Star Wars.*" [8] "Lucas' concept of the force was heavily influenced by Carlos Castaneda's *Tales of Power*, an account of a Mexican Indian sorcerer, Don Juan, who uses the phrase 'life force.' " [9]

More important, however, Lucas researched mythology, fairy tales, and social psychology for his story. Explains Lucas, "I had also done a study on . . . the fairy tale or myth. It is a children's story in history and you go back to the *Odyssey* or the stories that are told for the kid in all of us." [10] He also further remarked that "You just don't get them any more, and that's the best stuff in the world—adventures in far-off lands. . . . I wanted to do a modern fairy tale, a myth." [11] "Lucas, a dedicated student of mythology attempted to get fairytales, myths, and religion down to a distilled state, [by] studying the pure form to see how and why it worked." [12] He supports the need to do so by his association that "There is a whole generation growing up without any fairytales. . . . And kids need fairytales—it's an important thing for society to have for kids." [13]

Cultural Mythology in Star Wars

As has been noted by other critics, the Star Wars trilogy draws heavily upon a number of cultural myths, such as the American western, England's King Arthur and the era of knightly chivalry, and Japanese Shogun warriors.[14]

The costuming and decor of Luke's family farm, seen in *Star Wars: A New Hope*, provide a curious combination of the old and the new. Luke's white belted jacket is reminiscent of the garb worn by a Shogun warrior or a karate master. Obi-Wan Kenobi's rough-spun, floor-length hooded gown, however, clearly echoes medieval dress, or more specifically, the robe of a druid priest. Such costuming choices, therefore, remind the viewer of Arthurian legend, evoking Luke as a young Arthur, and Obi-Wan as Merlin, his shaman/tutor. The family farm is also very rough hewn and medieval in form, constructed of hand-hewn stone walls, arched doorways, and dirt floors. At the same time, however, the farm, complete with numerous "droids," "speeders," and high-tech farm machinery, is also very modern or postmodern, placing the film squarely in the sci-fi genre.

The story of Luke Skywalker's coming of age parallels King Arthur's childhood and emergence into adulthood. We learn, in the first film, that Luke, like Arthur Pendragon, is being raised in relative obscurity by his aunt and uncle and does not know his parents or their fate. Luke naturally possesses a compelling desire, like young Arthur, to learn his parentage. When Luke finds Obi-Wan Kenobi, it is as if Arthur has found his Merlin. Obi-Wan not only tells Luke of his "noble" Jedi parentage; he also gives Luke his father's light saber, instructs him in its use, and introduces him to the idea of the Force. This, of course, is very similar to the role that Merlin plays for a young King Arthur, revealing Arthur's royal parentage, preparing Arthur for the role of king, and arranging for Arthur to win Excalibur, the famous sword with which he rules England.

The medieval or Arthurian frame of reference for the fantastical world of this trilogy is also evoked in the first episode when the Rebels fight to protect, Princess Leia, who is saved by Luke. Luke, a young "knight," uses his light saber, a weapon of the age of chivalry, to rescue her from her prison cell. The order of the Jedi knights is also reminiscent of King Arthur's Knights of the Round Table.

The Star Wars trilogy draws heavily on Western mythology as well. Han Solo, as his name implies, is the classic loner western hero. A solitary figure, he shares his confidences only with his sidekick Chewbacca (acting as Tonto to Han's Lone Ranger). Han only looks out for "number one," and thus is not the cause-joining type. Throughout the majority of the first episode, for example, his involvement in Princess Leia's rescues stems only from his hope of a big reward. He is a "gun for hire" and a bounty hunter who only enters the drama when he is paid a hefty price by Luke and Obi-Wan to transport them to the planet Alderon. That Obi-Wan and Luke meet Han in a seedy outlaw bar, reminiscent of the saloons of the Old West, only reinforces the cowboy myth. Later in the first film, the tension in Han's love-hate relationship with Princess Leia provides much of the film's comic relief while also reinforcing the loner cowboy motif. Han Solo is a solemn character who may get involved with women for fleeting sexual gratification, but never for love or a committed

relationship.[15] Thus, both Luke and Han represent versions of the hero who must, over the course of the trilogy, grow up. Although coming of age for Luke will require a much more complicated and philosophically profound type of transformation, Han has some important lessons of his own to learn—most notably, how to care not only for something larger than himself, like a commitment to the Rebel cause, but also more deeply for others, specifically Luke, who becomes like a brother, and Leia, who becomes his heart's desire.

The Hero Quest

Luke Skywalker comes of age on the distant outpost planet of Tatooine, a place where nothing exciting ever happens. Like Dorothy in *The Wizard of Oz* and George Bailey in *It's a Wonderful Life*, Luke longs for "greener pastures" and adventures unavailable to him at home. We learn, for example, in *Star Wars*, that he wants nothing more than to leave the family farm in order to attend the "academy." His uncle refuses to let him go, however, claiming that he needs Luke's help for the harvest. Luke is devastated.

Campbell, referring to the hero's "call to adventure," notes that the hero

Luke Skywalker (Mark Hamill) in shock, after returning home from a visit to "Old Ben Kenobi" to find that his aunt and uncle have been murdered and his family farm has been burned to the ground. Although we learn, prior to this moment, that Luke longs for greener pastures and to exchange his ordinary world for the extraordinary, like many quest heroes before him, he at first refuses the "call to adventure." Even after Luke witnesses, along with Obi-Wan, the hologram plea for help from Princess Leia stashed in R2D2's memory bank, even after Obi-Wan gives him his father's light saber, Luke still refuses to leave Tatooine in order to help the Rebels in their fight against the Empire. It is only at this moment, when he realizes that the Empire's Storm Troopers have murdered his aunt and uncle and that his home is no more, that he accepts the call to adventure to fight against the Empire. Courtesy of the Museum of Modern Art—Film Stills Archives.

is either "lured, carried away, or else voluntarily proceeds, to the threshold of adventure." [16] Luke, like many quest heroes before him, despite his desire to exchange his ordinary everyday world for the extraordinary, at first refuses the "call to adventure." Luke, for example, only encounters Obi-Wan Kenobi by accident when he is forced to leave the farm in search of R2D2, the runaway droid that had left in search of Obi-Wan. Even after Obi-Wan rescues Luke and C3PO from the Sand people and brings them back to his house; even after Luke witnesses, along with Obi-Wan, the hologram plea for help from Princess Leia stashed in R2D2's memory bank and even after Obi-Wan gives him his father's light saber, Luke still refuses to leave Tatooine in order to help the Rebels in their fight against the Empire. Luke's reluctance to accept the "call to adventure" is evident, for example, in the following exchange:

Ben: You must learn the ways of the Force if you're to come with me to Alderon.

Luke: Alderon? I'm not going to Alderon. I'm gonna go home. It's late and I'm in for it as it is.

Ben: I need your help, Luke. She [Princess Leia] needs your help. I'm getting too old for this sort of thing.

Luke: I can't get involved. I've got work to do. It's not that I like the Empire. I hate it. But there's nothing I can do about it right now. It's such a long way from here.

It is only when Luke returns home to find his family farm a heap of smoldering ashes and his aunt and uncle murdered by the Empire's Storm Troopers that he accepts the call to adventure to fight against the Empire.

Luke's "initiation into a source of power," the second phase in the hero quest, involves learning to control the Force and to use it for humanity's good. Luke's initiation actually occurs at numerous points throughout the trilogy, most notably in the first and second films when he trains with two different Jedi masters, Obi-Wan Kenobi and Yoda.

Luke's first introduction to the Force and the order of the Jedi knights occurs in his first meeting with Obi-Wan Kenobi. Kenobi gives Luke his father's light saber, saying, "Your father wanted you to have this when you were old enough, but your uncle wouldn't allow it. He feared you might follow old Obi-Wan on some damn fool idealistic crusade like your father did." Later in the conversation Obi-Wan explains the order of the Jedi knights and introduces Luke to the Force, explaining, "the Force is what gives the Jedi his power. It's an energy field created by all living things, it surrounds us, it penetrates us, it binds the galaxy together." The Force is a powerful "source of power" that will allow Luke, once he learns to use it, not only to destroy the Empire's Death Star in *Star Wars*, but also to ensure the future of humanity in *The Return of the Jedi*.

Obi-Wan continues Luke's training as a Jedi in their journey to Alderon on Han Solo's spaceship. As Luke practices using his light saber against a "remote" electronic opponent, Obi-Wan reminds him, "Remember, a Jedi can feel the Force flowing through him."

Luke:	You mean it controls your actions?
Obi-Wan:	Partially, but it also obeys your commands.
Han:	Hokey and ancient religions are no match for a good blaster at your side.
Luke:	You don't believe in the Force, do you?
Han:	Kid, I've flown from one side of this galaxy to the other. I've seen a lot of strange stuff, but I've never seen anything to make me believe that there's one all-powerful force controlling everything. There's no mystical energy field controls my destiny. It's all a lot of simple tricks and nonsense.
Obi-Wan:	I suggest you try it again, Luke, and this time let go your conscious self and act on instinct. (Obi-Wan puts a helmet on Luke.)
Luke:	With the blast shield down I can't even see. How am I supposed to fight?
Obi-Wan:	Your eyes can deceive you. Don't trust them. Stretch out your feelings. (Luke successfully strikes two blows to the remote.)

You see. You can do it. . . . You've taken your first step into a larger world.

In this scene we are introduced to the idea that the Force requires intuition, instinct, a turning inward, and the help of the unconscious. Thus, this hero's "source of power" connects him to spiritual and nonrational ways of knowing and being in the world.

In the second film, *The Empire Strikes Back*, Luke begins to understand what it means to turn inward to find his source of power when he trains with the Jedi master Yoda on Dagoba. Dagoba, a swamplike jungle, is continually bathed in mist and overrun by tangled vines and roots. Luke calls it a "slimy mudhole." It is an extremely organic place, appearing as a single living, breathing organism. It is also a place lost in time, a throwback to a primeval beginning. Time on Dagoba seems to stand still. As such, the planet offers Luke a respite or pause from the blistering battles and swirl of events occurring elsewhere in the universe. Dagoba's liminal and organic qualities are in direct contrast to the sharp angles, shiny metallic gleam, and technological speed demonstrated by the battling Empire and the Rebel forces. To reinforce this contrast, the scenes on Dagoba are intercut with scenes of events on the Death Star and on Han Solo's spacecraft, thus heightening our awareness of the differences between the realm of the spiritual/nonrational—represented by Dagoba—and the scientific/technological—represented by the Empire and the Rebel Forces.

Very cavelike or enclosing, Dagoba can also be seen as a metaphor for the unconscious. Like Jonah in the "belly of a whale," Dagoba speaks to the notion that the hero's place of transformation often occurs in a cave, an enclosure, or an underground location. Thus Dagoba represents a liminal space into which the hero must descend in order to seek enlightenment or transformation. Speaking to R2D2, Luke calls Dagoba "a really strange place to find a Jedi master," adding, "This place gives me the creeps. Still, there is something very familiar about this place." Luke's comment that Dagoba is "really strange" yet "very familiar" speaks to the notion that the hero, when he enters into an adventure, as Campbell notes, "journeys through a world of unfamiliar yet strangely intimate forces, some of which severely threaten him (tests), some of which give magical aid (helpers)." [17] On Dagoba, Luke will not only find a magical helper in the form of Yoda, but he will also be severely tested, not only in his Jedi training, but also when he meets his father, Darth Vader, in a dream.

When Luke first meets Yoda, however, he does not recognize him as a Jedi master, but rather treats him as an annoying pest. Even when Yoda offers his help, Luke replies, "I don't think so. I'm looking for a great warrior." Replies Yoda, "A great warrior? Wars do not make someone great." Luke, as yet untrained in the ways of the Force, judges people and things by their appearances rather than their true nature. He looks outward rather than inward.

We see further evidence of this when Luke joins Yoda for dinner. Yoda's house is a cave, so enclosing that Luke cannot even stand up, further reinforcing the idea that places of transformation are often caves or underground locations where the hero is forced to assume a passive state of receptivity. While Yoda prepares the meal, Luke complains, saying, "I just don't understand why we can't see Yoda now." Yoda admonishes him by saying, "Patience, for the Jedi it is time to eat as well." Continues Luke, "How far away is Yoda—will it take us long to get there?" "Not far, Yoda not far," explains Yoda, adding, "patience, soon you'll be with him." Finally, however, Luke's temper erupts as he exclaims, "I don't even know what I'm doing here. We're wasting my time." Yoda turns aside, as if talking to himself, and says, "I can't teach him. The boy has no patience. He is not ready." As Obi-Wan appears, Luke realizes that he is already talking with Yoda and immediately tries to change Yoda's mind about his training. Yoda protests, explaining to both Luke and Obi-Wan, "A Jedi must hold the deepest commitment. The most serious mind. This one, a long time have I watched. All his life as he looked away to the future, to the horizon. Never his mind on where he was. What he was doing. . . . adventure, hah! excitement, hah! A good Jedi craves not these things." Yoda's comments about Luke's untrained mind speak to the Zen Buddhist idea of the importance of living in the present, without desire or regret. In Zen philosophy all life exists in an eternal now, with no future or past. Yoda's comments also speak to the idea that the hero's enlightenment often occurs in a liminal world (like Dagoba) and in a state of passive receptivity. For example, in another scene when Luke asks Yoda how he will know the "good side from the bad," Yoda replies, "You will know. When you are calm, at peace, passive. A Jedi uses the force for knowledge and events, never attack."

Luke spends a good deal of time on Dagoba, training with Yoda to improve both his physical strength and his mental control. With time, Luke becomes more confident in his understanding of the Force and in his use of it to move and levitate objects. A final "trial" for Luke to pass, however, or a final step in his training involves using the Force to raise his spaceship from the swamp where it is mired. Unsuccessful at doing so, however, Luke complains to Yoda that he cannot do it because "it's too big":

Yoda: Size matters not, look at me. Judge me by my size, do you? And where you should not for my ally is the Force and a powerful ally it is. Life creates it, makes it grow. Its energy surrounds us and finds us. Luminous beings are we, not this crude matter. You must feel the Force around you. Here, between you and the tree, the rock, me everywhere. Yes, even between the land and the ship.

Luke: (disgusted) You want the impossible. (Luke walks away. Yoda uses the Force and raises Luke's ship out of the swamp.)

Luke: I don't believe it!

Yoda: That is why you fail.

The goal of the hero's quest, or the hero's boon, is to see beyond the division of the "here and now" of consciousness and to realize, as Campbell explains, that "you and [the] other are one, that you are two aspects of one life, and that your apparent separateness is but an effect of the way we experience forms under the conditions of space and time." [18] The hero, in other words, "suggest[s] that behind that duality there is a singularity over which this plays like a shadow game." [19] Yoda's explanation of the Force speaks to this notion of the unity of time, space, and being. As a Jedi master, and as Luke's shaman/mentor, he attempts to initiate him into this understanding. Luke, however, fails due to a lack of belief. Working from a rational scientific perspective, which asserts gravity's role in keeping objects on the ground, Luke cannot possibly image how Yoda can raise a spaceship through force of will. Luke, in other words, cannot comprehend the power of spiritual/nonrational ways of knowing and being in the world, or, as Christ teaches, he has not yet learned the idea that "faith can move mountains." Yoda's levitation of the ship also exhibits qualities of a Zen master able to harness and move "Chi," the "Force" in this case being another word for "Chi energy."

Luke has actually failed a number of important tests on Dagoba. The first is when he judges things by their appearances and does not recognize Yoda as a Jedi master, and later assumes that Yoda is too small to raise Luke's ship from the swamp. The second failure is when he acts impatiently and fails to understand that enlightenment occurs in passive or liminal states of consciousness that open the hero to new possibilities. The third failure (which I discuss in the next section) occurs when Luke insists on taking his weapons into the cave and, acting out of fear and aggression, "slays" his father/Shadow-self. His final failure is a failure of belief—in himself, in Yoda, and in the Force.

The Father Quest in the Star Wars Trilogy

Luke's coming of age, in part, is a quest to find his father, or more specifically to find the father-potential inside of him. Such a journey is particularly complicated for Luke since his father, Darth Vader (literally "dark father"), is the embodiment of evil or "the dark side." Vader, like Obi-Wan, was a Jedi knight, a protector of the light. But like the archangel, who fell from heaven to become Satan, Darth Vader was "seduced by the dark side." As a result, for Luke, finding his father—and indeed he only discovers him half-way through the second film—also means facing his Shadow (those parts of himself that he most fears) or coming to grips with the potential for evil inside of him.

In one interpretation, the Star Wars trilogy treats good and evil as absolute and incompatible—one is either an Empire Storm Trooper or a member of the Rebel Alliance; one either works for the Force or against it. A more complex reading of the trilogy, however, views good and evil as inextricably linked. From such a perspective, Luke's Jungian task, growing up or becoming "individuated," not only requires finding his father but also facing his Shadow. It just so happens that in Luke's case his father is his Shadow. If Luke runs from his Shadow/father, he remains a child. If, however, he responds to Vader's temptation to join him and rule the universe, Luke will become consumed by the dark side. Luke's hero quest, therefore, is to confront his Shadow, neither running from it nor being consumed by it, but rather finding a way to integrate this Shadow-potential into his life. In this sense, Luke, the hero of the trilogy, is a mixture of both good and evil impulses. And Darth Vader, a central villain of the trilogy, despite his evil nature, possesses the potential for good as well. For both characters, this enlightenment occurs as a result of Luke's completion of the father quest, most clearly evidenced in three separate scenes from the trilogy. The first occurs in *The Empire Strikes Back* in a cave on Dagoba when Luke confronts his father's image and "slays" Vader/himself. The second occurs at the end of *The Empire Strikes Back* when Luke and Darth Vader battle and Vader cuts off Luke's hand. The third scene is the final confrontation and reconciliation between the two of them occurring at the end of *Return of the Jedi*. Each of these scenes is discussed in what follows.

Luke's first confrontation with Darth Vader occurs during the course of his training as a Jedi knight on Dagoba. After a long day's training, the following exchange occurs between Luke and Yoda:

Luke: There's something not right here. I feel cold death.
Yoda: That place is strong with the dark side of the force. A domain of evil it is. In you must go.
Luke: What's in there?
Yoda: Only what you take with you. (Luke straps his blaster and his light saber around his waist.) Your weapons, you will not need them.

Luke disregards Yoda's advice about his weapons and takes them anyway. Like Aeneas descending into the underworld to confront his father's shade, Luke descends into a cave on Dagoba to confront his own father. The cave is filled with roots and vines. A python guards the gate and hisses at him as he passes. The film changes to slow motion as Darth Vader appears. Luke pulls out his light saber and the two lock swords. Luke, in a brutally strong stroke, cuts off Vader's head. Vader's masked head rolls to the floor in front of Luke, and as Luke watches, Vader's black helmet explodes to reveal Luke's face staring back at him with a lifeless stare.

According to Campbell, in the hero's journey into the realm of the extraordinary he often "encounters a shadow presence that guards the passage [to that adventure]. The hero may defeat or conciliate this power and go alive into the kingdom of the dark (brother-battle, dragon-battle, offering, charm), or be slain by the opponent and descend in death (dismemberment, crucifixion)." [20] The shadow presence that Luke confronts in a "father-battle" (rather than a "brother-battle") is Darth Vader. Interestingly enough, Luke both "defeats . . . this power" and is at the same time "slain" by this power. He is "dismembered," or more specifically decapitated, by his own sword. The snake at the gate, a traditional symbol of knowledge that shatters Adam and Eve's innocence in Paradise, signifies the self-knowledge that will change Luke forever, no longer allowing him the innocence of childhood. (And indeed, over the course of the film, Luke's attire changes from white in the first film, to brown in the second, to black with patches of white in the third film.)

Yoda's response to Luke's question about what is waiting for him in the cave—"Only what you take with you"—refers to the idea that our Shadow is

ourselves, or rather those parts of ourselves that we most fear. Since the hero's ultimate goal is enlightenment, Self-knowledge begins with self-knowledge. Thus, the hero's first battle at the gate of the unconscious, in Jungian terms, is the battle with his Shadow-self. Luke fails this test and slays his father (Shadow) primarily because he fears becoming his father (Shadow), or being consumed by the dark side. He acts, in other words, out of fear and hate—both passions that drive Darth Vader, and ultimately almost consume every bit of good that Vader possesses.

Although Luke fails this test, Yoda makes it clear that Luke will only complete his hero quest and come of age as a Jedi knight when he confronts his father and acknowledges his father-potential. As Yoda says to Luke in *The Empire Strikes Back* at the end of his second visit to Dagoba to finish his training, "No more training do you require. Already know you that which you need." Responds Luke, "Then I am a Jedi." "Not yet," retorts Yoda, "One thing remains. Vader—you must confront Vader. Then, only then, a Jedi will you be, and confront him you will."

Such a meeting between Luke and Darth Vader occurs at the end of *The Empire Strikes Back* when a solitary Luke invades Vader's ship to face him. As they lock in battle, Vader says to Luke, "Your destiny lies with me, Sky-walker. Obi-Wan knows this to be true. . . . Obi-Wan has taught you well. You

The "second" meeting in the Star Wars trilogy between Luke Skywalker (Mark Hamill) and Darth Vader (David Prowse; the voice of James Earl Jones) near the end of *The Empire Strikes Back* when a solitary Luke invades Vader's ship to face him. As they lock in battle, Vader says to Luke, "Your destiny lies with me, Skywalker. Obi-Wan knows this to be true. . . . Obi-Wan has taught you well. You have controlled your fear. Now release your anger, own your hatred and destroy me." Luke, having learned an important lesson of Jedi (Zen) training, refuses to yield to his anger and his hatred. Walking the thin line between the passions of desire and fear, he refuses to kill his father. Although they engage in swordplay, Luke seems to primarily defend himself. Luke's coming of age, in part, is a quest to find his father, or more specifically to find the father potential inside of him. Such a journey is particularly complicated for Luke since his father; Darth Vader (Dark Father) is the embodiment of evil or "the dark side." Vader, like Obi-Wan, was a Jedi knight, a protector of the light. But like the Archangel, who fell from heaven to become Satan, Darth Vader was "seduced by the dark side." As a result, for Luke, finding his father, and indeed he only discovers him during this battle scene with his father, also means facing his Shadow (those parts of himself which he most fears), or coming to grips with the potential for evil inside of him. Courtesy of the Museum of Modern Art—Film Stills Archives.

have controlled your fear. Now release your anger, own your hatred, and destroy me." Luke, having learned an important lesson of Jedi (Zen) training, refuses to yield to his anger and his hatred. Walking the thin line between the passions of desire and fear, he refuses to kill his father. Although they engage in swordplay, Luke seems to primarily defend himself. Vader, however, proves stronger, and cuts off Luke's forearm. As Luke clings precariously to a platform extended high above a deep chasm leading to infinite space, we witness the following exchange:

Vader: There is no escape. Don't make me destroy you. Luke, you do not yet realize your importance. You've only begun to discover your power. Join me and I will complete your training. With our combined strength we can end this destructive conflict and bring order to the galaxy.

Luke: I'll never join you.

Vader: If you only knew the power of the dark side. Obiwan never told you what happened to your father.

Luke: He told me enough. He told me you killed him.

Vader: No, I am your father.

Luke: No, no, it's not true. That's impossible.

Vader: Search your feelings; you know it's true. Luke, you can destroy the Emperor. He has foreseen this. It is your destiny. Join me and we can rule the galaxy together as father and son. Come with me. It is the only way.

Luke answers by letting go. We watch as he spirals downward through tunnel after tunnel of seemingly endless space. Finally, however, he grabs a cross-shaped antenna extending out of the bottom of the battleship. Below him is the vast emptiness of space. Clinging to this metal cross, he calls out, as if forsaken, "Ben! Ben! Leia! Hear me, Leia."

This scene echoes Christ's temptation by Satan in which Satan tries to convince Christ to worship him by offering him a chance to rule the world. Christ, like Luke, refuses to join "the dark side." The scene also ends, of course, in a tableau of Christ's crucifixion. Once again, "the hero may defeat or conciliate [the] power and go alive into the kingdom of the dark (brother-battle, dragon-battle, offering, charm), or be slain by the opponent and descend in death (dismemberment, crucifixion)." [21] This second meeting between Darth Vader and Luke Skywalker echoes the first meeting in the cave on Dagoba, except that now it is Vader who defeats Luke in a "father-battle" (rather than a "brother-battle") and "dismembers" him—when he cuts off Luke's hand—while metaphorically crucifying him as well.

This meeting is also significant because Luke learns that Vader is his father, which raises a question of the extent to which he is like his father. If the father quest is, in part, finding the father in order to discover one's father-potential, then Luke's hero's quest now involves reconciling his propensity for good with his newly acknowledged propensity for evil.

The final meeting between Luke and his father, in the third film of the trilogy, is, in some ways, a reversal of their previous encounter. Luke invades the newly fashioned Death Star to once again confront Darth Vader. As they once gain lock light sabers, the following conversation ensues:

Luke: Your thoughts betray you, father. I feel the good in you, the conflict.
Vader: There is no conflict.
Luke: You couldn't bring yourself to kill me before and I don't believe you'll destroy me now.

Luke proves stronger this time and cuts off Vader's hand. We see a close-up, from Luke's point of view, of wires and gears dangling from Vader's severed arm. Luke looks down at his own mechanical arm. Luke refuses to fight and puts away his light saber. The Emperor takes advantage of his defenseless state and, using the Force, begins to electrocute him. Vader, at the last moment, intervenes and casts the Emperor into an endless chasm that appears to lead into the infinity of space. As Luke embraces his greatly weakened father, whose breathing has gotten noticeably harsher, the following exchange occurs:

Vader: Luke, help me take this mask off.

Luke: But you'll die.

Vader: Nothing can stop that now. Just for once let me look on you with my own eyes. (Luke takes off Vader's mask.)

Vader: Now go, my son. Leave me.

Luke: No, you're coming with me. I'm not going to leave you here. I've got to save you.

Vader: You already have. Luke, you were right about me. Tell your sister. You were right.

Thus, in this final meeting between Luke and his father, Luke refuses to kill his father, simply because he still loves him. Love, the most powerful force of all, allows Vader to be saved, and allows Luke to become a Jedi knight. Speaking of the hero's quest, Campbell notes that when the hero "arrives at the nadir of mythological round, he undergoes a supreme ordeal and gains his reward. The triumph may be represented as . . . his recognition by the father creator (father atonement) [or] his own divinization (apotheosis)." [22] For Luke, the "supreme ordeal" is facing his father/Shadow. This time, however, he does not run, nor does he succumb to the temptation to become his father/Shadow and join the dark side. Although Luke remains more human than machine—unlike his father who has become more machine than human—when Luke glances at his own technological arm it is as if he acknowledges his own propensity for evil. By the same token, when Luke removes his father's mask and we see his father's very human features, it acknowledges his father's propensity for good. Luke's reward—his hero's "triumph"—is two-fold. Looking upon Luke with his own eyes allows Vader to acknowledge Luke as his son, thus offering Luke "father atonement." Luke's second triumph, becoming a Jedi knight by facing his father, can be seen as a form of "divinization" or "apotheosis."

The Quest to Reconcile Science and Technology with Humanity and Spirit in Star Wars

The Star Wars trilogy is, of course, a member of the science-fiction genre; as such, it also plays out a version of the science and technology versus humanity and spirit quest. Speaking specifically of *Star Wars*, Campbell notes that the film "shows the state as a machine and asks, 'Is the machine going to crush humanity or serve humanity?' Humanity comes not from the machine but from the heart." [23] Perhaps the best example of the conflict between humanity

The Jedi master Yoda is perhaps the Star Wars trilogy's best representative of spiritual/humanist ways of being in the world. Yoda is so organic that he looks like a root or a tree branch. Being short, he is also close to the earth. With his large ears and eyes, and stocky stature, he appears dwarf-like as well. Yoda also lives on Dagoba, itself a natural or organic world. In *Return of the Jedi* we learn that Yoda is over nine hundred years old. Wise beyond counting as well as intuitive and connected to nature, Yoda as an old man/dwarf represents spiritual/nonrational ways of knowing. In his role as Jedi Master, Yoda has initiated generations of Jedi knights into the power of the Force, itself, a religion or philosophical system, like Zen Buddhism, based on an intuitive or nonrational understanding of being. Courtesy of the Museum of Modern Art—Film Stills Archives.

and the machine occurs at the end of *Star Wars* as Rebel fighter pilots attempt to fire a missile into the exhaust vent, the Achilles' heel of the technological monster that is the Empire's Death Star. Luke is the only fighter pilot with a chance of making the shot, all previous attempts having failed. As Luke makes his final approach to the target, Obi-Wan, speaking as a "spirit" guide, urges, "Use the Force, Luke. Let go. . . . Trust me." In response, Luke turns off his targeting computer and manually guides the missile that successfully destroys the Death Star. Using the power of the Force results in the triumph of humanity and spirit over science and technology.

The Jedi master Yoda is perhaps the trilogy's best representative of spiritual/humanist ways of being in the world. Yoda is so organic that he even looks like a root or a tree branch. Being short, he is also close to the earth. With his large ears and eyes and stocky stature, he appears dwarf-like as well. "In folklore," explains Jung, "the dwarf or the elf [is a] personification of the hidden forces of nature." [24] As previously discussed, Yoda also lives on Dagoba, itself a natural or organic world. In *Return of the Jedi* we learn that Yoda is more than 900 years old. According to Jung, the old-man archetype "represents knowledge, reflection, insight, wisdom, cleverness, and intuition on the one hand, and on the other, moral qualities such as goodwill and readiness to help, which make his 'spiritual' character sufficiently plain." [25] Thus, wise beyond counting as well as intuitive and connected to nature, Yoda as an old man/dwarf represents spiritual/nonrational ways of knowing. In his role as Jedi master, Yoda has initiated generations of Jedi knights into the power of the Force, itself a religion or philosophical system, like Zen Buddhism, based on an intuitive or nonrational understanding of being.

In partial contrast to Yoda, Luke Skywalker is a boundary-spanning figure. Although the Force is strong in him, and although he undergoes training as a Jedi knight, he is no stranger to technology. As a fighter pilot, he uses technology to complete his various missions. The droids, R2D2 and C3P0 are his closest friends. Although, as hero, he champions the goals of humanity and spirit, he is himself, like his father, part machine.

In contrast to Luke, Darth Vader has been so overtaken by technology that he has become a machine. When Luke asserts to Ben, in reference to his father Darth Vader, that "There is still good in him," Ben replies, "He's more machine now than man. Twisted and evil." Vader, however, is aware of the limits of technology. When one of the Empire's commanders, speaking of the Death Star, proclaims that it is "now the ultimate power in the universe," Vader admonishes him, saying, "Don't be too proud of this technological terror you've constructed. The ability to destroy a planet is insignificant next to the power of the Force."

Vader, although a technological monster, is human underneath his technological shell. As such, like Luke, he is a boundary-spanning figure. Although he has cast his lot with the Death Star and the Emperor's selfish desire to rule the galaxy, he still believes in the Force, and, as we see in the final film, there is a remnant of good in him as well. According to Campbell, *Star Wars* provides the same problem as *Faust*: "Mephistopheles, the machine man, can provide us with all the means, and is thus likely to determine the aims of life as well. But of course the characteristic of Faust, which makes him eligible to be saved, is that he seeks aims that are not those of the machine." When Luke unmasks his father, as Campbell notes, "he is taking off the machine role that the father has played. The father was the uniform. That is power, the state role." [26] When Luke says to his dying father, "I've got to save you," Vader replies, "You already have. Luke, you were right about me. Tell your sister. You were right." Thus, Vader can be saved because he ultimately "seeks aims that are not those of the machine," and does so when he saves Luke from the Emperor and reconciles his relationship with him.

The Grail Quest in the Star Wars Trilogy

Drawing as it does on Arthurian legend, it is not surprising that the Star Wars trilogy also tells a version of the Grail quest. "The theme of the Grail romance is that the land, the country, the whole territory of concern has been laid waste. It is called a wasteland. . . . It is a land where everybody is living an inauthentic life, doing as other people do, doing as you're told, with no courage for your own life." [27] The hero's primary task, therefore, is to restore the land to fertility, to reawaken hope, and to make life once again worth living.

In the Christian religion, Christ is the Grail, since his death and resurrection offers redemption for the sins of humanity. The literal Grail, from which all metaphorical Grails spring, is the cup of Joseph of Arimathea, from which legend says Christ drank wine at the last supper with his disciples, and which was used to catch the blood from his wounded side on the cross. Metaphorically, the Holy Grail "represents that spiritual path that is between pairs of opposites, between fear and desire, between good and devil." [28] In Arthurian legend, this Grail cup becomes the source of a year of questing for many of King Arthur's knights as they go in search of the vision that inspired Percival at Pentecost.

The galaxy, as the opening graphics of *Star Wars* tell us, is "faced with its darkest hour," and Luke and Leia are the destined saviors of their age. The current era of strife and endless battles between the Rebels and the Empire represents a continued bid, perhaps on both sides, for intergalactic dominance.

The Empire represents the forces that have made the galaxy into a wasteland. This is evidenced, in part, through the construction of not one, but two different Death Stars, technological marvels that announce the Empire's greatness while demonstrating its capability to destroy all planets and civilizations that do not bend to its will. The Emperor, like the Empire, is driven by greed, hate, and envy. His central desire, as denoted by his title, is to rule the galaxy. Thus, his overriding concern is for his own greatness and glory.

By contrast, the Jedi knights Yoda and Obi-Wan Kenobi, as adherents to the Force, represent a consciousness beyond the contemporary age that seeks to reunite all beings with the nonrational, mythical, and spiritual plane of existence. As Grail heroes, they see, for example, the spirit in all beings. As Yoda says to Luke, "Luminous beings are we, not this crude matter." Attuned as they are with nature, and the other, and divested of all passions, the Jedi see the unity of all things beyond the duality of the current era. And like all great prophets, they sacrifice self in order to achieve Self. This is demonstrated, for example, in *Star Wars*, when Obi-Wan lowers his sword, allowing Darth Vader to kill him. He says to Darth Vader just before he dies, "You can't win, Darth. You can strike me down. But I shall become more powerful that you can possibly imagine." On the one hand, Obi-Wan's individual human life is insignificant compared with all life. Or, to put it another way, since Obi-Wan is made up of the matter that flows through all life, his individual death has no impact on his life. Finally, as willing sacrifice, like Jesus Christ, Obi-Wan knows that by his death he will be reunited with the energy source from which all life flows, and if possible, will be even stronger in death than he was in life.

All three films in the trilogy make it clear that the order of Jedi knights is an ancient religion, significantly pre-dating the current age. For example, when Obi-Wan Kenobi gives Luke his father's light saber, the following exchange occurs:

Luke: What is it?
Obi-Wan: Your father's light saber. This is the weapon of a Jedi knight. Not as clumsy or random as a blaster. An elegant weapon, for a more civilized age. For over a thousand generations the Jedi knights were the guardians of peace and justice in the Old Republic, before the dark times, before the Empire.
Luke: How did my father die?
Obi-Wan: A young Jedi named Darth Vader, who was a pupil of mine until he turned to evil, helped the Empire hunt down and destroy the Jedi knights. He betrayed and murdered your father. Now the Jedi are all but extinct. Vader was seduced by the dark side of the Force.

This exchange makes clear that the era of the Jedi knights has long since passed away and that very few adherents to their teachings exist—Yoda, Obi-Wan, Luke, and Leia being the notable exceptions. Darth Vader, also a Jedi knight, forfeits his claim to this status, having been consumed by the "dark side." Although Vader still practices some of the ways of the force, such as intuition and using the Force to move objects and people, it is made clear that, contrary to its purpose, he uses the Force for evil rather than for good. Thus, the Jedi knights fight for a transformed world free from strife and hate. Although they represent an earlier era of consciousness (perhaps preconsciousness), they also represent future possibilities. Just as the myth of Camelot holds the promise of its own return, the Jedi knights, as Grail heroes, also represent a return to a more spiritual plane of consciousness.

Luke, as Grail king, is predominantly responsible for restoring the wasteland created by the endless battles between the Rebel Alliance and the Empire. This is evidenced in *The Empire Strikes Back* when Luke returns to Dagoba to complete his training. Yoda, on the verge of death, offers Luke one last admonition about the power of the Force and then reminds him of the Jedi's most important role, saying, "When gone I am, the last of the Jedi will you be. . . . Pass on what you have learned." Speaking of the hero quest, Campbell notes that "intrinsically it [represents] an expansion of consciousness and therewith of being (illumination, transfiguration, freedom)." The hero's "final work is that of return. If the powers have blessed the hero, he now sets forth under protection (emissary) . . . the hero re-emerges from the kingdom of dread (return, resurrection). The boon that he brings restores the world (elixir)." [29] As the Grail hero, Luke must ensure that the reign of peace and prosperity, represented by the thousand-generation rule of the Jedi knights, will return. His hero's boon, in other words, is to teach the culture to see beyond the division of here and now, and, through the teachings of the Force, attain enlightenment about the nature of all being. Luke, along with his twin sister Princess Leia, is charged with healing the sick and divided land. All Grail heroes, like Jesus Christ, who himself suffered grievous wounds as the perfect sacrifice for all sinners, are wounded heroes. Luke is no exception to this rule, having suffered for his people (through his dismemberment and his "father-battle"). Like a wounded King Arthur (himself a Grail hero sacrificed on the field of battle for his kingdom), Luke must teach the people that Camelot, or heaven on Earth, even if only dimly remembered, can be achieved again.

In sum, the hero quest, or the monomyth as Campbell often refers to it, is the central universal story in which the archetypic events of separation, initiation, and return are acted out. The hero, acting as cultural visionary/prophet/messiah, moves through these phases with the primary goal of healing the culture by his ability to transcend the dualities of human existence, seek unity from separation, and move culture to the next level of consciousness. Thus, the Star Wars trilogy plays out the battle for cultural transformation from the current era of consciousness, with its focus on science and rationality, to the next age of postconsciousness or transconsciousness, marked by a return to the spiritual plane of existence.

Problematizing the Star Wars Trilogy: Gender, Race, and Ideology

Despite its power as a spiritual tale of the evolution of consciousness, the Star Wars trilogy, by its conservative interpretation of the hero quest, offers a world with little place for women. With the notable exception of Princess Leia, all of the major characters are male, from the heroes (Luke and Han) to the Jedi masters (Yoda, Obi-Wan Kenobi, and Darth Vader), to the leaders of the Rebel and Empire forces. Even the potentially asexual characters of R2D2 and C3PO are played as male.

Drawing as it does on Arthurian legend, the trilogy also opens itself up to criticism in its portrayal of women. In the first film, for example, Princess Leia, like the typical fairy-tale princess, is held captive by the dark knight (Vader) and is powerless to save herself or the Rebel Alliance. Rescue requires the arrival of Luke Skywalker, who is destined to be Leia's knight in shining armor on many occasions. Leia again assumes this passive and powerless role in the second film of the trilogy when Jabba the Hut holds her captive. Not only must she again wait until Luke arrives, but she is also forced to play the degrading role of Jabba's palace whore, eternally chained to his throne while wearing a revealing belly dancer–like costume. Jabba's lecherous gaze, his constant lip licking, and his sexually suggestive belching emphasize her function as Jabba's sexual fetish.

Although Leia is portrayed as a fiery and feisty woman who clearly possesses a strong will, this persona is primarily developed to provide a "hard-to-get" challenge for Han Solo. A classic "taming of the shrew" dramatic motif, Leia's indomitable spirit simply presents Han with a more interesting conquest as he teaches her to love and bend to his will. Leia's primary function in the trilogy, in other words, is as Han's love interest, and in the first two films, before we discover that she is Luke's sister, Leia serves as both Luke's and Han's love object in a classic lover's triangle.

Not only is the Star Wars world almost exclusively male, it is almost exclusively white as well. With the notable exception of Landau Calrissian (Billy Dee Williams), all the characters are white. Even though James Earl Jones, an African-American actor, provides Darth Vader's voice, when Vader's face is finally revealed in the third film, a white actor plays him. Not surprisingly, Landau Calrissian, as a Judas figure, is portrayed as an outlaw who turns Luke, Han, and Leia over to Vader in order to protect his own selfish interests. Although he ultimately repents his evil ways and joins the Rebel Alliance, his main dramatic function is as a betrayer. Thus the only black character in the entire trilogy is portrayed primarily in a negative light.

The Star Wars trilogy has also been brought to task on ideological grounds. The film's mythic message that the nonrational and intuitive way of knowing is superior to the rational or logical way of knowing has been interpreted as a celebration of simplemindedness over deliberative thinking. An example would be when Obi-Wan Kenobi tells Ben to turn off his targeting computer in order to intuit the best moment to launch his missile at the Death Star. Film critics often pointed to this scene as offering the perfect metaphor for the 1980s Reagan ethos—an ethos of "homespun" truths, populist values, and simple-minded solutions to complicated problems. Kellner and Ryan, for example, provide an analysis of the trilogy as a fictional manifesto for President Ronald Reagan's conservative foreign-policy agenda, specifically a rationale for his Strategic Defense Initiative (SDI).[30] That SDI became known as the "Star Wars" defense initiative anecdotally reinforces this interpretation. Although I find this criticism of the film itself reductionistic in its failure to grasp the nature of the larger spiritual truths that the trilogy propounds, I acknowledge the potential danger of this interpretation.

The final chapter of this book provides a summary of the critical model developed throughout while also discussing the ideological implications of myth and mythic criticism. The chapter concludes with a discussion of the types of myths necessary as we move forward in the new millennium.

9
Myth, the Contemporary Moment, and the Future

The modern hero, the modern individual who dares to heed the call and seek the mansion of that presence with whom it is our whole destiny to be atoned, cannot, indeed must not, wait for his community to cast off its slough of pride, fear, rationalized avarice, and sanctified misunderstanding. "Live," Nietzsche says, "as though the day were here." It is not society that is to guide and save the creative hero, but precisely the reverse. And so everyone of us shares the supreme ordeal—carries the cross of the redeemer—not in the bright moments of his tribe's great victories, but in the silence of his personal despair.

—Joseph Campbell, *The Hero with a Thousand Faces*, p. 391

The idea of celebrating films that present a unified mythic vision—such as the perennial journey home—in the midst of the contemporary era of fragmentation and deconstruction could be viewed as anachronistic. And indeed, as Rushing explains:

The positions on the relationship of myth to cultural consciousness can be roughly divided into two opposing "camps"; skeptics for whom "false" and "consciousness" go together . . . and champions for whom "myth" is a nonliteral "truth"—a natural, meaningful, even beautiful expression of psychological and sociological orientations to reality.[1]

Those in the myth as false or ideological group take their cue from the writings of Karl Marx and Sigmund Freud and view "myth and ideology . . . as 'lies' or 'tricks of the mind' which mask the universal struggle for material advantages" or, in the case of Freud, sociopsychological adjustment. By contrast, those in the myth as "true" contingent see *some* myths as progressive and potentially liberating for a culture, while *occa-*

sionally viewing other myths as regressive or possibly restrictive.[2] While these two positions on myth can be marked out, as Rushing notes:

What is surprising, both outside and inside the field of rhetoric, is that neither camp pays much attention to the other. . . . Most mythic critics of cultural consciousness marginalize a significant realm of relevant scholarship, and neither perspective is affected by the other.[3]

Rushing and Frentz specifically address the "stand-off" between the two camps while attempting a partial reconciliation between them in a two-part essay entitled "Integrating Archetype and Ideology in Rhetorical Criticism." [4] Their project, in part, is to challenge the preeminence of the ideological turn in contemporary criticism, while rescuing the archetypal perspective from its current marginalized status. For the purposes of this discussion, what is most significant is their assertion that both ideological and archetypal criticism, at their core, have moral imperatives, and thus, may have more in common than is at first apparent. For the ideological critic the moral imperative involves "perform[ing] the morally significant act of fighting oppression by unmasking rhetorical strategies that maintain it." [5] The ultimate goal for many, although not all ideological critics is, of course, a classless society free from hierarchical structures and dominance relationships. For ideology theory, the heart of the problem is the ego or the assertion of the individual over the collective, predominantly a problem since the advent of capitalism. According to Rushing and Frentz, a moral commitment, be it of a different kind, also drives the psychological (Jungian) critic—the ego's or self's preeminence over the Self. The goal of this perspective is individuation, or psychological maturity "in which the ego is not destroyed, but eventually decentered to make way for the Self as the ultimate guide to moral action." [6]

Although both ideological and Jungian approaches assert the moral good of the collective, neither approach, Rushing and Frentz argue, offers a complete ethical solution to the problem of the ego:

For while Jung localizes the moral impetus in the archetypes, primarily the Self, Jameson [representing the ideological camp] positions his own utopian vision in the idealized social relationships arising from non-oppressive material conditions. But if one central ethical function of any adequate moral system is to liberate oppression, and if oppressions occur within the psyche as well as within the society, then any moral standard for criticism must address both domains.[7]

Rushing and Frentz, therefore, argue for a morally grounded criticism that not only unmasks textual practices that repress awareness of class and political oppression generally, but one that addresses repressions of the psyche as well. Specifically, the critic's moral charge would be to uncover textual practices that prevent or preclude what they call "cultural individuation." Although admitting that this formulation is tentative, they offer a sketch of what cultural individuation would look like:

> a culture moving toward individuation would struggle against oppression based upon economic class structure and other forms of hierarchic domination, and hence would progressively assimilate more and more of the cultural unconscious into awareness. Further we suggest that the ego-consciousness of individuals would expand outward to encompass a social collectivity which includes others as part of the Self; individuals would retain, but re-contextualize, their separate senses of self within this greater whole. Finally, while still maintaining their uniqueness, separate cultures would expand their identities outward into a more global, even universal, consciousness.[8]

In textual practice "narratives may implicitly advocate any number of courses of moral action in relation to the end point of cultural individuation. Those that imply a movement toward individuation would be judged as morally superior to those that imply a movement away from it." [9] From this perspective then, "master narratives" would not be viewed as either automatically repressive (as many ideological critics often view them) or automatically liberating (as many archetypal critics often do). Since universal archetypes are always manifest in particular cultural formulations, it may be that some manifestations, rather than working to move the cultural toward individuation, actually reinforce hierarchic relationships, and thus stymie a culture's evolution.

Rushing and Frentz, as they note, are not alone in asserting a moral imperative for the critic of narrative form. Walter Fisher, in his comparison of the "narrative paradigm" with the "rational world paradigm," argues that the rational world paradigm, the predominant mode of scholarly inquiry since the enlightenment, presumes that the world "is a set of logical puzzles which can be resolved through appropriate analysis and application of reason conceived as an argumentative construct." [10] This paradigm suffers, in Fisher's understanding, from an ability to see the way in which symbolizing is *both* rational and nonrational. In response, Fisher offers the narrative paradigm, which proceeds from the assumption that humans are storytellers acting on the basis of good reasons derived from experiences in the world. In this paradigm experience offers "a set of stories which must be chosen among to live the good life in a process of continual recreation." [11] In Fisher's words, narrative form "shapes morality by placing characters and events within a context where moral judgement is a necessary part of making sense of the action." [12]

I agree with Fisher, Rushing, and Frentz that moral judgments are necessary in any analysis of narrative form. Myths, neither true nor false, are rather more or less functional for interpreting the human condition and, thus, are more or less instrumental in moving a culture toward individuation. More specifically, I believe a mythic story that moves a cultural toward individuation meets the following criteria: it spontaneously arises from the culture in a fashion that speaks to human exigencies; it allows for the myth to change; it invites the audience to change; it encourages multiple interpretations of the myth; it invites multiple or competing stories to coexist in the same mythic universe; and it offers the grounds upon which it is to be tested or judged as liberating or functional. In what follows I discuss each of these briefly while noting films that either fulfill or fail the criteria listed.

Myths That Arise Spontaneously from the Culture

Mythic impulses, like visions, must arise spontaneously from the psyche of the individual or the culture and cannot be externally imposed. Campbell, discussing the artist's receptivity to this intuitive force, notes:

> Anyone writing a creative work knows that you open, you yield yourself, and the book talks to you and builds itself. To a certain extent you become the carrier of something that is given to you from what have been called the Muses, or in biblical language, "God." [13]

Even more important, however, mythic stories must speak to the exigencies of the human condition. Those stories that resonate with a culture do so because they have tapped into the unconscious energy in such a way that they address urgent questions of being and nonbeing. In Campbell's words:

> Since the inspiration comes from the unconscious, and since the unconscious minds of the people of any single small society have much in common, what the shaman or seer brings forth is something that is waiting to be brought forth in everyone. So when one hears the seer's story, one responds, "Aha! This is my story. This is something that I had always wanted to say but wasn't able to say. [14]

Jung refers to this intuitive receptivity to the Muse in terms of the dreamer/ visionary's responsiveness to the archetypes of the collective unconscious. According to Jung, archetypes:

> arise in a state of reduced intensity of consciousness (in dreams, delirium, reveries, visions, etc.). In all these states the check put upon unconscious contents by the con-

centration of the conscious mind ceases, so that the hitherto unconscious material streams, as though from opened side-sluices, into the field of consciousness.[15]

Both Jung and Campbell imply, in other words, that mythic material cannot be "scripted" or consciously constructed by the individual or culture at large. "Consciousness can no more invent, or even predict, an effective symbol than foretell or control tonight's dream." [16]

This would translate, for example, as an admonishment to screenplay writers against writing film scripts from prefabricated outlines of, for example, Campbell's distillation of the hero quest. This becomes a gray area for the film critic to trod, realizing, as I do, that George Lucas is very much aware of the power of myth and even acknowledges studying myths and fairy tales in his construction of the Star Wars trilogy. The Star Wars trilogy, as I have argued, is a powerful and effective interpretation of archetypal experiences. Despite this disclaimer, and despite the fine line the critic walks when making claims about the artist's intentions, I stand behind this position.

An example of the Hollywood film industry's unsuccessful attempts to "script" mythic stories illuminates this point. In the 1980s, Chris Vogler constructed an outline version of the central elements of Campbell's hero quest. According to John O'Leary, a freelance screenplay writer working in Hollywood at the time, the sketch was apparently championed by the heads of various studios and was frequently circulated to contracted screenwriters who were asked to use it in their plots. O'Leary notes that "You'd go to parties with writers and readers and everyone was, you know, kind of passing it around and talking about it." As far as he knows, however, nothing substantial ever came of it, and, for the most part, writers greeted the outline of the hero quest in a lukewarm fashion.[17] That Hollywood producers seriously considered using Campbell's distillation of universal myths speaks to their awareness of the power and potential popularity of such mythic stories for selling movie tickets. That such efforts to impose mythic elements on film scripts may have failed, however, may speak to the difficulty, if not the impossibility, of "consciously" tapping the "unconscious."

Myths That Are Open to Change

The mythic stories that are told in culture, although they may share certain universal qualities that do not change (and probably will not unless such universal exigencies as birth, growth, separation, death, and speculations on life-after-death change), must change in culturally specific fashions if they are to speak to the changing conditions and concerns of the culture. Myths that do not evolve are no longer useful and often fade away. A living myth, therefore, is a responsive myth. The American western myth is an example. This myth has evolved as the culture has changed, despite the fact that "the West" has been settled for almost a century now. The best examples of this myth are those that continue to engage some of the central philosophical debates with which the western and American culture still grapple, such as the tensions between the individual and the community and between the values of civilization and wilderness. Clint Eastwood's *Unforgiven*, for example, a revisionist western, rather than proclaiming the death of the western per se, instead proclaims the death of the western as ossified legend about absolute good and evil. By mixing these qualities up, the film deconstructs some of the potentially dangerous assumptions of the classical western, such as mythic regeneration through violence and the centrality of vigilante justice to civilization. Through the film's self-conscious, even reflexive orientation, viewers are invited to reflect on and critically discuss these and other ideologically problematic assumptions upon which the western is based. By the end of *Unforgiven* there are no new myths to replace the old ones; however, the one surety is that these age-old questions still remain, possibly waiting for the next western to tackle. Thus, cultural manifestations of archetypic material support cultural individuation to the extent these interpretations not only remain open to change, but also invite criticism of and change in the culture's mythic scripts.

The mythic critic can also ask to what extent does the story that is being told open up interpretive possibilities rather than close them down? To what extent does the myth allow for, even invite, multiple stories, with possibly different moral lessons for living, to coexist in the same mythic universe and possibly even inside of the same story. Jesus Christ, for example, taught the people through stories. The meanings of the stories that he told have been continually debated throughout time. Parable, like myth, by its very nature is an open form. Open not in the sense that absolutely any interpretation of meaning will do, but open in the sense that the range of interpretations of meaning is broader rather than narrower, polysemic rather than monolithic.

For example, when I recently discussed *E.T.: The Extra-Terrestrial* in a film class, I asked the students to define the central narrative experience, or what the story was about. One student said it illustrated the beauty of mystery and reminded her of how the rational and scientific world is compelled to dissect and analyze everything it doesn't understand and in so doing often destroys the beauty of it. Another student said it was about the power of friendship and reminded her of how she would do almost anything to help a friend. Still a third said it was about our need for home and how home, for her, represented a place of unconditional love and acceptance. While these interpretations are quite different, they are not incompatible moral lessons in the mythic universe of this film. *E.T.*'s polyvocal quality points to its status as a functional or living myth.

But possibly even more significant is the way in which this film, for example, even allows for potentially competing visions to coexist inside of the film as well as inside of the same mythic universe. *E.T.* clearly celebrates the realm of the intuitive and nonrational. Elliot and his brother and sister hide E.T. from adults in general and the scientists in particular because they know that as members of the rational world these adults will inspect, dissect, and ultimately destroy the mystery and beauty that is E.T. Although the magical, mystical nonrational realm is clearly emphasized in the film, the rational scientific realm, rather than being demonized, is also validated. Although the rational world plays the antagonist in the film, it is a benevolent adversary. The scientific-rational paradigm, in other words, although offering what may be seen as a competing vision to the nonrational/spiritual paradigm celebrated in the film, is, according to the film, simply a different, but not incompatible way of knowing.

In addition, *E.T.* and *Close Encounters of the Third Kind* not only spawned an entire decade of films about benevolent aliens and mystical musings on human-alien contact, such as we see in the film *Contact*; it also opened the door for competing visions of unfriendly aliens and apocalyptic musings as seen in such films as *Alien*, *Aliens*, and *Independence Day*. In other words, rather than defining and confining the genre of space fiction, *E.T.* may actually have contributed to its growth, change, and diversity. As such, effective mythic stories "open up" rather than "close down" interpretive possibilities while often inviting other, possibly competing versions of the myth to exist in the same culture or age.

By contrast, *The Lion King* provides an example of a mythic story that turns the circle of life specifically, and creation mythology generally, into a justification for hierarchy. Although Mustafa's and Simba's dominion over the beasts of the jungle and birds of the air offers a benevolent monarchy, it is a monarchy nevertheless. As I argued earlier, the film's anthropomorphic interpretation of the animal kingdom, based as it is on social Darwinism and assumptions about the natural order of things, invites application to the human world, applications that although instrumental, particularly in a capitalist society, may ultimately be morally detrimental. *The Lion King*, in other words, provides an example of a cultural interpretation of an archetypal myth that may close down, rather than open up, interpretive possibilities for audiences and for the culture at large.

Myths That Invite Change in the Audience

Dramatic movement, particularly as a result of the protagonist's arc or development over the course of the story, is a widely accepted criterion for judging the value of a narrative. So it is not a leap to say that liberating myths are those that allow for, and indeed invite, change in the audience as well. But what kind of change? Changes that move an individual or a culture toward individuation are the kind I have in mind. For example, as a result of hearing or seeing the story, the critic can ask, does the audience feel compelled to examine something about their lives, to see themselves or their actions in a new light—to better understand a relationship of a personal, cultural, or spiritual nature? That the Star Wars trilogy has been so widely received again and again by audiences all over the world invites the mythic critic to examine the mechanisms by which these films speak to our collective search for meaning and offer advice for our individual and collective spiritual journeys. The same could be said of such seemingly diverse films as *The Wizard of Oz* and *2001: A Space Odyssey*, the one a 1939 MGM fantasy film, the other a 1970s sci-fi classic. The popularity of these films may rest in their ability to reinterpret the quest for home in a fashion that speaks to our collective unconscious while also reinvigorating our private and collective searches for meaning and growth in an era of separation and fragmentation.

By contrast, a number of the films this book has discussed, while drawing upon mythic stories, such as the father quest or the sacred marriage quest, often fall prey to conservative or ideologically problematic interpretations of these quests. Such interpretations, rather than allowing or inviting the audience to change in ways that speak to our higher natures, may actually support status-quo visions of society that demean or constrict various groups' attempts at individuation, or may further reify hierarchical relationships in society. So, for example, although *It's a Wonderful Life* offers an endearing portrait of small-town life, celebrating the role of the good neighbor, the value of community consciousness, and the centrality of love to salvation, it can also be viewed as an indictment of women and minorities who challenge traditional or conservative visions of their "place" in society.

The same critique can be made of *Field of Dreams*, which, while offering transcendence to Ray and a community of believers on a baseball field where "dreams come true," signifies that this sacred space is a male domain and implies that a woman's place is also in the home, or at least not on a baseball field. The film may also be viewed as reactionary by its portrayal of the disappointments of the "Big Chill" generation, epitomized by Terence Mann. The film implies that the ideals for which that generation fought, such as world peace and equality and civil rights for women and minorities, are possibly unattainable or unrealistic. Myths, therefore, that invite audiences to change rather than crystallizing status-quo and often conservative visions may be deemed superior to those that do not.

Myths that Offer Grounds for Judgment

A functional myth should also offer the grounds upon which it is to be tested or judged as such. Myths potentially become dangerous when they assert a permanence that assumes both a disconnection from material conditions and insularity from critical discussion. Central to MacIntyre's discussion of narrative's moral impulse is that narrative as "a living tradition . . . is an historically extended, socially embodied argument, and an argument precisely in part about the goods which constitute that tradition." [18] Living functional myths, in other words, are those that not only acknowledge their contingent status and their implicit ideology, but also offer these up as grounds upon which they are to be tested. Fisher asserts that narrative rationality presumes the twin tests of coherence—does the story "stick together"—and fidelity— does the story ring true with what we know about how the world works.[19] But beyond these well-established tests of the narrative paradigm, the critic of myth can ask to what extent does the myth acknowledge its contingent, socially-historically–grounded status? To what extent does it acknowledge its own implicit ideology or way of knowing?

This is a difficult question for critics of American film, particularly since Hollywood films have a difficult time acknowledging their status as film, let alone their status as ideologically contingent. The best Hollywood myth-makers, however, rise to this challenge.

Stanley Kubrick's films, for example, although positing as their central dilemma the mythic search for higher intelligence and meaning in a universe, always ground this mythic vision in historically specific contexts, whether cold war relations, as in *Dr. Strangelove*, or American involvement in Vietnam, as in *Full Metal Jacket*. Not only historically grounded, Kubrick's films also acknowledge their status as film in a style that is both reflexive and intellectual and, at times, invisible and emotional. Drawing on Brechtian techniques of alienation, Kubrick's film style frequently pulls us in emotionally only to push us out intellectually. This back and forth movement creates identification—we come to care, for example, about these characters and their moral dilemmas—while also allowing self-conscious examination—of the act of filmmaking and viewing—and critical reflection—of the specific event portrayed. For example, although *2001* ultimately asserts the need for an evolution toward a higher state of consciousness, it does so using a film style that invites us to dwell on the construction of this thesis. This reminds us of the film's contingent status as film (a visual and auditory construction of the pro-filmic event) and as narrative (an interpretive version by one filmmaker, cinematographer, screenplay writer, and so on). *2001*, although speaking to the universal exigency for unity and meaning in a seemingly fragmented and meaningless world, acknowledges its version of this quest as contingent and socially and historically grounded. The film, in other words, nods to its own implicit ideology or way of knowing.

Gone with the Wind, by contrast, released at the height of the Hollywood industry's mastery of the studio system, unselfconsciously draws on the universal quest for home in a fashion that not only fails to acknowledge its contingent or historically grounded status; it also ultimately works to disguise or erase our awareness of these things. Plantation life, presented as an ideal, is celebrated in an aesthetic fashion verging on the fascistic. Although the film tells a version of the destruction of this racist system of privilege and hierarchy during the Civil War, because it does so against the backdrop of 1930s instability it speaks to the audience's desire for conservative or status-quo visions, regardless of the basis of those visions. Better the gracious order of plantation life and the benevolent rule of kind white masters, the film implies, than economic instability and uncertainly, regardless of whether that instability is brought on by a civil war or a stock-market crash.

In sum, although reliance on a single, unquestioned narrative can certainly be viewed as ideologically restrictive, labeling all myths as false consciousness in response denies the power and usefulness of myths for interpreting and continually re-creating the human experience. And, while it is true that moral impulse is the defining character of narratives, and, by extension, mythical narratives, this does not necessarily mean that all moral visions are necessarily insular, exclusionary, or static.

Myths in the Future

If myths then can be both functional or dysfunction, if they can either move an audience toward cultural individuation or away from it, what mythic visions do we need as humanity moves into the next millennium? What role do we need our myths to play? Rushing, speaking specifically of the "patriarchal co-optation of the feminine archetype" in *Alien* and *Aliens*, asserts in her conclusion that "The new myth for humankind needs to be a *quest*, not a *conquest*; its purpose, to *search* rather than to search and destroy." [20] Rushing and Frentz assert that such myths would invite cultures, while "still maintaining their uniqueness," to "expand their identities outward into a more global, even universal, consciousness." [21] Campbell reaches a similar conclusion regarding the shape of myths in the future. As he explains, "When you come to the end of one time and the beginning of a new one, it's a period of tremendous pain and turmoil. The threat we feel, and everybody feels — well, there is the notion of Armageddon coming, you know" [22] and this requires "myths that will identify the individual not with his local group but with his planet." [23] He goes on to explain that:

the only myth that is going to be worth thinking about in the immediate future is one that is talking about the planet, not the city, not these people, but the planet and everybody on it. . . . And what it will have to deal with will be exactly what all myths have dealt with — the maturation of the individual from dependency through adulthood, through maturity, and then to the exit; and then how to relate to this society and how to relate this society to the world of nature and the cosmos.[24]

What may be needed, in other words, are stories that help us see beyond the divisions of here and now — the seeming dualities of male and female, self and Other, technology and spirituality, and the human and the divine.

Notes

Chapter 1. Introduction

1. Joseph Campbell, *The Hero with a Thousand Faces* (Princeton, N.J.: Princeton University Press/Bollingen Series 17, 1972), 39.

2. Campbell, *Hero*; Joseph Henderson, "Ancient Myths and Modern Man," in *Man and His Symbols*. ed. Carl G. Jung (Garden City, N.Y.: Doubleday, 1964); Robert Jewett and John S. Lawrence, *The American Monomyth* (Lanham, Md.: University Press of America, 1988); Mayreen Murdock, *The Heroine's Journey: Women's Quest for Wholeness* (Boston: Shambhala, 1990).

3. Susan Mackey-Kallis, *Oliver Stone's America: "Dreaming the Myth Outward"* (Denver, Colo.: Westview/HarperCollins, 1996); Aldous Huxley, *The Perennial Philosophy* (New York: Harper Colophon, 1970); Mircea Eliade, *The Myth of the Eternal Return* (Princeton, N.J.: Princeton University Press, 1954); Janice Rushing in *"E.T.* as Rhetorical Transcendence," *Quarterly Journal of Speech*, 71 (1985): 190.

4. Carl Jung, *The Archetypes and the Collective Unconscious*, trans. R. F. Hull (Princeton, N.J.: Princeton University Press, 1990); Mackey-Kallis, *Oliver Stone's America*; Carol Pearson, *The Hero Within* (San Francisco: Harper and Row, 1986); Michael Washburn, *The Ego and the Dynamic Ground: A Transpersonal Theory of Human Development* (Albany: State University of New York Press, 1988); Ken Wilber, *The Atman Project: A Transpersonal View of Human Development*, (Wheaton, Ill.: The Theosophical Publishing House/Quest Books, 1980) and *Up From Eden: A Transpersonal View of Human Development* (Boston: New Science Library/Shambhala, 1986); Anthony Stevens, *Archetypes: A Natural History of the Self* (New York: Quill, 1983).

5. Robert Davies, James Farrell, and Steven Matthews, "The Dream World of Film: A Jungian Perspective on Cinematic Communication," *Western Journal of Speech Communication*, 46 (1982): 326–43; Geoffrey Hill, *Illuminating Shadows: The Mythic Power of Film* (Boston: Shambhala, 1992); Janice Rushing, "Mythic Evolution of the 'New Frontier' in Mass Mediated Rhetoric," *Critical Studies in Mass Communication*, 3 (1986): 265–96, and "Power, Other and Spirit in Cultural Texts," *Western Journal of Communication*, 57 (1993): 159–68.

6. Other examples include Janice Rushing, *"E.T.* as Rhetorical Transcendence" and "Evolution of 'The New Frontier' in *Alien* and *Aliens*: Patriarchal Co-optation of the Feminine Archetype," *Quarterly Journal of Speech*, 75, (1989): 1–24; Mackey-Kallis, *Oliver Stone's America*; Janice Rushing and Thomas Frentz, *Projecting the Shadow: The Cyborg Hero in American Film* (Chicago: University of Chicago Press,

1995); Dale Williams, "*2001: A Space Odyssey*: A Warning Before its Time," *Critical Studies in Mass Communication*, 1 (1984): 311–21; Joel W. Martin and Conrad E. Ostwalt, Jr., eds., *Screening the Sacred: Religion, Myth and Ideology in Popular American Film* (Boulder, Colo.: Westview Press, 1995.)

7. Janice Rushing and Thomas Frentz lay out the critical positions on these two views of myth; the one sees myth as icology or false-consciousness the other primarily views myth as liberating or enlightening. Rushing and Frentz attempt an integration between them in "Integrating Ideology and Archetype in Rhetorical Criticism," *Quarterly Journal of Speech*, 77 (1991): 385–406.

8. Jung, *Archetypes*, 279.

9. As Janice Rushing notes, "any so-called 'transcendent' myth which suggests that higher experience excludes the world is . . . a sham . . . transcendence is both a historical term and a transhistorical one" ("Cinema and Cultural Consciousness," presented at the Speech Communication Association Convention, Chicago, November 1986, p. 11). This is the case, because, as Rushing notes, "transcendence includes the lower levels and does not negate them" (p. 9).

10. Cf. *Essays on the Odyssey*, Charles H. Taylor, Jr., ed. (Bloomington: Indiana University Press, 1965). This concept is also discussed by Rushing in "*E.T.* as Rhetorical Transcendence," 190.

11. Cf. George Lord, "The Odyssey and the Western World," and Charles H. Taylor, Jr., "The Obstacles to Odysseus' Return," in *Essays on the Odyssey*.

12. Rushing and Frentz, *Projecting the Shadow*, 20.

13. Thomas Frentz and Thomas Farrell, "The Rhetoric of *The Exorcist*," *Quarterly Journal of Speech*, 61 (1975): 43.

14. Rushing, "*E.T.* as Rhetorical Transcendence," 188.

15. Rushing, "*E.T.* as Rhetorical Transcendence," 189.

16. Mackey-Kallis, *Oliver Stone's America*, 15.

17. Rushing, "*E.T.* as Rhetorical Transcendence," 189.

18. Rushing, "*E.T.* as Rhetorical Transcendence," 200.

19. Rushing, "*E.T.* as Rhetorical Transcendence," 198.

20. Jung, *Archetypes*, 160.

21. Martin Medhurst and Thomas Benson, *Rhetorical Dimensions in Media: A Critical Casebook* (Dubuque, Ia.: Kendall/Hunt, 1984), x.

22. Mackey-Kallis, *Oliver Stone's America*, 3.

23. Michael Marsden, John Nachbar and Sam Grogg, eds., *Movies as Artifacts* (Chicago: Nelson Hall, 1982), 6.

24. Although it is not the central focus of their analysis, Rushing and Frentz in "*Projecting the Shadow*" frequently point out various elements of the hero quest in the Star Wars trilogy. A 1998 Smithsonian Museum exhibit dedicated to the films and their attendant memorabilia has also acknowledged mythic elements in the films.

25. Janice Rushing and Thomas Frentz, "Integrating Ideology and Archetype in Rhetorical Criticism," *Quarterly Journal of Speech*, 77 (1991): 385–406 (from *The CommSearch Edition II* CD-ROM, p. 9).

Chapter 2. The Perennial Journey Home

1. Campbell, *Hero*, 35.

2. Campbell, *Hero*, 3.

3. Joseph Campbell, *The Power of Myth*, with Bill Moyers, (Apostrophe S Productions, Inc., and Alfred van der Marck Editions, 1988), 5. See also Anthony Storr, ed., *The Essential Jung*, (Princeton, N.J.: Princeton University Press, 1983), 71, 74, 83.

4. Campbell, *The Power of Myth*, 53; Cf. Huxley, *The Perennial Philosophy*, section XXIV, "Ritual, Symbol Sacrament."

5. Campbell, *The Power of Myth*, 62.

6. See, for example, Jung, *Archetypes*, 123; also Storr, *The Essential Jung*, part 4.

7. Kevin Thomas Curtin, "The Natural: Our *Iliad* and *Odyssey*," *Antioch Review* 43 (1985): 227.

8. Laszlo Versenyi, *Man's Measure: A Study of the Greek Image of Man from Homer to Sophocles*, as cited in Curtin, "The Natural," 226.

9. Jung, *Archetypes*, 157; see also p. 93, "Whether he understands them or not, man must remain conscious of the world of the archetypes, because in it he is still part of Nature and is connected with his own roots. A view of the world or a social order that cuts him off from the primordial images of life not only is no culture at all but, in increasing degree, is a prison or a stable."

10. Campbell, *The Power of Myth*, 71.

11. Campbell, *The Power of Myth*, 71.

12. Jung, at times, implies this position regarding the origin of myth in so far as he equates the psychological process of individuation with a culture's universal evolution toward transcendence, which is the focus of many myths. At other times he asserts that myths do not arise from physical nature. See, for example, "The archetype does not proceed from physical facts, but describes how the psyche experiences the physical fact, and in so doing the psyche often behaves so autocratically that it denies tangible reality or makes statements that fly in the face of it. The primitive mentality does not *invent* myths, it *experiences* them. Myths are original revelations of the preconscious psyche, involuntary statements about unconscious psychic happenings, and anything but allegories of physical processes" (*Archetypes*, p. 154, emphasis in original).

13. Campbell implies this position in his discussion of the differences in the myths told by hunting and gathering cultures versus farming cultures in *The Power of Myth*.

14. Doty provides an extended discussion of this biogenetic approach to myth in *Mythography: The Study of Myths and Rituals* (Birmingham: University of Alabama Press, 1986). See also Mary Douglas's *Natural Symbols: Explorations in Cosmology* (New York: Pantheon, 1970).

15. Cf. Rushing and Frentz, "Integrating Ideology and Archetype," for a discussion of archetypes as ahistorical and not necessarily grounded in experience or envi-

ronment (p. 4). Campbell implies a similar position in *Hero*, 257. See also Michael Osborn, "The Evolution of the Archtypal Sea in Rhetoric & Poetic," *Quarterly Journal of Speech* 63 (1977). Jung asserts this position as well; cf. *Archetypes*, 42–53.

16. Joseph Campbell seems to implicitly support this position in a number of his works; see, in particular, *The Power of Myth*. See also Huston Smith, *The World's Religions* (San Francisco: HarperSanFrancisco, 1991).

17. For an extended discussion of the functions of myth see Doty, *Mythography*, chapter 2. For a discussion of the relationship between universal and cultural myths, see Rushing, "Mythic Evolution of the 'New Frontier.' "

18. Campbell, *The Power of Myth*, 22–23.

19. Campbell, *The Power of Myth*, 72. Also see Michael Osborn's discussion of "culturetypes" and their relation to archetypes in "Rhetorical Depiction," in *Form, Genre, and the Study of Political Discourse*, ed. Herbert W. Simons and Aram A. Aghazarian (Columbia: University of South Carolina Press, 1986), 79–107.

20. For a thorough discussion of the various approaches to myth, broken down by their orientation (sociofunctional, ritualistic, biogenetic, psychological, literary/archetypal, semiotic/ideological, theological/religious), see Doty, *Mythography*.

21. Robert Rowland, "On Mythic Criticism," *Communication Studies*, 41 (1990): 101–16.

22. Cf. Claude Lévi-Strauss, *The Raw and the Cooked*, trans. John and Doreen Weightman (New York: Harper and Row, 1969), and "The Structural Study of Myth," in *The Structuralists from Marx to Lévi-Strauss*, ed. Richard T. DeGeorge and Fernande M. DeGeorge (Garden City, N.Y.: Doubleday, 1972), and *Structural Anthropology*, trans. Claire Jacobson and Brooke Grundfest Schepf (New York: Basic Books, 1963).

23. Bronislaw Malinowski, in "Myth in Primitive Psychology," writes, "Myth, as it exists in a savage community, that is, in its living primitive form, is not merely a story told, but a reality lived" (p. 100). Also, he says that "Myth fulfills in primitive culture an indispensable function: it expresses, enhances, and codifies belief; it safeguards and enforces morality; it vouches for the efficiency of ritual and contains practical rules for the guidance of man" (p. 202) (*Magic, Science and Religion and Other Essays* [Garden City, N.Y.: Anchor, 1948]).

24. Theodore Gaster, *Myth, Legend and Custom in the Old Testament* (New York: Harper and Row, 1969).

25. Huston Smith, *The World's Religions*.

26. Cf. Mircea Eliade, *Myth and Reality*, trans. Willard R. Trask (New York: Harper and Row, 1963), and *Myth of the Eternal Return*.

27. Huxley, *The Perennial Philosophy*.

28. Wilber, *Up From Eden* and *The Atman Project*.

29. Roland Barthes, *Mythologies*, trans. Annette Lavers (New York: Hill and Wang, 1972), *S/Z*, trans. Richard Miller (New York: Hill and Wang, 1974), and *Image—Music—Text*, trans. Stephen Heath (New York: Hill and Wang, 1977).

30. Jacques Ellul, "Modern Myths," *Diogenes*, 23 (1958): 23–40.

31. Cf. Dan Nimmo and James McCombs, *Subliminal Politics: Myths and Myth-makers in America* (Englewood Cliffs, N.J.: Prentice Hall, 1980); W. Lance Bennett, "Myth, Ritual, and Political Control," *Journal of Communication*, 30 (1980); and William F. Lewis, "Telling America's Story: Narrative Form and the Reagan Presidency," *Quarterly Journal of Speech*, 73 (1987): 280–302.

32. For a fuller discussion of the functions of myth, see Janice Rushing, "On Saving Mythic Criticism," *Communication Studies*, 41 (1990): 136–49.

33. Cf. Janice Rushing and Thomas Frentz, " 'The Deer Hunter': Rhetoric of the Warrior," *Quarterly Journal of Speech*, 66 (1980): 392–406.

34. Campbell, *The Power of Myth*, 32.

35. Campbell, *The Power of Myth*, 40.

36. Jung, *Archetypes*, 5; see also p. 155.

37. See also Jung, *Archetypes*: "Modern psychology treats the products of unconscious fantasy-activity as self-portraits of what is going on in the unconscious, or as statements of the unconscious psyche about itself. They fall in to two categories. First, fantasies (including dreams) of a personal character, which go back unquestionably to personal experiences, things forgotten or repressed, and can thus be completely explained by individual anamnesis. Second, fantasies (including dreams) of an impersonal character, which cannot be reduced to experiences in the individual's past, and thus cannot be explained by something individually acquired. These fantasy-images undoubtedly have their closest analogues in mythological types" (p. 155).

38. Campbell, *Hero*, 4; see also Jung, *Archetypes*: "Many of these unconscious processes may be indirectly occasioned by consciousness, but never by conscious choice. Others appear to arise spontaneously, that is to say, from no discernible or demonstrable conscious cause" (p. 154).

39. Campbell, *Hero*, 4.

40. Campbell, *Hero*, 257.

41. Campbell, *The Power of Myth*, 59; see also Jung, *Archetypes*: "Myths . . . have a vital meaning. Not merely do they represent, they *are* the psychic life of the primitive tribe, which immediately falls to pieces and decays when it loses its mythological heritage, like a man who has lost his soul" (p. 154).

42. "The people who can keep them alive are artists of one kind or another. The function of the artist is the mythologization of the environment and the world," in Campbell, *The Power of Myth*, 85.

43. Jung, *Archetypes*, 160.

44. Campbell, *The Power of Myth*, 58–59.

45. Davies, Farrell, and Matthews, "The Dream World of Film," 333.

46. Davies, Farrell, and Matthews, "The Dream World of Film," 332. Bruce Kawin also argues that the audience's relationship to the camera's perspective also makes the filmic experience rife with psychological implications, in *Mind Screen* (Princeton, N.J.: Princeton University Press, 1978).

47. Jung, *Archetypes*, 155.

48. Cf. Huxley, *The Perennial Philosophy*, chapter 13.

49. For the most recent culmination of their thinking on this idea, see Rushing and Frentz, *Projecting the Shadow*.

50. Rushing and Frentz, *Projecting the Shadow*, 41.

51. Erik Erikson, *Identity and the Life Cycle* (1959; rpt. New York: W. W. Norton, 1980), 108.

52. Cf. Huxley, *Perennial Philosophy*, chapters 2 and 13.

53. Jung, as cited in Rushing and Frentz, *Projecting the Shadow*, 41.

54. Mackey-Kallis, *Oliver Stone's America*, 17.

55. Mackey-Kallis, *Oliver Stone's America*, 17.

56. Mackey-Kallis, *Oliver Stone's America*, 18.

57. Jung, *Archetypes*, 167.

58. Mackey-Kallis, *Oliver Stone's America*, 20.

59. As cited in Rushing and Frentz, *Projecting the Shadow*, 39.

60. Mackey-Kallis, *Oliver Stone's America*, 20–21.

61. Campbell, *The Power of Myth*, 126.

62. Campbell, *The Power of Myth*, 126.

63. Rushing and Frentz, *Projecting the Shadow*, 37. For a fuller treatment of transconsciousness, see also David Ray Griffin and Huston Smith, *Primordial Truth and Postmodern Theology* (Albany: State University of New York Press, 1989); Huxley, *The Perennial Philosophy*; and Wilber, *Up from Eden*.

64. Rushing and Frentz, in their attempts to reconcile postmodern and modern understandings of the sovereign rational subject, elaborate on what a de-centered ego in transmodernity would look like: "Both modernism and postmodernism fixate upon the sovereign rational subject as the center of the self. Given that modernism canonizes the ego and postmodernism attempts to decenter it, this statement may seem wide of the mark. But both strains of thought—the one through glorification and the other through vilification—consider the ego, not the soul, to be the seat of the self. In modernism the ego becomes God. In postmodernism, when the ego is destroyed, so is God" (p. 24). "Postmodern thought has not put an end to Spirit, but merely repressed it into unconsciousness" (p. 25). "But it is hubris, not only to crown the rational subject as sovereign, but also to think that we can destroy Spirit. One must play God to kill God. Spirit was here before we were, and it will go on existing. . . . It is the human imperative, we believe, not to banish the ego, but to reestablish its links with its simulations and its soul" (p. 27).

65. Campbell, *The Power of Myth*, 48.

66. Campbell, *The Power of Myth*, 48.

67. Campbell, *The Power of Myth*, 50; see also Campbell, "Creative Mythology," *The Masks of God: Creative Mythology* (Arkana: Penguin Books, 1991), 347, 649–56, and on the nature of duality, 78–79.

68. Campbell, *The Power of Myth*, 51.

69. "The transcendent does exactly that—transcendent means to 'transcend,' to go past duality" (Campbell, *The Power of Myth*, 50).

70. Campbell, *Hero*, 38; the entire book is an extended elaboration of the hero quest. See also Campbell, *The Power of Myth*, 122–63.

71. Campbell, *Hero*, 35.

72. Campbell, *The Power of Myth*, 123.

73. Jung, *Archetypes*, 135–36; for greater elaboration, see 3–74 and 275–354. See also Anthony Stevens, *Archetypes: A Natural History of the Self* (New York: Quill, 1983), 31–32, and Rushing and Frentz, *Projecting the Shadow*, 34.

74. Campbell, *The Power of Myth*, xv.

75. Campbell, *The Power of Myth*, 110.

76. Campbell, *The Power of Myth*, 49.

77. Campbell, *The Power of Myth*, 136.

78. Campbell, *Hero*, 245–46.

79. Campbell, *Hero*, 246.

80. For an extended discussion of the similarities among creation myths of various cultures, see Campbell, *The Power of Myth*, 42–54, 56, 114–15; *The Masks of God: Occidental Mythology* (Arkana: Penguin Books, 1991), 76–86, 85, 102–5, 111–12, 206, 112, 420–21, 157–58, 192, 200–206; *The Masks of God: Creative Mythology.*

81. Campbell, *The Power of Myth*, 42.

82. Campbell, *The Power of Myth*, 45.

83. For an elaboration of the sacred-marriage quest, see Campbell, *The Power of Myth*, 200–203, and *Hero*, 109–20, 250–51.

84. Stevens, *Archetypes*, 155.

85. Campbell, *Hero*, 116.

86. For a fuller elaboration of the father quest, see Campbell, *The Power of Myth*, 129, 138, 166.

87. For a fuller treatment of the Grail quest, see Julius Evola, *The Mystery of the Grail: Initiation and Magic on the Quest for the Spirit*, trans. Guido Stucco (Rochester, Vt.: Inner Traditions, 1994); Campbell, *The Power of Myth*, 195–200, 217, 218, and the Grail king, 112, 116, 197, 198; Campbell, *The Masks of God: Creative Mythology*, part 3.

88. Evola, *Mystery of the Grail*, 35.

89. For greater elaboration of the Arthurian Grail motif, see Evola, *Mystery of the Grail*, 31–37.

90. Campbell, *The Power of Myth*, 196.

91. For the most recent culmination of their thinking on this idea, see Rushing and Frentz, *Projecting the Shadow*.

92. Campbell, *The Masks of God: Occidental Mythology*, 21–22.

93. Campbell, *The Masks of God: Occidental Mythology*, 86.

Chapter 3. Reframing Homer's *Odyssey*

1. M. I. Finley, *The World of Odysseus* (New York: Viking Press, 1969), 3.

2. Finley, *The World*, 11.

3. Finley, *The World*, 3.

4. Finley, *The World*, 4.

5. This concept is also discussed by Rushing in "*E.T.* as Rhetorical Transcendence," 190.

6. George D. Lord, "The *Odyssey* and the Western World," in *Essays on the Odyssey*, ed. Charles H. Taylor, Jr. (Bloomington: Indiana University Press, 1963), 37.

7. Lord, "The *Odyssey*," 37.

8. Lord, "The *Odyssey*," 37.

9. Lord, "The *Odyssey*," 36–37.

10. George E. Dimock, "The Name of Odysseus," in *Essays on the Odyssey*, ed. Charles H. Taylor, Jr. (Bloomington: Indiana University Press, 1963), 60.

11. Dimock, "The Name," 60–61.

12. Dimock, "The Name," 58.

13. Dimock, "The Name," 59.

14. In a somewhat different but not incompatible reading of Odysseus' loss of identity, Campbell argues that "Nobody" or "no name" represents a necessary loss of ego-consciousness in order for Odysseus to transcend to the realm of impersonal deeds. More specifically, "no name" represents "self-divestiture at the passage to the yonder world: because he did not assert his secular character, his personal name and fame, Odysseus passed the cosmic threshold guardian, to enter a sphere of transpersonal forces, over which ego has no control" (*The Masks of God: Occidental Mythology*, 167).

15. Charles H. Taylor, Jr., "The Obstacles to Odysseus' Return," in *Essays on the Odyssey*, ed. Charles H. Taylor, Jr. (Bloomington: Indiana University Press, 1963), 88.

16. Taylor, "The Obstacles," 88.

17. Campbell, *The Power of Myth*, 51.

18. Taylor, "The Obstacles," 95.

19. Taylor, "The Obstacles," 89.

20. Taylor, "The Obstacles," 96.

21. Taylor, "The Obstacles," 97.

22. Taylor, "The Obstacles," 97.

23. Taylor, "The Obstacles," 97–98.

24. Taylor, "The Obstacles," 98.

25. Taylor, "The Obstacles," 98.

26. Taylor, "The Obstacles," 98–99.

27. Taylor, "The Obstacles," 99.

28. Taylor, "The Obstacles," 99.

29. See, for example, Rushing and Frentz, "Integrating Ideology," 6, for a detailed discussion of this idea.

30. Campbell, *The Masks of God: Occidental Mythology*, 164. Campbell also reads the *Odyssey* in light of the universal hero quest; see, for example, 164–77.

31. *Odyssey*, trans. Robert Fitzgerald (New York: Random House Vintage Books, 1989), book II: lines 49–69.

32. *Odyssey*, book I: lines 324–50.

33. Taylor, "The Obstacles," 99.

Chapter 4. The Sacred Marriage Quest in American Film

1. Campbell, *Hero*, 109.

2. Campbell, *The Power of Myth*, 116.

3. Campbell, *Hero*, 110–11.

4. Campbell, *Hero*, 111.

5. Campbell, *Hero*, 111.

6. Campbell, *Hero*, 119.

7. Antiphons for the Feast of the Assumption of the Blessed Virgin Mary (August 15) at Vespers, from the *Roman Missal*.

8. Janice Hocker Rushing, "Evolution of 'the New Frontier' in *Alien* and *Aliens*: Patriarchal Co-optation of the Feminine Archetype," *Quarterly Journal of Speech*, 75 (1989): 1–24.

9. Campbell, *The Masks of God: Occidental Mythology*, 80.

10. Campbell, *The Masks of God: Occidental Mythology*, 7.

11. Campbell, *The Masks of God: Occidental Mythology*, 44.

12. Rushing, "Evolution of 'The New Frontier," 3–4.

13. Campbell, *The Masks of God: Occidental Mythology*, 21.

14. Edward Whitmont, *The Return of the Goddess* (New York: Crossroads Books, 1986), viii.

15. Campbell, *The Masks of God: Occidental Mythology*, 22.

16. Campbell, *The Masks of God: Occidental Mythology*, 21.

17. Rushing "Evolution of 'the New Frontier,' " 5–7.

18. Campbell, *The Masks of God: Occidental Mythology*, 17.

19. Campbell, *The Masks of God: Occidental Mythology*, 15.

20. Campbell, *The Masks of God: Occidental Mythology*, 15.

21. Campbell, *The Masks of God: Occidental Mythology*, 29.

22. Campbell, *The Masks of God: Occidental Mythology*, 29–30.

23. Rushing, "Evolution of 'the New Frontier,' " 5–7.

24. Campbell, *The Masks of God: Occidental Mythology*, 26–27.

25. Marc Angelaccio, *Baseball: The American Mythic Narrative*, unpublished honors thesis, Villanova University, Spring 1997, p. 90.

26. Angelaccio, "Baseball," 90.

27. Campbell, *Hero*, 49–58.

28. The idea of Ada's piano as her voice can also be read as a reflexive commentary on the role of the film for the filmmaker. Jane Campion not only directed but also wrote *The Piano*. As such, the film itself, for Campion, like the piano for Ada, can be seen as a metaphor for the filmmaker's voice. Campion may speak through her films in ways she might not speak with her everyday voice.

29. Campbell, *Hero*, 119.

30. Campbell, *Hero*, 114.

31. Campbell, *The Masks of God: Occidental Mythology*, 158.

32. For an extending discussion of this issue, see Virginia Woolf's *To the Lighthouse*; in particular, see Woolf's treatment of Lily, the painter.

33. John Berger, *Ways of Seeing* (New York: Penguin Press, 1991).

Chapter 5. The Father Quest in American Film

1. Campbell, *The Power of Myth*, 166.

2. Campbell, *The Power of Myth*, 166.

3. Campbell, *Hero*, 136.

4. See, for example, Campbell's discussion of "father atonement" in *The Power of Myth*, 166; and "Hero," 147.

5. Campbell, *The Power of Myth*, 107.

6. Campbell, *The Power of Myth*, 106.

7. Campbell, *Hero*, 136.

8. Campbell, *Hero*, 136–37.

9. Campbell, *Hero*, 147.

10. Matthew 26:11.

11. Roger Aden, "Back to the Garden: Therapeutic Place Metaphor in *Field of Dreams*," *Southern Communication Journal* 59, 4, (1994): 307.

12. *Variety* (1989, Nov. 8), 6.

13. *Variety* (1990, May 2), 130.

14. Aden, "Back to the Garden," 308.

15. G. Grella, "Baseball and the American Dream," *Massachusetts Review*, 16, (1975): 562.

16. Marc Angelaccio, *Baseball: The American Mythical Narrative* unpublished honors thesis, Villanova University, 1997, 27–28.

17. Conrad Ostwalt, *After Eden: The Secularization of American Space in the Fiction of Willa Cather and Theodore Dreiser* (London: Associated University Presses, 1990), 26.

18. As cited in Robert Jewett and John S. Lawrence, *The American Monomyth* (New York: Anchor Press/Doubleday, 1997), 171.

19. Ostwalt, *After Eden*, 5.

20. As cited in Jewett and Lawrence, *The American Monomyth*, 172–73.

21. As cited in Jewett and Lawrence, *The American Monomyth*, 172–73.

22. Ostwalt, *After Eden*, 28.

23. Aden, "Back to the Garden," 309.

24. Jewett and Lawrence, *The American Monomyth*, 170.

Chapter 6. The Search for Home During the 1930s

1. Campbell, *The Power of Myth* and *Hero*.

2. Rushing and Frentz, "Integrating Ideology," 10.

3. Richard Selcer, "Home Sweet Movies: From Tara to Oz and Home Again," *Journal of Popular Film and Television*, 18, no. 2 (1990): 53.

4. Selcer, "Home Sweet Movies," 54.

5. Selcer, "Home Sweet Movies," 54.

6. Selcer, "Home Sweet Movies," 55.

7. Selcer, "Home Sweet Movies," 57–58.

8. Selcer, "Home Sweet Movies," 60.

9. Selcer, "Home Sweet Movies," 53.

10. David Payne, "*The Wizard of Oz*: Therapeutic Rhetoric in a Contemporary Media Ritual," *Quarterly Journal of Speech*, 75 (1989): 25–39.

11. Selcer, "Home Sweet Movies," 56.

12. Lynette Carpenter, " 'There's No Place Like Home': *The Wizard of Oz* and American Isolationism," *Film History*, 15, no. 2 (May 1985), 39.

13. Henry M. Littlefield, "*The Wizard of Oz*: Parable on Populism," *American Quarterly*, 16 (1964): 47–58.

14. Harvey R. Greenberg, *The Movies on Your Mind* (New York: E. P. Dutton, 1975), 13–32.

15. Payne, "Therapeutic Rhetoric."

16. Carol Pearson and Katherine Pope, *The Female Hero in American and British Literature* (New York: R.R. Bowker, 1981), 68–71.

17. In his essay "Home Sweet Movies: From Tara to Oz and Home Again," Selcer explores home as a central concept in both *The Wizard of Oz* and *Gone with the Wind*. He claims that home was an idea with particular significance in the 1930s American psychological landscape. He claims that both films retell this myth "in a way that touched 1939 audiences on a deep, personal level, even if they did not understand why" (53–54). In both *Gone with the Wind* and *The Wizard of Oz*, according to Selcer, "The threat to the rural American home from catastrophic disaster, whether natural or manmade, is at the heart of both films. Each in its own way perfectly captured the mood of the times and elevated the ideal of home to new mythic heights. It was more than coincidence that after nine years of the worst depression in American history, these two movies were released at the same time, became two of the biggest box-office draws of the decade, and ultimately two of the most popular films of all time" (55–56).

18. Thomas Pauly, "*Gone with the Wind* and *The Grapes of Wrath* as Hollywood Histories of the Depression," in *Movies as Artifacts*, ed. Michael Marsden, John Nachbar, and Sam Grogg, Jr. (Chicago: Nelson-Hall, 1982), 165.

19. David O. Selznick, *Memo from David O. Selznick*, ed. Rudy Belmer (New York: Viking Press, 1972), 212.

20. Selcer, "Home Sweet Movies," 56.

21. Selcer, "Home Sweet Movies," 56.

22. Pauly, "Hollywood Histories," 165.

23. Pauly, "Hollywood Histories," 169.

24. Jeffery Richards, "Frank Capra and the Cinema of Populism," *Political Criticism* (1980), 65–78.

25. Richards, "Frank Capra," 66.

26. Richards, "Frank Capra," 66.

27. Richards, "Frank Capra," 66.

28. Richards, "Frank Capra," 65.

29. A number of secondary contrasts related to the quest for home are also set up in the film, specifically between owning vs. renting, Bailey Park vs. Potter's Field, Bedford Falls vs. Pottersville, life vs. death/suicide, simplicity/innocence vs. big-city sophistication, marriage vs. spinsterhood, and the working man vs. the college man; see, for example, Richards, "Frank Capra."

30. Selcer, "Home Sweet Movies," 54.

Chapter 7. Modern Challenges in the Home Quest

1. Campbell, *The Power of Myth*, xiv.

2. Rushing, in "*E.T.* as Rhetorical Transcendence," points out the metaphysical qualities in *E.T.*, specifically analyzing the film in terms of Perennial philosophy and Jungian psychology. As such, my analysis of the film is indebted to hers.

3. Jung, *Archetypes*, 159.

4. Jung, *Archetypes*, 161.

5. Jung, *Archetypes*, 162.

6. Jung, *Archetypes*, 174.

7. Jung, *Archetypes*, 164.

8. Jung, *Archetypes*, 356.

9. Jung, *Archetypes*, 357.

10. Jung, *Archetypes*, 384.

11. Jung, *Archetypes*, 130.

12. Rushing, in "*E.T.* as Rhetorical Transcendence," points out numerous mandalas in the film.

13. Jung, *Archetypes*, 159.

14. Jung, *Archetypes*, 161.

15. Jung, *Archetypes*, 162.

16. Jung, *Archetypes*, 164.

17. Jung, *Archetypes*, 164–65.

18. William Wordsworth, "Ode: Intimations of Immortality from Recollections of Early Childhood," in *British Literature, Vol. II: 1800 to the Present* (Lexington, Mass.: D.C. Heath & Co., 1974), 73.

19. Jung, *Archetypes*, 178.

20. Rushing, in "*E.T.* as Rhetorical Transcendence," summarizes Jung's ideas (in *Flying Saucers: A Modern Myth*, trans. R. C. Hull [Princeton, N.J.: Princeton Uni-

versity Press, 1978]) regarding the prevalence of childlike aliens in society: "Jung found that the UFO inhabitants were often rumored to stand about three feet high, to be weightless, and to look vaguely like humans or 'technological angels'—sometimes dwarfs with enormous heads bursting with intelligence. . . . Sometimes they were carrying out a cautious survey of the earth, but typically avoiding contact with humans. They obviously had superior technology, and were occasionally feared as destroyers of the planet. More often, however, they were credited with superior wisdom and moral goodness which would enable them to save humanity" (p. 194).

21. Although I have independently reached many of my conclusions regarding *E.T.*, my analysis of the film is indebted to Janice Rushing's "*E.T.* as Rhetorical Transcendence."

22. Rushing, "*E.T.* as Rhetorical Transcendence," 41.

23. Jung, *Archetypes*, 222.

24. Jung, *Archetypes*, 158.

25. Rushing, "*E.T.* as Rhetorical Transcendence," 40.

26. Rushing also points out E.T.'s child/old man appearance in "*E.T.* as Rhetorical Transcendence," 39.

27. Rushing also points out E.T.'s physical and spiritual connection to nature in "*E.T.* as Rhetorical Transcendence," 39.

28. Jung, *Archetypes*, 222.

29. Rushing, "*E.T.* as Rhetorical Transcendence," 40.

30. The similarities between Elliot and E.T. have been pointed out by Rushing ("*E.T.* as Rhetorical Transcendence," 39) and others.

31. Matthew 28:20, King James Version.

32. Wordsworth, "Ode: Intimations of Immortality," 73.

33. Jung, *Archetypes*, 171.

34. Campbell, *The Power of Myth*, 42.

35. J. Agel, *The Making of Kubrick's 2001* (New York: New American Library, 1970), 10.

36. J. Baxter, *Stanley Kubrick: A Biography* (New York: Carroll and Graf Publishers, 1997), 26.

37. An exception to this is Dale Williams, "*2001: A Space Odyssey*: A Warning Before Its Time," *Critical Studies in Mass Communication*, 1 (1984): 311–21. Williams notes the transcendent qualities in *2001* as well as the presence of wholeness themes. Hunter, Kaplan, and Jaszi note that the film deals with three stages of human progress: evolutionary, technical, and spiritual ("Review of *2001: A Space Odyssey*," in J. Engle, ed., *The Making of Kubrick's "2001"* [New York: New American Library, 1970], 215–22.)

38. R. P. Kolker, *A Cinema of Loneliness: Penn, Kubrick, Coppola, Scorsese, Altman* (New York: Oxford University Press, 1980), 72.

39. Kubrick's attention to the compositional possibilities of the film frame can no doubt be traced to his love of photography. With the receipt of a Graflex camera for his thirteenth birthday, photography started as a hobby for Kubrick, but, as LoBrutto notes, it quickly became an obsession. Not only was he his high school's official pho-

tographer, Kubrick also worked for four years as a photographer for *Look* magazine before turning his attention to filmmaking (V. LoBrutto, *Stanley Kubrick: A Biography* [New York: Penguin Books, 1997], 10.)

40. Kolker, *A Cinema of Loneliness*, 75.

41. Williams also notes this connection in "A Warning Before Its Time," 317.

42. Williams, in a Burkean analysis of *2001*, also notes the separation and hierarchy theme in the film ("A Warning Before Its Time").

43. Williams, "A Warning Before Its Time," 319.

44. See, for example, Mackey-Kallis, *Oliver Stone's America*, chapter 5, for an extended discussion of this idea.

45. Jung, *Archetypes*, 384.

Part III. Synthesis

1. Rushing and Frentz, in *Projecting the Shadow*, although it is not the central focus of their analysis, frequently point out various elements of the hero quest in the Star Wars trilogy. A 1998 Smithsonian Institution exhibit dedicated to the films and their attendant memorabilia has also acknowledged mythic elements in the films.

2. Janice Rushing and Thomas Frentz, "Integrating Ideology and Archetype in Rhetorical Criticism," *Quarterly Journal of Speech*, 77 (1991): 385–406 (from *The CommSearch Edition II* CD-ROM, p. 9).

Chapter 8. The Star Wars Trilogy

1. Dale Pollock, *Skywalking: The Life and Films of George Lucas* (Hollywood, Calif.: Samuel French Trade, 1990). The background material that follows, unless otherwise noted, comes from Pollock's book.

2 Harrison Ford (Han Solo) was actually cast by accident. As the story goes, Ford was installing a door in Francis Ford Coppola's new office at Goldwyn Studios when he saw Lucas for the first time since he had played a bit part in Lucas' *American Graffiti*. Lucas asked Ford to help him out by reading opposite some of the actresses he was auditioning for Princess Leia. The rest, as they say, is history.

3. Pollock, *Skywalking*, 184.

4. Pollock, *Skywalking*, 185.

5. Pollock, *Skywalking*, 186–87.

6. Pollock, *Skywalking*, 215.

7. Pollock, *Skywalking*, 215.

8. Pollock, *Skywalking*, 142.

9. Pollock, *Skywalking*, 140.

10. Paul Scanlon, "The Forces Behind George Lucas," interview with George Lucas, *Rolling Stone*, August 25, 1977, p. 43.

11. Stephen Zito, "George Lucas Goes Far Out," *American Film*, April 1977: 13.

12. Pollock, *Skywalking*, 134.

13. Pollock, *Skywalking*, 139.

14. See, for example, Andrew Gordon's "*Star Wars*: A Myth for our Time," in *Screening the Sacred*, Joel W. Martin and Conrad E. Ostwalt, Jr., eds. (Boulder, Colo.: Westview Press, 1995), 73–82.

15. Gordon also notes some of the similarities between Star Wars and the classic western in "*Star Wars*: A Myth for Our Time," 76–77.

16. Campbell, *Hero*, 245.

17. Campbell, *Hero*, 246.

18. Campbell, *The Power of Myth*, 110.

19. Campbell, *The Power of Myth*, 49.

20. Campbell, *Hero*, 245–46.

21. Campbell, *Hero*, 245–46.

22. Campbell, *Hero*, 246.

23. Campbell, *The Power of Myth*, 18.

24. Jung, *Archetypes*, 158.

25. Jung, *Archetypes*, 222.

26. Campbell, *The Power of Myth*, 18.

27. Campbell, *The Power of Myth*, 196.

28. Campbell, *The Power of Myth*, 196.

29. Campbell, *Hero*, 245–46.

30. Douglas Kellner and Michael Ryan, *Camera Politica: The Politics and Ideology of Contemporary Hollywood Fiction* (Bloomington: Indiana University Press, 1988).

Chapter 9. Myth, the Contemporary Moment, and the Future

1. Rushing, "Cinema and Cultural Consciousness," 1.

2. See Janice Rushing and Thomas Frentz, "*The Deer Hunter*: Rhetoric of the Warrior," *Quarterly Journal of Speech*, 66 (1980): 392–406, as an example of an analysis that attempts to point out both the progressive and regressive qualities of myth in this film.

3. Rushing, "Cinema and Cultural Consciousness," 3.

4. Rushing and Frentz, "Integrating Ideology and Archetype"; Thomas Frentz and Janice Rushing, "Integrating Ideology and Archetype in Rhetorical Criticism: Part II: A Case Study of Jaws," *Quarterly Journal of Speech*, 79 (1993): 61–81.

5. Rushing and Frentz, "Integrating Ideology and Archetype," printed in *Comm-Search Edition II* CD-ROM, p. 1.

6. Rushing and Frentz, "Integrating Ideology and Archetype," 6.

7. Rushing and Frentz, "Integrating Ideology and Archetype," 6.

8. Rushing and Frentz, "Integrating Ideology and Archetype," 6–7.

9. Rushing and Frentz, "Integrating Ideology and Archetype," 9.

10. Walter Fisher, "Narration as a Human Communication Paradigm: The Case of Public Moral Argument," *Communication Monographs*, 51 (1984): 4.

11. Fisher, "Narration," 8.

12. William Lewis, "Telling America's Story: Narrative Form and the Reagan Presidency," in *Readings in Rhetorical Criticism*, ed. Carl Burgchardt (State College, Pa.: Strata Publishing, 1995), 302.

13. Campbell, *The Power of Myth*, 58–59.

14. Campbell, *The Power of Myth*, 58–59.

15. Jung, *Archetypes*, 155.

16. Campbell, *Hero*, 389.

17. Personal communication, June 7, 1999; Christopher Volger has since published *The Writer's Journey: Mythic Structure for Writers* (Studio City, Calif., Michael Wiese Productions, 1998) based on this outline from Campbell.

18. Alasdair MacIntyre, *After Virtue*, 2nd ed. (Notre Dame: University of Notre Dame Press, 1981), 222.

19. Fisher, "Narration."

20. Janice Rushing, "Evolution of 'The New Frontier' in *Alien* and *Aliens*: Patriarchal Co-optation of the Feminine Archetype," *Quarterly Journal of Speech*, 75, (1989): 21.

21. Rushing and Frentz, "Integrating Ideology and Archetype," 6–7.

22. Campbell, *The Power of Myth*, 17.

23. Campbell, *The Power of Myth*, 24.

24. Campbell, *The Power of Myth*, 32.

Index

Acknowledgments

A number of individuals need to be mentioned for their support of this book. I especially extend heartfelt thanks to my editor, Patricia Smith, for believing in the project, and for encouraging me to persist through each phase of the book's various incarnations. Her patience was boundless. Special thanks to my department chair, Teresa Nance, for supporting the sabbatical that allowed me to move foward decisively on early drafts of the book, and to Villanova University for making this sabbatical available.

I also gratefully acknowledge the work of several anonymous reviewers, who always provided constructive and insightful feedback about the manuscript. They surely helped to make this a much better book. Thanks also to the members of the "Omphalos" reading group, who asked provocative questions about Chapter 4, and ultimately pushed me in some new and interesting directions with this chapter. Special thanks to Nancy Covington for her dedicated help in picking out the film stills for the book.

Finally, to my husband, Kyriakos Kallis, I express undying gratitude for being an equal partner in the raising of our two boys, William and Alexander. Doing his fair share of child rearing and encouraging and believing in my work made the book a joy to write.